In His Majesty's Footsteps

A Personal Memoir

In His Majesty's Footsteps

A Personal Memoir

Vasit Dejkunjorn

Translator
Busakorn Suriyasarn

Editor
Christopher G. Moore

Heaven Lake Press

15086722

Distributed in Thailand by:
Asia Document Bureau Ltd.
P.O. Box 1029
Nana Post Office
Bangkok 10112 Thailand
Fax: (662) 260-4578
Web site: www.heavenlakepress.com
E-mail: editorial@heavenlakepress.com

First Published in Thailand in 2006
by Heaven Lake Press
Second printing, June 2006
Printed in Thailand

Original title: *Roy Phra Yugalabaht*
Copyright 2001 © Matichon Public Company Limited

Jacket design: Jae Song
Jacket photograph with gracious permission of His Majesty.
Front flap photograph with gracious permission of His Majesty.
Back cover photograph (Grand Palace): Ralf Tooten © 2006
Author's photograph: Christopher G. Moore

The permission to use the photographs used in the book has been arranged by the
author in co-operation with the photographer, Suthat Phatanasingh, a former Daily
News photographer, who was assigned to photograph the Royal Court activities.

ISBN 974-94125-8-3

ACKNOWLEDGEMENTS

When the opportunity presented itself to translate Pol. Gen. Vasit Dejkunjorn's highly popular Thai edition of *In His Majesty's Footsteps*, we seized it with no hesitation. Given the scarcity of books in the English language that have intimate accounts about the extraordinary and widely admired Thai monarch, King Bhumibol Adulyadej, we believed this was exactly the kind of book that deserved an English audience.

This book was made possible by the efforts and contributions of many people. First, we thank the author Pol. Gen. Vasit Dejkunjorn for the opportunity to present his work to the wider audience it deserves and for his support and assistance throughout the project, including in acquiring the rights to use the photographs. We are indebted to Thanpuying Putri Viravaidya, Deputy Principal Private Secretary to His Majesty the King and the Royal Household Bureau for graciously allowing us to use the front cover photograph of His Majesty.

The translation process was as much enjoyable as it was challenging. Dr. Busakorn Suriyasarn, with the help of Pairoh Sripattanatadakoon, spent many months translating the memoir, and checking and rechecking the numerous names and terms concerning royal and religious rituals and ceremonies as well as military ranks and units. Their carefulness and professionalism are greatly appreciated. Thanks are also due to Helen Court for her copyediting work, Paweena Plangpawat and Thomtong Tongnok for their diligent proofreading and assistance in compiling the glossary and index, and Duangruetai Sattayavivad and Khwanruethai Jiamsomboon for their indispensable support in the book production process.

Finally, we are grateful to Ralf Tooten for his photograph, which appears on the back cover of the book, and to Khun Suthat Phatanasingh, a former Daily News photographer who was assigned to photograph the Royal Court activities, for granting permission to use his photographs. Edward Stauffer worked diligently to create the design and layout for this book, drawing upon his years as a publishing industry professional.

Any errors or mistakes in the text are the sole responsibility of the editor.

Christopher G. Moore
Editor
22 May 2006

1

It was a hot and humid afternoon in April of 1967 at Marigadayavan Royal Residence on the royal beach of Cha-am. I was resting in a room that was probably once—over a hundred years ago—an office of a court staff in the reign of King Mongkut. By now the room and the rest of the palace was old and in disrepair. His Majesty King Bhumibol Adulyadej had generously granted the Border Patrol Police permission to use the palace ground for training exercises and certain quarters as offices and dormitory.

I was then a police lieutenant colonel in Special Branch but had been assigned to teach history and political theories to the Border Patrol Police since 1963—the year the battle between the Thai authorities and the communist insurgents was beginning.

My relationship with the Border Patrol Police, though not exactly accidental, was certainly unexpected. Earlier that year I had been involved in setting up a northeastern Special Branch field office. As a commanding officer, I was visiting several of my subordinates who were undergoing training courses in radio communication at the BPP's Aerial Reinforcement Unit (BPP PARU), more widely known as the PARU Camp.

During one of these visits, I had an opportunity to meet Pol. Lt-Col. Pranetr Ridhipachai, deputy commander of the BPP PARU, who was at the time attending the Army Staff School. He was also serving in the secret service, which regularly took him to Laos.

In the short time that Dep. Cdr. Pranetr and I got to know each other, we discovered quite quickly that we agreed on a lot of things. The most important was the need to educate and train the police force in the

1

fight against rising communist insurgencies: how our police needed to understand what communism was really all about, the danger it posed to Thailand and the reason for our resistance against it, otherwise they would just blindly follow orders and not see the bigger picture. We both understood the critical need for an education campaign against communist brainwashing and propaganda against democracy.

That was how the history and political theories class for police began and how I became the first lecturer. I began lecturing police officers, especially those in the PARU and other BPP units, and eventually also the provincial police.

My teaching career took me all over the country and sometimes across national borders. I went wherever my students were. More than a few times I laid beside them in the line of fire in the battlefields. Once I witnessed a great loss: we lost an entire unit of parachutists to the enemy.

That afternoon at Marigadayavan, I was training yet another class of BPP officers. We, teachers and students, all had the afternoon off from training and were enjoying our downtime until the next training day. During that time, Their Majesties King Bhumibol and Queen Sirikit were staying at Klai Kangwol Palace in Hua Hin, Prachuab Khiri Khan, twenty-six kilometers from Cha-am.

The close relationship between HM King Bhumibol and the BPP, especially the PARU, was well-known in uniformed circles. I had known with quiet envy for some time that when HM the King was at Klai Kangwol Palace, paratroopers would on occasion be given audience and invited to dinner. Many were lucky to be in an intimate royal audience and some were even given the king's own special amulets. These called Somdej Chitralada (Might of the Nation), were much sought after by police and soldiers. I dreamt of being blessed with one someday.

In fact I had already had two opportunities to be in the audience of the king and the queen: the first time when I received my bachelor's degree in political science at Chulalongkorn University in 1952, and the second in a play in front of the royal audience in 1959 or 1960. (At the time I was still a major. The play was entitled 'Luuk Khun Luang' ('The Lord's Sons'), written by MR Kukrit Pramoj, who also played the leading character 'Khun Luang'. I played the youngest son of the

Khun Luang. My mother in the play was played by the late Khun Supan Buranapim.) However, those two audiences I had were not intimate. I had no direct conversation with either the king or the queen.

Like many Thais, I dreamt of a once-in-a-lifetime chance to be in an intimate audience of the king and the queen—to be in the presence of and to be directly spoken to by Their Majesties. Therefore, as could be imagined, I was ecstatic when a police officer ran to me—highly ecstatic himself—and said that the king and queen would be coming for a brief stay at Marigadayavan and all the officers were ordered to get in uniform for the royal reception. I put on my uniform immediately. I recall that I was in a green field uniform that afternoon, the standard uniform for border patrol police training.

The royal limousine was driven in slowly and parked away from the officers' reception line. I noticed that the king was the driver. The king and queen, both casually dressed, got out of the limousine and walked toward us. The royal couple stopped at the head of the reception line to allow Dep. Cdr. Pranetr to announce a royal reception.

As is the tradition, the proper royal language for 'introduction' could be uttered either by the individuals who were in the audience or by another person. There were a lot of officers in the reception line that afternoon and one individual introduction at a time would take too long. Because Dep. Cdr. Pranetr knew all of us well, he would do the introduction of the officers whom His Majesty stopped to greet.

When it came my turn—the king stopped in front of me—Dep. Cdr. Pranetr uttered (as speaking for me), 'I, Police Lieutenant Colonel Vasit Dejkunjorn' as I was standing straight and solemn in a salute. What I didn't expect was that the king did not move on right away but said to me, 'What are you doing here?' My entire person felt numb and I thought I was going to faint, as I realized that the king initiated a *direct* conversation *with me*. After I regained my composure, I responded, 'I am here to teach the Border Patrol Police, sir.'

Since that moment and throughout the night I felt as though I had been floating in a dream. I couldn't believe that not only had I a close audience with the king, but that the king himself also spoken directly to me. By the end of that week, another dream of mine came true. All police officers on duty in Hua Hin, including all of us at Marigadayavan, were invited to a royal audience and dinner.

When the royal couple traveled to a provincial royal residence, an invitation to Saturday dinner was customarily extended to royal staff in the entourage, civil and military officials who provided security, as well as key local personalities and business people.

Dinner at Klai Kangwol Palace was usually served buffet style in a courtyard in front of Piam Sook Royal Residence. If it rained, dinner would be served indoors in Sala Roeng, a pavilion. Dinner guests were free to sit wherever they liked, but a separate table for eight was set for Their Majesties and six special guests. Before I could pick up a plate and join the other guests for the buffet, a lady in waiting came to inform me that the king had invited me to join his table. I was to sit on the right of Queen Sirikit.

If my family had known that I was being invited to sit at the same table with the king and queen, they would say I had a lot of good karma. But they would have no idea how frightened I was by it that evening. I followed the other special guests to the table. The king and queen were already seated, the king at one end and the queen at the other. Before being seated, I followed the others by prostrating on the ground before the king and then the queen. Fortunately I knew the appropriate prostration, which was not to open the palms to touch the ground and before moving them up slowly over the head—the palms-opening prostration is reserved for Lord Buddha only. A royal page seated me. Once seated, I found myself still mentally reciting a mantra—my habitual practice to fend off nervousness.

Whoever has been in a personal audience of Queen Sirikit knows that Her Majesty has such exquisite charm and is such a comforting conversation partner, with a beautiful voice and gracious smiles. Although it was the first time I had had a conversation with Queen Sirikit, I felt such comfort that I almost forgot about the butterflies in my stomach.

2

Dinner was served at Their Majesties' table. I still remember to this day that the first course was chicken, baked western style and that we had to use forks and knives. I had studied in America so using forks and knives and western table manners were not alien to me. I thought I would do all right that evening.

Then again, it was hard not to be overwhelmed by the experience. Lo and behold as I was meticulously cutting the tiny pieces of chicken, one jumped from my plate and landed squarely in front of the queen's. It was bad, but it could have been worse. It could have landed *on* Her Majesty's plate!

In any event, as I was in some sort of an altered state—definitely horrified—a scenario was running though my head: perhaps I could dive in the ground underneath the dinner table and never emerge again in this lifetime—just what Phaya Decho in the historical drama 'Phra Ruang' might have done. But then I realized I wasn't Phaya Decho and I couldn't dive in the ground underneath a dinner table, or anything else, for that matter. I froze, at my wit's end. The royal pages who were serving dinner could have come to my rescue but they were too far away. Finally, after what seemed like a lifetime, I decided to rescue myself. I reached my hand out to fetch that piece of chicken back and dropped it on my plate.

All that time, if Queen Sirikit had witnessed anything she did not let out any hint. She continued to speak with others and me at the table as if nothing had happened. Needless to say, my appetite was not so great after the flying chicken incident. All I can remember now about the next course was that it was Thai food. The rest of the meal became just a blur. I moved the food around on the plate to keep an appearance that I was eating.

Although my appetite was not so receptive, my ears were. From listening to the royal couple's conversation at the dinner table, I learned for the first time how concerned they were about the well-being of the Thai people. The king and queen asked in particular about the people they had just visited. Those of us at the table, civil servants, military officials and policemen like me, were asked about our duties and activities. I realized that dinner was probably a good source of intelligence for the royal couple.

At the end of dinner, we all rose and again prostrated on the ground as the couple left the table. The king joined the band on the stage, and the queen moved to another table to chat with a group of people and to enjoy the music.

The Aor. Sor. Band got its name because the band regularly played on Aor. Sor. radio, the king's private station, which was located in Chitralada Garden. The abbreviation Aor. Sor. stands for Amphorn Palace, one of the Chakri throne halls, located in Dusit Royal Palace. All members of the band were amateurs: all had a day job, some in civil service and others in business. The band members, including the king, got together every weekend. They played jazz—the king's favorite—as well as Thai and western contemporary music. The band singers were also amateurs and volunteers. What I had not known before was that there were also *volunteered* singers.

I got that piece of knowledge firsthand when the lady in waiting, MR Benjawan Chakrabandhu, came to deliver the queen's invitation to me to go up the stage and sing. I was not so terrified this time because I happened to have been born into a musical family—both my father and mother played and sang classical Thai songs. I was used to being volunteered and forced to sing in public from childhood and always kept myself in tune. In the bathroom, that is. I accepted the queen's invitation and more than willingly walked up on stage, prostrated before the king, and whispered to Khun Manratana Srikranon behind the piano 'Lao Duang Duean'—my best song.

From that night on, whenever the Aor. Sor. Band played at dinner I was always invited to sing. To keep pace with the invitations, I had to relearn other songs besides 'Lao Duang Duan'. Invitation to dinner at the Klai Kangwol Palace came almost every weekend when the royal couple came to Hua Hin. Also, whenever they wished to have a visit with the subjects in Hua Hin and nearby districts, I was often asked to provide security during their mission. Because I was not directly responsible for security at the time, I had to ask for permission from my superiors for each mission.

Road conditions in Hua Hin were not good in those days. Except for Phetchkasem, which was the main road, all were unpaved dirt. The rugged surface and potholes could make travel very challenging. Land Rovers and Jeeps were the best transportation for the road conditions.

In my first security service, I was in an open jeep, the leading vehicle in the royal procession. The king was driving a Land Rover. Jeeps were official police vehicles in those days. Although still in usable condition, they were anything but new and were in short supply. They had been donated by an American agency USOM (United States Operations Mission) to police units operating in remote areas. The procession was moving rather slowly on the potholed roads. The jeep leading the motorcade, in which I was riding, had a near accident and almost flipped over. Fortunately no one was hurt. Later the king purchased several jeeps for Naresuan Camp's official use.

Admittedly, being occupied with security, I found it hard to pay full attention to all the details of the king and queen's activities. But like most others, I could not help but notice that Their Majesties were always generous with their time and in allowing the people to have opportunities to interact intimately with them. The people in Hua Hin and nearby districts were mainly farmers. They knew that the king and queen would pass where security officers were waiting, and would therefore come with fruits and vegetables from their farms to offer to their beloved monarchs. The king was usually driving and would stop at every point where the villagers were waiting. My job as a security police officer in the motorcade was to radio the king ahead of each waiting point. The security car would usually stay a bit further ahead and keep a distance, while other security police got out of the car to provide security to the royal couple.

In fact, providing security for Their Majesties during their rural mission was more like facilitating the audience for the local subjects who were so excited and eager to meet their king and queen. Also, there were a lot of gifts to carry that were presented to by the populations to the king and queen from each visit. The gifts were mostly fruits and vegetables. Because there were so many, it wasn't possible for Their Majesties to take all back to the royal residence. A portion was usually taken back to the royal kitchen and the rest usually went to the needy, students and patients in local schools and hospitals.

During the royal visits, security officers like me had to have a quick eye and a quick mouth. We divided the job to watch the left or the right side of the road. Whenever any of us spotted anyone waiting for the king and queen on the roadside, we would immediately radio all cars in the procession. Other than people, there were also potholes and animals crossing the road to watch out for.

We were particularly mindful with the animals, because it was a common knowledge that the king and queen were both fond of animals. It was Their Majesties' policy that the procession would always give way to the villagers' pets or occasionally wild animals to finish their journey across the road before the procession could continue. So it is fair to say that the royal missions were usually anything but speedy, and there were many, many stops along the way. I remember in the following year we were down south in Narathiwat. Shortly after the procession left Thaksin Palace—near the Tan Yong mountain range—Their Majesties' car stopped for a pair of cobras to cross the road.

Not long after I began providing my security service during royal visits in the Hua Hin district and nearby area, I began to accompany the royal couple to other provinces as well. Royal missions to remote provinces sometimes began with official ceremonies, but usually ended with a visit with the local populations. If there were military or police units operating in the area (usually in the battlefields in those days), they would get a royal visit as well.

Royal missions also involved several forms of transportation. Usually it was a Royal Thai Air Force aircraft from the palace, then by helicopter to the airport nearest possible to the destination, and finally by car to the final destination if the place of visit was not accessible by helicopter. At the outset of my service to Their Majesties, I had no idea that it would be taking all kinds of transportation and that 13 years later I will have racked up almost as many flying miles as an average pilot and frequent-flying passenger.

On 16 December 1968, I accompanied Their Majesties to the opening ceremony for the Thailand-Laos high voltage electricity transmission, which took place in a pavilion on a raft in the Mekong River, on the invisible border of Thailand (Nong Khai) and Laos (Vientiane). It was a significant event because it was one of the rare occasions when the monarchs of both countries were present, King Bhumibol of Thailand and King Sawang Wattana of Prathet Lao.

That was the first that I accompanied Their Majesties to such an event and the only time to Laos border. Their Majesties left Don Muang Airport for Nong Khai Airport and then traveled by car to the awaiting royal boat that the water police had prepared. Two police officers were designated to provide security on that royal mission, myself and Pol. Col. Pranetr Ridhipachai who was then the commander of the BPP PARU, also known as Naresuan Camp. (Pol. Col. Pranetr became a police general and a deputy-general to the Royal Thai Police Department at the end of his career in the civil service.) Pol. Col. Pranetr and I were not only proud but also very excited that we had a chance to work in Isan, a strategic area rife with communist insurgencies.

I recall that we were standing on the either side of the royal boat, each holding an M-16 in the ready position. I don't remember exactly now who was on the right and who was on the left, but what I certainly remember is that shortly after we assumed our bodyguard standing position, we received a royal instruction to do away with our menacing way and adopt a more friendly outlook. We were told that the king and the queen wished to have a welcoming and respectful meeting with the neighboring Laotian monarch.

I learned to grasp diplomacy through observing the royal couple's interactions with their Laotian counterparts. Because I was born in Isan and my father was actually from Nong Khai, I always had a sense of special affinity with the Lao people who, in my view, were our brothers and sisters. The Lao people shared similar language, culture and customs with the people of Isan and northern Thailand. Given my personal empathy, I could not help but feel so excited and pleased to see such close, warm, and genial relations between the two monarchs.

3

Not long after I had begun providing security for the royal couple, my duty changed. I was assigned to a duty station in Hua Hin, Prachuab Khiri Khan for two years, from 1967 to 1968.

As I mentioned, my official position was with Special Branch, which was then merely a command unit, not the headquarters like it is today. My teaching assignment to the Border Patrol Police was an additional duty. I was only called to teach history and political theories during training. This changed in 1967 when the Communist Suppression Operation Command (CSOC)—initiated a mobile training project for civilians in the sensitive areas. The purpose was to train armed self-protection skills to villagers in the sensitive areas. I was asked to head the training team, and accepted.

An Army rehab center, located on Phetchkasem Road about 6 to 7 kilometers from the center of Hua Hin district in Suan Son Patiphat was converted to a People's Assistance Teams Training Center. Sakon Nakhon province was our first training site. The first class of selected volunteers were all men, and women joined in the following classes as we expanded to other provinces, including Nakhon Phanom, Ubon Ratchathani and Prachuab Khiri Khan.

At the time the political situation was volatile in several provinces in Isan, the north and in certain parts of the south. There were frequent clashes between the communist insurgents and the authorities, causing injuries and loss of life on both sides. The villagers were undoubtedly afraid for their lives, particularly those in areas where there was constant fighting. They did not have the luxury to choose to side with either the insurgents or the authorities, but had instead to yield to whoever had more power and more powerful weapons at any given time.

In my new duty I had more opportunities to work with the police paratroops and consequently more chances to accompany the king and queen on their missions to a number of sensitive areas, including those with ongoing fierce fighting. It was evident that the royal couple thought little of their own safety and put their priorities on the well-being of their subjects. That made it all the more worrying for us. Coordination among civilian, police and army officials needed to be stepped up for tighter security to the king and queen during some very difficult and dangerous missions. Initially, as one of the security officers, I did not realize the extent of difficulties in providing royal security in such circumstances. I began to fully appreciate the demands of the job only after I began working full-time in a permanent position in palace security.

Prachuab Khiri Khan was already home of People's Assistance Teams training centers of both the police and the military. The army had an infantry center in Pran Buri and the police force had the Naresuan Camp right across from Klai Kangwol Palace in Hua Hin. The training center, also in Hua Hin, was added to the list, making Prachuab Khiri Khan a province with a complete set of army, police and civilian training centers.

Because the troops, and sometimes civilians, were carrying out difficult and often dangerous duties, the royal couple regularly visited them in the training camps as well as in their stations. Their visits were a real morale boost for all involved. Many troops, especially those with border patrol duties, were sent to different parts in the country. Some lost their lives while on duty. Most of those killed were sent back to Hua Hin, which was considered the 'home' of the BPP PARU, for royally sponsored cremation.

The war with the communist insurgents was indeed a strange war. Communism was a foreign ideology. It was imported to Thailand by foreigners who disseminated this ideology behind the scene through a group of

Thais. Yet, they were successful in causing serious and violent conflicts among the Thai people, who took up arms to kill one another.

It is this kind of war that was strange to me because on the surface it looked like a Thai civil war, but in fact there were the 'big brothers' behind the scene, the United States behind the Thai government and China and the Soviet Union behind the communists. The communists were able to expand the areas of conflicts to several provinces. The curious thing was the apathy of most Thais outside the areas of insurgencies. They didn't seem to care about what was going on between the government and the communist insurgents. It was not uncommon to find people enjoying festive activities while soldiers were laying holding their guns in the battle just in the next town.

There was no clear line of engagement and there were no clear enemies and allies in that war. The only clarity was the loss of lives on both sides—all of them Thai. On the one side, there were the military and police and later civil servants and civilian volunteers who joined the force. On the other side, it was the communists, known as the communist insurgents. Armed communist insurgencies began around 1961. When I began serving King Bhumibol and Queen Sirikit in 1967, the situation had worsened considerably, but royal visits continued as before without regard to whether the destination was on the front line.

The king and queen visited both the authorities and the villagers in each area. They were particularly concerned about the safety of those involved in the fighting against the insurgents, because there were always losses and injuries. They always asked about the state of the equipment available for the troops. In the beginning of the crisis, it was evident that the tools and equipment for the military and police were quite limited, insufficient for their needs. Most weaponry was old and outdated. Although the American soldiers were using the small automatic AR-15 (which later became known as M-16) in the Vietnam War, the Thai soldiers had very few of those at hand.

I can't recall which American army officer or which unit provided an M-16 to the king, but I remember that the king was very much interested in the workings of that type of weapon. His Majesty would disassemble the M-16 to study the parts and the mechanics of it. In no time, he was able to assemble the parts back together and repair broken M-16s. During the many visits to the front line, upon learning that some weapons were not functioning and parts were not available for repair, the king would take all the M-16s that were out of order back to repair. The good parts of many broken M-16s were put back together with his own hands and the soldiers and police got some of their M-16s back in good order.

Once I took the good guns back to the policemen in Pitsanulok. Just before we could land, the helicopter on a police base on the outskirt of Nakhon Thai district, we were hit from the ground. It was the first time I was shot while on duty for His Majesty. One of our technicians got a hit in the face, but we were able to get away from the firing shots and landed on a base inside the district instead.

Police helicopters were merely transport vehicles and were not equipped with weapons other than the lone automatic attached on the side. When we encountered enemy firing from the ground, there was nothing we could do but fire back with the side automatic and leave the scene as soon as possible. Upon learning about the incident, the king asked MR Debharidh Devakul, who was an engineer, to mount an automatic on the helicopter where the pilot could fire at the front as well. The newly installed automatic was put to several tests. We test-fired in the sea in Cha-am and in the firing range in Prachuab Khiri Khan. The tests came out satisfactory.

Shooting became another interest of the king and the queen and they both were good shots. On their numerous visits to the police and military camps, the couple could be found in the shooting range, observing or joining the practice. The children were also taught to shoot different types of guns. On one evening, His Majesty was at the firing range in Naresuan Camp. After having fired a round from the M-16, I ran to target to check the results and was not surprised to see all shots inside black circle on the target (as I knew by then that HM was a very good shot). I ran back to HM and, after a quick salute, said proudly and loudly, 'All shots dead on target, sir.'

The king asked, 'How many shots?' I didn't count the number but I knew that there were twenty in each magazine of an M-16, so I responded right away, 'Twenty, sir.' The king looked at the gun in his hand and turned it back and forth a few times and then looked up at me and smiled and then said, 'This is incredible. I put in eighteen but it could actually fire twenty.' From then on I became extremely precise with words. If I didn't know, I'd say I didn't know and quit relying on just pure wit.

The king also had a keen interest in ham radio. A smallest portable short-wave receiver in those days was at least a foot long, taking at least eleven large flashlight batteries. Weighing as much as a rifle, it was difficult to carry. But for police and soldiers, it was worthwhile. The radio range was rather short. Although I was once able to radio Chiang Rai from Phetchaburi, it was probably a fluke. Long-range radio would require even larger and heavier equipment.

The king enjoyed staying in touch with many (mostly state) radio stations. He was presented with many sets of small receivers, one of which was said to be waterproof. A witness related to me later that upon hearing the claim, the king asked for a big bowl of water and proceeded to put the so-called waterproof set in it. It so happened that it was really waterproof as claimed. That special radio receiver got itself a royal nickname 'The Water Machine'. The Water Machine eventually became my very own radio set while I was serving the king until I retired from palace security duty.

4

The Royal Thai Police Department gave the king a personal call ID frequency 'Kor Sor 9', which became something of a sacred word in the ham radio community.

His Majesty told a story about an apparently bored or depressive rank and file provincial policeman who made a career out of lamenting on air about his life of hard luck. Feeling sorry for the man, one day the king sent the loquacious policeman a Wor 16 (meaning a request to test signal) and identified himself as Kor Sor 9. Upon receiving the call, the policeman—probably thinking his ham radio fellow was joking with him—pleaded the caller to stop such an unbecoming trick and stop violating a person 'in a high place'. It took several affirmations by the king for the lucky policeman to realize that it was in fact the very person 'in a high place' himself who called.

The wonder of technology and mechanics had captured King Bhumibol's interest since childhood. He built his own first set of radio receiver while studying in a university in Switzerland. His Majesty found pleasure in putting together and fixing parts of radio receivers. But, like other hobbies, assembling and fixing the radio sets gradually lost its status as a leisure activity and became yet another routine task with practical purposes for others.

His Majesty's earnest interest in using radio to communicate with government offices motivated officials as well as civilians to pay more attention to this technology in their fields. There is no doubt that the king was a pioneer in radio communication in Thailand. In fact, he was often among the first to embrace new technologies, from computers to pagers to cellular phones to the Internet.

❖

In every cool season (Thai winter usually begins in late November and ends in February), the royal household moved to Bhubing Palace in the northern city of Chiang Mai.

Initially, like everyone else, I thought that the annual move was nothing more than a winter vacation for the royal family. But I came to see that the move was more like a change of base of operation for the household. The king, the queen and the royal children continued to carry out their normal duties and would fly down to Bangkok if the duties called for it. If Klai Kangwol Palace was the base of field operation for the lower central and upper southern regions, Bhubing Palace was the base of field operation in the north.

Situated on the mountain top twenty-four kilometers from the base of Doi Suthep, Bhubing is the second oldest royal palace of the Chakri Dynasty after Klai Kangwol in Hua Hin. All of the structures in Bhubing were built in Thai style. There were residences for the royal members, guests, the household and palace security staff.

When I first came to Bhubing, I was not yet part of the palace security force, so I had to stay in a hotel in Chiang Mai and would go up to Bhubing only when summoned. By Thai standards it was usually quite cold on top of Doi Suthep in December, so I had to pack the winter clothing I would for a trip to a foreign country with a cold climate.

The king and queen usually spent the afternoons visiting people in the communities. I was still in my thirties at the time and thinking that I'd done enough field activities that accompanying Their Majesties to remote hill tribe villages accessible by only 4-wheel drive vehicle and on foot would be no problem. How wrong I was. My legs were in pain for days after the first trip that I had to walk up and down hill after hill to a hill tribe village. Their Majesties, on the other hand, were quite, a lot fitter than yours truly and had no complaints. This, I figured, could probably be explained by the fact that the royal couple jogged every evening. The children sometimes joined them. Queen Sirikit usually had an additional aerobic exercise session after each jogging session.

The realization that I wasn't quite so fit as I thought I was effectively motivated me to begin my own exercise regimen that I keep up with regularly today.

❖

There was a particular reason in the king's interest in the Thai hill tribe minorities in the north, who are known as *chao khao,* or the people who live on mountains. Growing opium was the main source of livelihood for several hill tribes, thanks to the climate in Thailand's mountainous north, which was so good for growing for this crop. This was, of course, against the law and government policy aimed to suppress and eradicate opium production and punish growers and traffickers. The king realized that stopping opium production was easier said than done for the hill tribe people, for whom growing opium had been a way of life for generations. Moreover, the people of the mountains were practically caught in the debt trap of the middlemen. They took out goods on credit from the village shopkeepers, the middlemen, and paid for them in opium. The goods–opium exchange rates were not exactly in the villagers' favor. At the end of the year, the opium growers were no more than a few thousand baht richer and not in a good bargaining position. It would be hard to find buyers directly and the risks of getting arrested by police were too great for villagers without the right connections.

Convincing the villagers to abandon opium for other cash crops was by no means an easy task. It required a clear government policy direction and serious and sustained efforts in implementing the policy. Frequent changes of government generally does not lend itself to continuity in policy implementation, especially when a new government came in by coup d'etat as was so often the case throughout the decades of Thailand's military dictatorships. In this kind of political environment, the much revered monarchy presented, arguably, the most stable and the best placed institution to carry out such a difficult and important task—to change the thinking of the people and the way they had lived for generations.

I witnessed for the first time in 1967 how the king and queen worked with such passion for the cause of the hill tribe people. Their Majesties worked hard to understand the way of the people of the mountains. Gently and patiently, they appealed to the people the benefits of abandoning opium for alternative crops. I had no idea at the time that this work would turn to be a decades-long mission.

Helicopters were the best way to reach very remote hill tribe villages in those days. The Royal Thai Air Force managed to build a small airstrip near the palace for the royal family. In the surrounding areas of the Bhubing Palace in the Suthep-Pui mountains were a number of Hmong villages where the king and queen were regular guests.

Usually around 4.30 p.m. the car would wait for the royal couple at the front gate of Bhubing and the Special Branch Police and the highway police would lead the motorcade and the provincial police follow it. In cases of a royal mission to a remote area that usually fell under the jurisdiction of the border patrol police, the BPP would lead the royal motorcade because they were more familiar with the terrain.

Also, in unofficial missions like this, the king and queen and occasionally the royal children, would dress casually or in camouflage, suitable for mountain hiking. The roads on the mountains, if there were any, would be dirt roads built by the Forestry Department. The only sensible vehicles were 4-wheel drive Jeeps, Land Rovers and Range Rovers.

As I mentioned, the king loved to drive his own car. His Majesty was a very safe and focused driver—appropriately changing gears and keeping control of the driving speed, always in touch with the road conditions. But, strangely enough, I found myself often mentally strained in His Majesty's car and much more relaxed in other cars. In all fairness, it couldn't really blame the king's careful and conscientious driving for my stress. What I probably should put the blame on was my self-imposed—and needless—eagerness to mentally help the king drive from the back seat. Not that the king needed any help.

Besides their guns, the royal security police also had to carry were logs to wedge the wheels in, literally, the many uphill struggles when the cars needed a low-tech push uphill. The heavy-duty job was to clear the road obstacles.

5

O ne of the things that impressed me during the years prior to
my full-time service for His Majesty in 1970 was the highly
commendable Border Patrol Police. Throughout the years I taught
the history and political theories classes to the BPP, I was heartened
by the dedication and courage of the men in the BPP forces. This was
especially true with those in the Police Aerial Reinforcement Unit
(PARU). My classes followed my students even to the front line, where
I witnessed many of them sacrificing their lives in the fight against
the communists. So inspired, I decided to take a parachuting class in
Naresuan Camp.

Parachuting was nothing new to me—as a spectator, that is. Certainly, having had many paratroopers as students, I had seen a number
of them jumping off the plane, falling feet first to the ground without
getting shortened to death. What's more, I was on the Thai-American
Friendship Foundation fundraising committee and part of a number of
parachute shows we organized across Thailand to raise funds to build
schools. Sometimes I had to get on the plane with the parachutists. My
attitude about parachuting at the time was not particularly enthusiastic.
Every time I saw people jumping off the plane in droves—albeit with
proper equipment—into the air for the sole purpose of risking their lives
to land on the ground, I could not help thinking that they did not seem
altogether mentally sound. Let's face it, normal and mentally healthy
people would figure out that the airplane would have to land at one
point, making jumping off it quite unnecessary.

In any event, over the years I had developed a strong bond with my
paratrooper students. I taught them that the victory of communism in

20

Thailand would mean the destruction of the pillars of our society—our nation, our religion and our king. Therefore, fighting communism was an honorable duty. If it meant sacrificing our lives, it would be for the good of the nation. Hearing myself preaching this to my students over time, I realized that it was only fitting that I, as their teacher, exhibited the courage I tried to inspire in them. If they could jump off the plane, then I should have the courage to jump off the plane as well.

My friends who heard about my taking a parachuting class started to gossip: 'Vasit enjoyed brainwashing his students so much that he brainwashed himself, too,' they would say. Because I had the rank of a police lieutenant colonel and a position as a teacher, I was considered a special student. Two teachers were assigned to me: the late Khru Somjit Dhanyachoto, who was responsible for training me on the ground (he held the rank of a police lieutenant colonel before passing on), and Khru Somnuek Krisanasuwan, who gave me training in the air (he retired with a rank of a police colonel).

I will not go into details of the difficulties of my parachuting training. But I do say that I am forever indebted to both teachers. They helped me build my self-confidence until eventually I was able to make a plunge like others and learn to solve problems without panic when the parachute malfunctioned.

Their patience for me was also admirable. Having a full-time job meant that I could train only during my spare time, so my practice was sporadic. According to Khru Somjit, I spent the longest time on ground practice in the history of the school. It took me two years before I could start air training.

The regular duty that consumed most of my time was training civilian volunteers to work in various operation units to protect villagers in combat. The training camp in Suan Son Patiphat in Hua Hin was located on the west side of Phetchkasem Road, amidst terrain well suited for combat simulation—a large forest on unpopulated foothills. Sometimes real bullets were used in the training. Camp personnel and trainers had accommodation in the camp area. Staying away from home was pretty much my way of life. Throughout my service in the police force, I lived more or less like a nomad, moving from one place to the next to wherever the duty called. This time my temporary home was a small bungalow in Suan Son Patiphat.

By that time I had had some experience in combat training. Like most other boys, I had basic military training in secondary school. As an adult, I had some guerilla fighting experience during my time in the Seri Thai movement at the end of World War II, and professional police training in the New York City Police Academy and the FBI National Academy. The parachute police school in Naresuan Camp would be the first and only Thai police institution in which I would train. A group of teachers from the parachute police school made up part of the training team at the camp. They taught weapon handling and strategic fighting in combat. I certainly learned a lot from them about combat operations.

As the palace got news that I was teaching paramilitary forces in the training camp, Queen Sirikit paid a visit. By that time, there were already some young women joining in this paramilitary force; some were still teenagers. Most of these young women, mostly from Isan, had finished secondary school and had received training nursing from the Ministry of Public Health. After having finished the training course from the camp, these young women returned to their home villages in the northeast. During several years thereafter I continued to carry out the queen's patronage to them, delivering to them much-needed goods.

In December 1967, the CSOC changed the name of the People's Assistance Teams Training Center to the Training Center for the Village Defense Teams. All the personnel, including teachers and trainers, were officially transferred to this new center, although they didn't have to move physically. The governor of Prachuab Khiri Khan, Khun Prayad Samarnmitra, was appointed its director. (Khun Prayad was later killed in an ambush in Chiang Rai). I was appointed deputy director of the training division and had to move from my old office in Suan Son Patiphat to a new building in Muang district in Prachuab Khiri Khan. I remained there until early 1969, when the CSOC relieved me of my duty.

However, my karma with training and security did not end there. Before the end of 1968, a position in the palace police force would become vacant because a senior officer was about to retire. I received an inquiry from the palace, whether I would consider taking the position, if it became vacant. My response was that I would if it were His Majesty's wish.

Before beginning to serve His Majesty fulltime, I felt that I needed more professional experience. By that time, I had served for a number of years in Special Branch and had worked extensively with the border patrol police. What I lacked was experience as a provincial police officer. Since my time as chief of Chiang Rai Special Branch field office several years before, I had known Pol. Maj-Gen. Thep Supasamit who was then the commander of Provincial Police Region 5 in Lampang (He later became assistant secretary-general of the Royal Thai Police Department and retired as a police lieutenant-general). I had much affection for Pol. Maj-Gen. Thep and respected him like my big brother. I actually called him *Phi* (Big Brother) Thep. I contacted him and told him that I wished to apply for a position in Region 5.

Quite naively, I assumed that my official transfer would be simple: Pol. Maj-Gen. Thep, the commander, submitted a request for me to transfer to his jurisdiction and it would be readily approved. As it turned out, the Provincial Police Headquarters found Pol. Maj-Gen. Thep's request for my transfer 'a little problematic' (which meant the request was denied). However, Phi Thep told me that there was another way: he could request instead for my transfer to the Joint Civilian-Police-Military Intelligence Center of Region 5, which was one of the intelligence units established by the CSOC. Throughout the country, there was one center in each regional police jurisdiction. Each joint information center was an intelligence unit for each district and was usually staffed by personnel 'on loan' from various military forces, the Royal Thai Police Department and government offices. The center for Region 5 was located in Chiang Mai. There was no hesitation on my part to move to a new temporary home: Chiang Mai's Suriwong Hotel.

Work at the joint information center was mainly paperwork, specifically, intelligence analysis. After a while I realized that the job wasn't exactly what I had in mind and that I wasn't going to be very useful in my security work for the king. I consulted Pol. Maj-Gen. Thep and told him frankly that I needed field experience. My Big Brother obliged. Now I was stationed in the Third Army Forward Headquarters as liaison police officer. I got what I asked for; situated in Chiang Klang (then)

23

subdistrict in Nan province. The Third Army was a front region that could really offer me a real field experience—a battlefield experience.

Sharing its eastern border with Laos, Nan was among the provinces hardest hit by communist insurgency. Despite underdeveloped road and transportation systems between Thailand and Laos in that region, the geographical proximity made it possible for the Lao comrades to send assistant troops to help their Thai counterparts and for the Thai comrades to escape from the Thai authorities to hide inside the Lao border.

As a liaison police officer, I had no direct responsibilities to fight communist insurgents but I did have opportunities to see up close anti-insurgency operations by police, military and civilian forces. This experience provided me helpful insights into future situations.

Despite my having moved far away, occasionally I was called to serve the king and queen during their stay at Bhubing Palace in Chiang Mai. I continued to send intelligence briefings to His Majesty the King on a regular basis. Two years earlier I had become a Special Branch superintendent, and because of this I had to travel back to Bangkok at least once a month to submit my living expenses of the month to the finance division and to collect next month's allowance. Another and no less important reason for the monthly trip to Bangkok was to submit a monthly report to my superior as input for meetings with foreign counterparts.

Once, while I was in Bangkok, the commissioner of the Central Investigation Bureau (CIB), Pol. Lt-Gen. Pojna Phekanantna was invited to speak about CIB activities at the Police Detective Training School. But because the commander was tied up with another engagement, I was asked to speak in his place.

I was quite familiar with the Police Detective Training School because I had taught many classes there at one time. During my return to speak this time, I was struck by the question from several police cadets as to whether they would receive additional pay for having completed the course.

I still had that question in my mind, when, some time later, the head of the class asked me to write an article for the class's graduation book. I gave him a brief article, entitled 'What is Police Detective Training School?' I had no idea that that little article would offend some readers so much that the Royal Thai Police Department would investigate me.

6

The article 'What is Police Detective Training School?' published in the Class 18 graduation book had an element of satire—a writing style I was good at. It began something like this: 'The Police Detective Training School was another good place to take naps, but it was no ordinary napping place because if one manages to nap through the end of the course, one will be granted a certificate by the good Royal Thai Police Department.'

The satirical introduction was intended to grab the attention of the readers (i.e. my own students). The rest of the article would address the main point, which was the privilege and responsibility that come with an opportunity to be educated at a prestigious institution. I wanted to both remind the graduates that the purpose of their education was to learn and equip them with the necessary skills and knowledge to do their job effectively and professionally—not to get additional payment or any other personal benefits. I also wrote that policemen who advance in their career through fate without help of knowledge and skills are no different from mannequins in police uniforms.

These words evidently hit a raw nerve in certain people. One, I later found out, who seemed the hardest hit was the director of the Police Detective Training School himself, the late Pol. Maj-Gen. Prasert Thanadpojanamatya. Pol. Maj-Gen. Prasert filed a complaint with the Royal Thai Police Department, accusing me of tarnishing the reputation of the Police Detective Training School, urging that I be punished.

The Royal Thai Police Department dutifully appointed an investigation committee, whose chair was no other than the late Pol. Lt-Gen. Jamras Mandhuganond, who was then deputy director-general of the

Royal Thai Police Department and a former CIB commissioner. So, in effect, Pol. Lt-Gen. Jamras was my boss and not just any boss, but the one who often asked me to temporarily leave the jungle to write reports for him in English.

I wrote my own testimony, in which I said I had had no intention of slandering the school and that the article had been published in a graduation book circulated only internally. My writing was a message from a teacher to former students, though my style of writing may have been a bit unconventional. In my defense, I quoted three police officers who testified that the article was beneficial rather than damaging to the school.

These witnesses were Pol. Lt-Gen. Pojna Phekanantna, the CIB commander (who asked me to give the talk in his place in the first place), Pol. Maj-Gen. Thep Supasamit, commander of Provincial Police Region 5 and my boss at the time, and Pol. Col. Pranetr, the BPP PARU superintendent. What I omitted from the testimony to the committee was the fact that my three witnesses were actually in stitches with laughter while reading my article.

As it turned out, the investigation committee did not call any of the three but instead several of the plaintiff's witnesses, some of whom were students of the graduating class for which I wrote the article. The committee finally concluded the investigation and recommended a disciplinary action for my 'inappropriate conduct'. The police department decided to give me a light sentence, which was to put me on probation.

In a practical sense, being put on probation is indeed a light sentence, in that it is like being told: 'We are not going to punish you this time but don't ever do the same thing again, or else.' However, for anyone in the police force, being put on probation means a lot; as a disciplinary action, it leaves an ugly, permanent mark in your personnel file (unless one manages to get it expunged). In my case, the probation was recorded and without any details other than that I 'behaved inappropriately'.

Because I felt that I had behaved appropriately and did not want to have it recorded otherwise in my file, I filed an appeal with the police department under the Ministry of Interior. And because the Ministry of Interior rejected my appeal, I exercised my right to file my appeal directly with the prime minister.

During this time, the Royal Aide-de-Camp Department sent a request for my appointment as a royal court security police officer to the police department. The request was a secret. To this day, I still don't understand why such a request had to be made in secret (even to the person concerned) because once the news has reached the second or third ear, it is no longer a secret. I learned about it during a trip back to Bangkok to submit my monthly expense and receive the next month's allowance. I was at the time based in the Third Army Forward Headquarters in Chiang Klang subdistrict, Nan.

As it turned out, I knew more than I was supposed to. Without my knowledge, the police department objected to the request of the palace, reasoning that I was a valuable asset to the Royal Thai Police Department with many very important duties, such as serving in the security committee in SEATO (Southeast Asia Treaty Organization) and being the editor of *Tamruad* (*Police*) magazine. In the response of the police department, it was not mentioned that although I carried out a number of important duties I was given permission to work for the CSOC headquarters. Neither did the response state that the valuable officer in question has just been investigated and disciplined for 'inappropriate conduct'.

Many years later I learned that in addition to the objection to the request for my appointment, the police department actually recommended a first police lieutenant for the appointment in my place.

It didn't take long for me to come to a conclusion that there must be someone who really did not want me in court security—for whatever reason. But what worried me was realizing if that certain someone could say no to the palace, they must be very powerful indeed. If that certain someone were displeased at the possibility of my appointment, this could spell trouble for my work and would inevitably affect His Majesty the King if I were to be appointed.

I thought about the matter for several days and finally decided to write a letter to the king. The letter was sent from the jungle in Chiang Klang to someone I could trust to personally hand to His Majesty. In the letter I told His Majesty that I would like to avoid causing any conflict between His Majesty and those who did not want me as a royal court security police officer. I did not have any particular ambition to be in the royal court police or in the inner circle of the royal palace. I was perfectly willing to take another position that would allow me to serve His Majesty, although not as closely.

❖

I continued to work as a liaison police officer in Chiang Klang. In this job I had rare opportunities to see up close counterinsurgency operations by the military, especially the army. After a short while, I became aware of a worrying fact: if this battle were to become war it would be a war of only a group of soldiers, the police, and a small population in the north. There was no dispute that the government and the army were, considering the sizable budget and weaponry, firmly behind the Third Army. However, the understanding of the real situation was sorely lacking, which in turn undermined the effectiveness of the counterinsurgency efforts.

I say this because, though communist insurgencies were being fought fiercely and people were losing their lives in the hot zones, life in the cities—even in Nan, Chiang Rai and other provinces—was going on as if nothing were happening. People continued having fun and spending conspicuously on entertainment. What was particularly bad for the morale of the troops were the images of the commanders busily entertaining themselves. Such images were there in the newspapers for all, including troops on the front line, to see.

Amidst fierce fighting against the communist insurgency, I visited a paratroop operation unit on an isolated mountaintop at the Thai-Lao border. The geography of this paratroop base was rather precarious—quite well exposed to the enemy's attack. I was dropped off by a helicopter, which needed a safer place for landing. I would have to radio the pilot to return to pick me up. The members of the unit were all my former students. Once I got off the helicopter, the head of the unit swiftly took me behind cover because the chance of getting hit by snipers increased with every minute of exposure.

The first word out of the mouth of the unit head, a police sergeant, was, 'So good of you to come visit us, Ajarn.' He wanted me to talk to his men. The problem was the police troopers under his command were refusing to do their patrol duty.

Only those who have performed it can appreciate the stress of patrol duty on the battlefront. A strong and stable base of an operation unit gives a sense of safety and a level of comfort for the troops, but an immobile base is highly vulnerable. The longer a base is immobile, the less chance there is of knowing the movements of the enemy. The enemy also has an advantage to move more freely.

It is therefore imperative that the troopers do their patrol duty, which is not different from going out to ask for a fight with the enemy. You need to know where the enemy is and to assess their capacity. But patrolling is a high risk in itself. The first step the troopers take out of their base, they are exposed to ambush, landmines and other dangers. Going on a patrol is therefore not only a test of the troopers' knowledge of weapons and combat strategy, but it is also a test of the patrollers' mettle.

The problem was obvious. Not going out on patrol meant that the unit was a sitting duck. The enemy had the advantage to attack, which had happened with other battlefronts. Once it became known that a BPP PARU fell, the morale of the police, military and paramilitary troopers would certainly be affected.

When I asked the sergeant's men why they didn't want to patrol, a police corporal unfolded a newspaper. On the front page was a picture of the director-general of the Royal Thai Police Department (Pol. Gen. Prasert Rujirawongse) in his official white uniform dancing with a lady. The police corporal said as he and his mates were risking their lives fighting the insurgents in the battle, the commander was enjoying his time on the dance floor. 'Does this mean he doesn't care if we live or die? What are we fighting for?' he asked.

I spent about two hours explaining to my former students the peculiarity of fighting against communism. In this war the enemy didn't come charging in waving his flag, as you would expect in a traditional warfare. Instead, the enemy gradually expanded the battleground by infiltrating little by little and pitting Thais against each other. This is done in such a quiet and ingenious way that the general Thai population was not aware of the real danger. Life outside the battlefield continued as normal. In this kind of situation—I tried to put a nice spin on what was not very defensible—the commander needed to go along with the rhythm of life outside. I pointed out to the men the fact that the newspaper had reported the party in which the director-general of the police department attended was a fundraising event, and in that kind of situation it was not unusual that there might be dancing. It could even be said that he was doing his job—one that was different from that of the foot soldiers. Then I explained to them the importance of doing their job, patrol duty. Once they settled down and seemed to have understood the point, we went on a patrol.

Upon returning from that trip, I became even more convinced that the top-level government and military executives really had little understanding of the real magnitude of the situation and dangerously underestimated the capability of the communist insurgents. They were still indulging in personal pleasures. In my view, what the country had to do to overcome the communists was to unite and mobilize all its resources. Awareness campaign was sorely needed. The first group of people to start with was government leaders and commanders of the troops.

7

L ife at the Third Army Forward Headquarters in Chiang Klang, Nan was lonely, especially for a liaison police officer like me who didn't have any direct involvement in the battleground fighting.

My superior then was Third Army Forward Commander Gen. Prasarn Raengkla, who was also the chief of staff of the Third Army. I had two colleagues, a soldier and a police officer, Col. Sa-ngat Charn-wathitanont the chief of staff of the Third Army Forward Headquarters and Pol. Lt-Col. Pimol Jaraksa, another liaison officer from Dara Rasmee Camp. Both were my senior in terms of age and school class. The latter I had known for a long time.

I had a lot of time on my hand as a liaison officer, so I took the time advantage to study the army operations. I reviewed the documents at headquarters and made several observation trips to the army and police bases in the area. From the desk review and field observation, it wasn't difficult to see that neither the police troops and soldiers on the front line got much attention from their superiors in Bangkok. And all the troops were fighting a personal war within.

I would never forget the dark and quiet in the night there. The longer I stayed, the more sympathy and respect I had for all the soldiers. If it weren't for their determination and courage to fight the enemy, I am not sure if we, as a country, would have made it through those difficult times.

A young American first lieutenant served at the time as an advisor to the Third Army Forward Headquarters. I learned a lot from this hard-working young man, including how to disassemble an artillery piece and reassemble it on a helicopter. This technique helped increase efficiency of the artillery soldiers in the Third Army Forward Headquarters and became used widely there.

During that time I was assigned to carry another duty, which was to give lectures on history and political theories to hill tribe volunteers and Lao soldiers. I was glad to find out that my Isan mother tongue, the northeastern Thai dialect so similar to Lao language, was hugely useful in teaching my Lao students.

In this assignment I had a wonderful opportunity to travel across many mountains in the north to many hill tribe communities and to Laos, where I met many young people who would later become leaders in the country. One of these was Col. Witoon Ya-sawasdi, who was then a commander of the unconventional forces in Laos.

Once, during a helicopter flight from Chiang Mai and Chiang Klang, Nan, we encountered a big rainstorm. The pilots increased the altitude to about 8,000 feet to get above the storm. About an hour later, we were in Nan but the storm was still in force. The pilots tried to dive through the thick clouds but visibility was bad and the ground was nowhere in sight. Fearing that we would hit a cliff, the pilots decided to take us up above clouds again. The problem was—as we would find out later—that the pilots forgot to increase the rotation speed of the engine before taking the aircraft to higher altitude. So, instead of shooting through the clouds, we suffered an engine failure and the helicopter went on a free fall. All the pilots could do was to keep it in flight.

It was not until the helicopter fell down to about 2,000 feet and the ground came in sight that the pilots were able to gain control by increasing the rotation speed and pulling ahead at a speed over 120 Knots. We managed to land safely at the Chiang Klang Airport and I was able to arrive at my meeting on time.

The pilots that day were Pol. Cap. Pisit Nantapaet and Police First Lt. Supoj Siripool. I had my whole life flashing over my eye. I'm certain that I wasn't alone in thinking that we were all going to die in a crash, judging from the sound of everyone praying for dear life. Khun Pisit told me after the incident that he thought we were as good as dead during the freefall.

My last act before the imagined impending death was to hold on to the one Buddha amulet I had hanging on my neck, calling frantically upon the five divinities I always prayed to: Buddha, Dharma, Sangha, HM the King and HM the Queen. The amulet that I was holding onto dearly was given to me by HM the King one evening after dinner at Klai Kangwol Palace. This amulet—Somdej Chitralada, Might of the Nation—was made by King Bhumibol himself. Usually the amulet was given on request but sometimes this special amulet was given as a gift to military and police officers by the king.

I still remember the sensation on that night at Klai Kangwol when the king gently placed the amulet on my palm; the amulet felt hot as though it had just been taken out of an oven. There were nine of us (eight police officers and a navy officer) that night who were given this amulet by the king.

His Majesty later related to me that the process of making this amulet did not involve use of any ovens or heating equipment. The amulet was made of soil from many sacred places all over the country, flowers offered by his subjects, and the king's own hair. These three elements were mixed together with latex and molded without heating. The mold was made by a very important sculptor, the late Ajarn Paitoon Muangsomboon, who was later honored as a national artist in visual arts (sculpting).

After we were all handed the amulet the king told us that before we performed a *puja* ritual blessing on the amulet we should *pid thong* (affix a gold leaf) on the amulet. But only on the back—*pid thong lang phra*. The king explained that the act of *pid thong lang phra* was an analogy: a self-reminder that good deeds were not for display and that the good deeds were the reward in themselves.

As the nine of us were walking out of Klai Kangwol that night, I said to my fellow officers that a winning lottery ticket could end with '99', considering that there were nine of us and the king was the ninth reign in the Chakri Dynasty. I have no idea if any of us chanced a lottery ticket with '99' ending number but I did not because that was not my kind of thing. The winning lotto on that round did end with '99'!

33

I affixed a gold leaf on the back of my Somdej Chitralada amulet and put it in a locket. Somdej Chitralada became the only amulet I wear on my neck.

I had been away from HM the King for about a year, always on the move. Upon my return to the palace, I was brimming with happiness to be in his audience again but also feeling a certain amount of frustration. I had been on some very demanding and dangerous duties—there were times when I almost lost my life—but I felt that the police department did not recognize my contribution and dedication to the job. At least not even a token appreciation in terms of increased salary for a long time. After dinner, before His Majesty turned in, I told him that there was something I wanted. 'What do you want?' he asked. I said bravely that I would like to affix the gold leaf on the *front* of Somdej Chitralada. His Majesty asked me why. I answered honestly that ever since His Majesty gave me Somdej Chitralada, my career had been nothing but difficult and dangerous and, worse yet, that the police department had never given me any raise.

His Majesty's words of consolation that night became a guidance, which I have taken to heart: 'Do your duties the best to your ability and do not be concerned about rewards; success of the duties are their own rewards.' Since then I was no longer troubled by lack of recognition or rewards from the police department in my professional career.

The news about my appointment as a royal court security police officer had quieted down. The position was becoming vacant in October 1969 and the search for a new replacement should have started. I thought there was nothing I could do about this matter. The king had already instructed the Royal Aide-de-Camp Department to send a request for my appointment to the police department. If the Royal Thai Police Department disagreed with my appointment and made another recommendation, it was prerogative of the department. And if the Royal Aide-de-Camp Department accepted the alternative choice, it would be forwarded to the king, who would make a deliberation. The entire matter was beyond my control, but what I knew I would never do was to plead with anyone for the appointment.

Then came the Prime Minister's Office order dated 3 April 1970 appointing me as a royal court security police officer effective 6 March 1970. At the time I had one important piece of task unfinished at the 5th Joint Civilian–Police–Military Intelligence Center. The task was to pick up a leading communist insurgent who had decided to turn himself in. This insurgent was active in Chiang Rai province. I had promised the commander of the CSOC Region 3 (which was the same as Third Army) Lt-Gen. Samran Phaetayakul that I would bring in this insurgent.

I informed Lt-Gen. Samran of the order for my appointment but affirmed him that I intended to follow through with my promise, but I would, first, have to report for duty to Chief Aide-de-Camp General, Adm. MC Galwalnadis Diskul and he would have to send a request for permission for me to take part in this special mission.

Because Lt-Gen. Samran was not willing or able to send such request, I went ahead with reporting for my new duty at Klai Kangwol in Hua Hin where the king was staying at the time. It was 27 April 1970. I remember this date because it was the birthday of the Naresuan Camp, an important day of celebration for all the border patrol police personnel. Another thing that made this day quite memorable was what my new boss said to me in no uncertain term: 'You should know that no one wants you here except the king.'

Oddly enough, I was quite proud and relieved to hear that welcoming remark: proud that my appointment was His Majesty's wish and relieved that it was His Majesty's alone, as my new boss made it more than clear that it was not his personal wish. So, this made it quite easy for me to do my work and to give my undivided loyalty to none other than the king himself.

As I left my post in the Third Army Forward Headquarters in Nan, a few people had to take up the unfinished task I left behind. The Chiang Rai governor, Khun Prayad Samarnmitra, an officer from the Third Army, Col. Chamnian Meesanga and the superintendent of Chiang Rai Provincial Police, Pol. Col. Sridej Poompraman, had to pick up the communist insurgent as previously arranged. I heard the terrible news when on duty with the king in Chulalongkorn University that the three good men had been killed in an ambush while traveling to pick up the insurgent.

8

The news of assassination in the north hit me hard, particularly because I had known the three men quite well. I had worked with Col. Jamnian in the Third Army and had known Khun Prayad since he was governor of Prachuab Khiri Khan. I served as Khun Prayad's deputy when he was the director of Training Center for the Village Defense Teams, while I was deputy director of the training division. As for Pol. Col. Sridej, he and I had been colleagues for almost 10 years, ever since he served as provincial police captain of Chiang Rai's Muang district (and I was chief of Chiang Rai Special Branch field office). During the few years of my posting in the north we had also worked very closely, staring death in the face more than a few times but managed to come back out alive together.

The king had also known the three gentlemen well, especially Khun Prayad, who had served both the king and the queen closely during his term as governor of Prachuab Khiri Khan. On 3 November of that year (1970) the king and the queen went to a Buddhist temple, Wat Jed Yod, in Chiang Rai to make a *kathina* offering (to offer robes to monks after the three months of dwelling in the monastery during the Buddhist Lent in the rainy season). In this trip the royal couple also paid respect to the late Pol. Col. Sridej, whose body was kept at the wat. The family and friends of the late police colonel considered the royal visit a great honor.

For all the appointments and transfers I had had in my career there was no special sentiment and conditions. I had always taken any new position as an important and natural part of my job. However, being appointed a royal court security police officer was different. It came with a great amount of pressure and a huge magnitude of responsibility. Not only that I had to provide security to the king, but also the queen and their children. I was aware from day one of the job that there would be no room for mistakes. Even the smallest mistake could have an immeasurable impact on both the destiny of our country and the integrity of my life and career. I was given the job to protect the people most revered by the people of Thailand.

Before I became part of the palace security team, my lifestyle was no different from those of other police and military officers. Leisure and entertainment among families and friends were part of everyday life. But in this job, given the magnitude of my responsibility, I realized there was no more room for these activities, especially those that could undermine my judgment like drinking.

The palace environment made easy the transition to my new lifestyle. All my new colleagues from all three military forces seemed to me so peaceful, composed, and focused individuals. I would find out not long after that the source of this peacefulness and focus was His Majesty the King, and that the regular practice of meditation and earnest adherence to the Buddhist teachings among the court personnel were inspired by the king's personal practices of both.

I myself, though born a Buddhist, had not been a good Buddhist practitioner. I might have red more books on Buddhism than my peers, especially those written by the late reverend Buddhadhasa Bhikkhu, and I might have sporadically tried to practice but laziness often had the better of me. Here, given the earnest atmosphere in the palace, I felt both interested and compelled to return to the Buddhist way. I quietly began practicing meditation again and searched for more understanding on Buddhist teachings from books and tapes. It is fair to say that signing on to the palace security job was an important character reform for me.

My duty as a court security police officer, as stated in the Royal Court Police Officer Act, included providing security to the royal family as well as carrying out given royal commands. The first royal command

I received in this duty was to serve as a bodyguard to a royal family member who would become an important national hero, MC Vibhavadi Rangsit.[1]

Thanying Vibha—or Dame Vibha, as I called her—was a daughter of Prince Pittayalongkorn[2] and MC Pornpimolpan (Worawan). Thanying Vibha had a well-known brother from the same parents, MC Bhisatej Rajani, the current director of the Royal Project. Thanying Vibha was married to MC Piyarangsit Rangsit, son of Prince Khunchaiyanat Narendhara.

Before my first audience with Thanying Vibha, I was aware that she was a writer and had written a number of novels and articles under a penname of Wor Na Pramualmark. Then, when I had an opportunity to attend the royal court, I discovered that Thanying Vibha was also the queen's lady in waiting, accompanying the royal couple on trips both inside the country and abroad since 1957.

Thanying Vibha was regularly entrusted to perform royal duties by both the king and the queen and many of her duties included visiting remote communities in the south, north, and northeast. My first mission with Thanying Vibha was to Surat Thani and later to other provinces such as Nakhon Si Thammarat, Phattalung, Phuket, Krabi and Songkla. Judging from my experience in the north and the northeast, the situation in the south was no less volatile. The communist insurgents in the south were armed and organized and often engaged in fighting with authorities. Ambushes on authorities were not uncommon. The intensity of communist insurgencies in Surat Thani was comparable to that in Chiang Rai and Nan in the north and Sakon Nakhon and Nakhon Phanom in Isan or the northeast.

The traveling style of Thanying Vibha was down to earth like that of the royal couple. Ground was a preferred mode of transportation and helicopters were used only when necessary. This is because ground transportation allowed for better contact with the people and better observation of how the populations really lived.

---

[1] MC Vibhavadi Rangsit became Her Royal Highness Princess Vibhavadi Rangsit after her sudden death in 1977.

[2] Prince Rajani Chaemcharas or 'Nor.Mor.Sor' was the founder of the Rajani family.

In most of Thanying Vibha's missions to the south, we usually traveled by train from Bangkok to the capital *amphur* or district of a province and used the capital *amphur*, usually Amphur Muang, as our base, from which we would travel by any means to the destination villages, by car, motorcycle, boat, or on foot. If traveling by car was possible, the cars were usually afforded to us by the Department of Health.

Like in the missions of the royal couple, there was always a medical team of doctors, nurses and medics to provide medical check-ups and services to the people in the communities visited by Thanying Vibha's mission. Because I dressed in plain clothes, I was often mistaken to be a doctor by the villagers and I would be given a new nickname 'Doctor Vasit.'

The easy-going, friendly and down to earth style of Thanying Vibha made her popular among both the local officials and the villagers. Her ability to connect so well with the locals had the opposite effect on the communist insurgents in the area who preferred to see the local people more disenfranchised rather than being united through frequent presence of a royal member. It was not difficult to discern danger from the atmosphere or the little incidents that happened during the mission.

Once in Phra Saeng district, our motorcycle caravan was brought to a halt by a big log lying across the road. After a little investigation, it appeared that it could not have got there either by itself or by a storm but had instead been intentionally put there by someone (who fortunately did not remain there to confirm our theory). The able bodies in the group gathered the muscles to remove it and we continued on our way, each clinging to our individual chauffeur on the back of a motorbike.

Going on missions to the areas rife with communist insurgency, one had to walk a fine line between responding to security and safety concerns and keeping the mission as practical and as enjoyable as possible. At times, we had no choice in the mode of travel or accommodation. When we did not travel by car or on motorbike, we went by boat and sometimes stayed over night by the riverbanks. One of those times was our mission to Baan Ta Khun and Khiri Nikhom districts. A number of local villagers came to have an audience with Thanying Vibha. Both the mission and the villagers appeared to have enjoyed the lively conversation and no one showed any sign of wanting to go home. Rather late in the evening as the sun was setting, Thanying finally asked the villagers how they were going to get home. They weren't going home that night, they said, because it would be too dangerous with tigers prowling about in the nighttime. So everyone ended up staying on the riverbank with Thanying that night.

Going on a mission with Thanying could also be full of natural dangers: hiking on steep mountains and waterfalls was not unlike taking obstacle courses in a competition. Once we almost lost a doctor, Doctor Sawasdi, who fell down a waterfall but fortunately ended up in a pond. The district chief of Khiri Nikhom had built a little thatch for Thanying Vibha to stay by this waterfall that would later be named after her, 'Vibhavadi Waterfall'.

I served Thanying Vibha for over two years until September 1972, when I was asked to follow the king and the queen to Phra Saeng district. The communist insurgents in the area made it clear that the royal visit was not welcome. We were ambushed and lost one police officer.

In Prasaeng I got my first glimpse of HM the King's philosophy of development. In a visit to a temple, the structure of which was nothing more than four poles and a tin roof, the abbot asked the king for a new temple. One could imagine the discomfort for both monks and laypeople in the rainy season. The king responded positively to the abbot's request for the new temple and everyone was imagining a new temple built from the beautiful Fine Arts Department's official design, but that was not to be. The new temple would be built on the existing structure with the new materials—wood, tin and nails—from the king.

From this example, I would come to understand that the king's development policy was based on local sustainability that would be gradual, rather than drastic. A new, more elaborate temple constructed according to the Fine Arts Department's artistic design would not be suitable in an impoverished village where the villagers lived in modest and makeshift houses.

After returning from that trip, we were told that a few villages had not received any or all of the goods that were to have been delivered to them from the king. I went back on helicopter with the superintendent of Border Patrol Police 8th Subdivision, Pol. Col. Wipas Wipulakorn, to deliver the goods to make up for those that did not arrive. As we were having lunch with the villagers in Baan Sai-khrob in Kian Sa subdistrict, some whispered to us that there were several communist insurgents in the party. Pol. Col. Wipas and I did not waste any time. We immediately stopped eating and left the scene. Not long after our departure, we received news on radio that the insurgents had taken the policemen at the party hostage and confiscated all their guns.

9

Besides being an accomplished author of novels and feature articles, Thanying Vibha was also an avid student of history and archaeology. Following her on royal missions was like attending a mobile school.

With only a little stimulation, my personal interest in the subjects flourished. Thanying Vibha taught me how to study ancient Chinese pottery and how to distinguish archaeological findings from mundane broken pots. I spent quite a bit of time looking at the ground while following her and picking up a number of broken pieces of old pottery—many simply old and some worthy of attention. Thanying Vibha was a patient teacher. She said when I showed broken pieces to her, 'Keep them. No one would break good pots for you to study.' After a while, I learned to read the different characteristics of Chinese pottery from the Song, Ming and Qing dynasties.

Around this time, the young Her Royal Highness Princess Sirindhorn, the second daughter of the royal couple, became interested in archaeology, particularly in Chinese pottery. When I returned from a trip with Thanying Vibha I always brought home pieces of old china for the princess to study. After so many trips, the ladies in waiting started to complain that the princess's quarters in Chitralada Palace were filled with broken pots and asked me not to give her any more.

Thanying Vibha had a favorite drink on the road, Earl Grey with bergamot flavor. I always brought my little field diesel cooker and by default became the designated tea-maker. Once I made tea during an afternoon visit at the house of the *kamnan*, head of Tambon Ta-khun, in a jungle in the southern provaince of Surat Thani. For some reason unknown to me the cooker caught on fire as I was lighting it with a match. The flame shot so high that the thatch roof caught fire. Fortunately the floor was sandy and I managed to put out the fire with the sand before the house of the good *kamnan* burnt to the ground.

Traces of fighting between authorities and communist insurgents were visible along the roadside as we were moving around Surat Thani, but that did not seem to arouse any fears in Thanying. Although she realized that there were insurgents in the villages she visited, but to her it did not matter what side they were on. As she once told an audience during a talk—someone asked her to relate her experience with communist insurgents—that she had no story to tell. To her, people in need were people in need, no matter what ideology they subscribed to. She said, 'especially in a flood, I never thought who was who because everybody needed food and clothing and they could all get sick just the same. So all the rescue package was meant for everyone who needed help in a crisis.'

Given Thanying Vibha's interest in archaeology, stopping at interesting archaeological sites was part of her visits around the country. Among many pilgrimages, we once visited Wat Takian Bang Kaew in Phattalung province to make an offering to the Buddha's relics in a pagoda in the temple. The villagers told a story that the relics in this temple were originally from Sri Lanka and were to have been taken to Wat Boromathat in Maung district, Nakhon Si Thammarat, but somehow the pilgrim, after reaching the shore, got lost and went east instead.

As the story goes, once the pilgrim reached the base of the Sonchai Mountain, he learned that the pagoda in Nakhon Si Thammarat, in which the relics were supposed to be kept, was already finished. So he decided to build a new pagoda for the relics in Phattalung, which became Wat Takian, which later became Wat Kian. (The word 'ta' was dropped from the name for some inexplicable reason.) If the story was true the pagoda in Wat Takian Bang Kaew would have been from the same era as the pagoda in Wat Boromathat in Nakhon Si Thammarat.

In the yard of Wat Takian Bang Kaew were remnants of old Chinese pottery. Thanying Vibha thought that there might have once been a Chinese community there, especially given how near the sea it was, it could have been a seaport for Chinese merchants.

Another temple in Phattalung to which I followed Thanying Vibha on a pilgrimage was Wat Don Sala in Kuan Khanoon district. This temple wasn't an archaeological site but the home of a monk of remarkable importance in Phattalung and the nearby provinces, the late Phra Ajarn Nam Kaew Chandra. During our visit, the *bot*—a building in which Buddhist ceremonies are performed—was under construction. As soon as Thanying Vibha informed the king that the temple was being built, the king decided to make a contribution: the design and construction of the temple's gable. Two important artists were appointed: Ajarn Luang Pisal Silapakarm to do the design and Ajarn Paitoon Muangsomboon, a national sculptor, to oversee the construction of the gable. Pol. Col. Wipas Wipulakorn and I were both designated, again, to take Ajarn Paitoon back and forth between Bangkok and the temple until its new *bot* was done. The king and the queen visited the new temple on 26 September 1972.

After the Day of Great Sorrow in October 1973 I was assigned to coordinate between the Sanya Dharmasakti government and the students' representatives, so the king asked me to put my duty to Thanying Vibha on hold. Even so, around the end of 1973 Thanying made a special request for me to follow her on a social welfare mission to the poor Karen communities in Sri Satchanalai district in Sukhothai province. The Karen lived in a couple of very remote villages and the 'roads' could not really be called roads but tracks, which snaked around a number of variable sizes of bumps and holes. We traveled by Land Rovers. One of the cars was once stuck in a large hole and the villagers had to help getting the car back on the road.

The final destination for that trip was Baan Mae San. We could have made it there by helicopter, but for some reason Thanying Vibha chose to trek. It was one the most challenging 12-kilometer treks I had ever experienced. One of the interesting things we learned when we finally made it to the village was that all—literally all—the villagers had the same last name, 'Khang Khiri'. Indeed, although it wasn't so uncommon for villagers to come from the same clan and sharing the same *sae* (Chinese word for last name), it was quite unusual for every single person in the whole village to have the same adopted Thai last name. It turned out that the last name (which aptly translates to 'perched on the mountain') was given to the villagers at the same time by the district chief.

The poverty of the Karen villagers was evident. Without even rice, they were poorer than even the poorest peasants. Their standard of living was more akin to that of hunter-gatherers. Their main staple included wild potatoes and whatever edible roots and plants they could find in their village and in the wild. The load of rice that was sent ahead of the mission under royal patronage was already exhausted. When we arrived, the villagers warmly welcomed us, the visitors, with little that they had—young coconuts. After the round of welcome, the guests saw another manifestation of poverty in the village in the dogs charging to the leftover coconuts. It was the first time I had ever seen dogs eating coconuts!

As representative of the king and as a royal member herself, Thanying Vibha brought in each of her visit not only a sense of caring and warmth to the villagers, but also drew attention from local authorities to the welfare of the villagers. During the visit to this Karen community, she managed to persuade an educated local villager who once worked as a schoolteacher to agree to teach the children. She personally offered him an annual stipend in addition to the teacher's salary he would receive from the government.

Another Karen village visited on that trip was Baan Huay Tom in Li district, Lamphun. Thanying Vibha and I had been there once before. The Karen in this village migrated from other provinces and, according to the villagers, followed a monk to settle there. The monk was Kruba Chaiwongsa Pattana and seemed to have had special affection and respect from the Karen, although he was a northern Thai native. Able to speak their language, this monk taught the villagers about Buddhism and preciousness of life. The Karen villagers eventually became devout Buddhists and strict vegetarians.

Probably due to the villagers' strict vegetarian diet, at the time of Thanying Vibha's second visit, they appeared less than healthy; their skin had a distinct yellow tint from lack of protein. Upon returning from that mission, Thanying Vibha informed the king of the villagers' problem.

Shortly after the royal couple returned to Bhubing Palace, they visited the Karen village and introduced the variety known as mung bean to the villagers. From then on the villagers started growing mung bean, which would become an important source of protein.

Thanying Vibha was a devout Buddhist herself and seriously practiced meditation. There were two teachers from whom she took instruction: Phra Maha Veera Dhavaro, an ascetic monk, also known as the 'Black Monkey Ascetic' of Wat Taa Sung, Uthai Thani, who later received a royal title, and Kruba Dhammachai of Wat Tuung Khaow Puang, Mae Taeng district, Chiang Mai. Thanying Vibha related to me about her progress in meditation practice: Once her mind was no longer grasping, completely peaceful, she could feel her body elevating above the floor. Sometimes when she had finished her meditating session, she would find herself at a different place from where she started in the room.

Thanying Vibha was a kind of person who put the well-being of others before her own. The morning of 16 February 1977 was like any other day, in a police helicopter on the way to a remote village. As the helicopter was flying above Wiang Sra district in the southern province of Surat Thani, news came on the radio that two border patrol troops had been critically injured in a skirmish with communist insurgents.

Upon hearing the news, Thanying Vibha instructed the pilot to drop-off her two teachers at a *wat* in Baan Song. She would go with the helicopter to pick up the two injured troops, take them to the hospital and then return to pick up the two monks. But as the helicopter was making a descent, it was hit by heavy gunfire from the insurgents on the ground. One shot penetrated the body of the helicopter and hit Thanying Vibha. Miraculously, others were safe. With the helicopter heavily damaged, the pilot had to make an emergency landing at a school in Baan Song village. In the time it took another helicopter to arrive to take her to Surat Thani Hospital, Thanying Vibha took her last breath. Just before she died, Thanying Vibha asked her two teachers to say farewell to her beloved king on her behalf. She had, she explained, to move on to 'nippana'. According to the people who were there, Thanying's last words were: 'I could see it now. It's so bright, so beautiful.'

At that moment Thailand lost one royal member who loved her country and her people more than her own life.

❖

During Thanying Vibha's last mission, I was on duty in the northern palace in Chiang Mai. The same evening of hearing the sad news, I accompanied HRH Princess Sirindhorn to Bangkok to pick up Thanying Vibha's body. A funeral service was arranged the following day at a temple where Thanying Vibha regularly practiced her meditation—Wat Benjamaborphit.

I saw her for the last time at the bathing ceremony. In my profession, I had seen a lot of death and crying at funerals but this was not my habit. But for Thanying Vibha, I was unable to hold down my tears. I broke down crying when I saw her in front of the king and the queen. The overwhelming sadness was beyond my restraint.

On the wreath from the king placed in front of Thanying Vibha's casket were written four lines from a song, a royal composition, 'The Ultimate Dream':

Determined to right the wrong
Devoted to the mother land 'till the end in ashes
Prepared for death that will be by integrity outlasted
Remembered as gold leaves behind the Buddha

On the queen's wreath was a poem:

Then came the day
When so much sadness and sorrow filled my heart
Enemies took away your breath
But not your bravery, Dearest Vibhavadi

The royal cremation for Thanying Vibha was arranged at Wat Thepsirin Tharawat on 4 April 1977. On that day Thanying Vibha was honored with a new title, Her Royal Highness Princess Vibhavadi Rangsit. She also received The Most Illustrious Order of the Royal House of Chakri and The Most Illustrious Order of the White Elephant.

10

The political situation was highly volatile during the time I began my tenure as a royal court police officer in 1970. Communist insurgencies were becoming rampant in the original red zones in the north, northeast and the south and spread over to the central region. Armed insurgents crept closer to Bangkok. Skirmishes and random guerilla attacks against the authorities were sporadic in Suphan Buri, Phetchaburi and Prachuab Khiri Khan.

As I have mentioned, I was aware of the royal couple's concerns for the precarious political situation but I only came to see the real depth of their concerns and dedication to the well-being of the people in my capacity as a palace security officer. I found myself accompanying them to the most dangerous places to take care of the people in the greatest need of help—authorities suffering casualties and villagers terrorized by violence. Rescue packages—food, medical assistance and other necessities—were quickly dispatched to the crisis zones. These material necessities lifted up the spirit of the people, but what seemed to be equally, if not more, important was a sense of security that was embodied in the presence of their revered king and queen.

Of course, a security standard procedure required that an area always be cleared ahead of every royal visit. And more vigilance for travel to the 'red' zones—areas with heavy communist infiltration. However, it didn't take a security expert to know that there is no such thing as complete security and absolute safety. We knew that in certain areas the insurgents had so well infiltrated the populations that it was hard to separate friends from enemies. So, every travel to the red or even the 'pink'—semi-infiltrated—areas gave me and other security officers huge worries. This is not to say that royal visits to the non-red and non-pink zones were free from danger. There was no place for complacency. Security officers had to assume that danger was always lurking. It could come from anyone, anywhere, at any time, and in any form.

It wasn't so worrisome when we had time to coordinate with the military, police and local authorities and clear the area in advance but, because crises were by their nature unscheduled, many visits were sudden and ad hoc. I don't know how other security officers cope with their worries. I dealt with mine with premature gray. Within only one year into the palace security job my hair became completely gray. I was only a few months into my fortieth birthday.

The first big test for me as a palace security officer was the opening ceremony for Sawan Pracharaksa Hospital in Nakhon Sawan on 20 July 1970. The royal couple arrived in the afternoon in the Nakhon Sawan Airport to an official welcome by soldiers, as was customary. Then they were on their way to the city of Nakhon Sawan.

I didn't know whose idea it was to arrange for the royal motorcade to cut right through the center of the city's largest market, but presumably this was done out of good intention to allow local residents to have intimate audience with their king and queen. Even then Nakhon Sawan was a large and heavily populated city. Roads inside the city were narrow and tall buildings were tightly packed along each side of the road in the market. From security point of view it was the farthest thing from safety—a disaster. The market should have been avoided at all costs.

I began to realize that the motorcade was going through the market when I saw that Their Majesties' car had already gone inside the market, the masses of people eagerly waiting on each side of the road and more looming ahead. My intuition told me that something bad was going to happen.

The problem started when people on the front rows on both sides of the road were pushed forward by those in the back, who also wanted to catch the glimpse of their king and queen. Those in the front rows as a result willingly or unwillingly moved closer to the royal limousine. Policemen and boy scouts providing security reinforcement could only helplessly watch and be pushed along by the massive waves of people.

In no time the motorcade was brought to a standstill, completely surrounded by tens of thousands of people. It was the worst security nightmare come true.

As soon as the royal limousine came to a complete stop, the royal security guards and myself, the only police officer assigned for that trip, got out of the car and hurriedly pushed our way amidst the sea of people to Their Majesties.

What I didn't expect to see was that His Majesty got out of the car and shortly thereafter was followed by Her Majesty. The faces of the royal couple were full of compassionate smiles as they warmly greeted the eager masses with no hint of any concerns for their own safety.

The royal guards and I decided to do what we thought best: we locked hands to make a human fence around the royal couple and prevented anyone from getting too close. It was a challenging task, given such weighty waves of people who seemed to have yielded to the formidable impulse to touch their king and queen. The waves of people were so strong that the king's private secretary (ML Thaweesanti Ladawal) was lifted of the ground and ended up on top of the hood of the royal limousine. The royal couple greeted the people and slowly made their way toward the hospital on foot, while the security guards and police made their best attempts at providing security. Finally, they arrived at Sawan Pracharaksa Hospital and the following masses were stopped at the front gate of the hospital.

I had long wondered about the real utility of the swords that police officers and soldiers carried as part of their official uniforms in royal audience. The mystery was solved for me that day when the sword on Second-Lt. Pol. Gen. Nitya Sukhum was bent almost double. I doubted if he could even manage to take it out of its scabbard again.

As the royal couple reached inside the hospital ground the opening ceremony began. Following the opening ceremony, the royal couple was given a tour of the hospital by the director, starting from the lower to the upper floors. The hospital had six floors and only one or perhaps two small elevators. After the king and the queen and a few people got inside, there was no room left in the elevator. I had a choice of waiting for the elevator to come down or running up the stairs to the sixth floor.

❖

At only forty, I figured I still had youth and strength on my side. With the rigorous physical training I had with the border patrol police in stock, running up six flights of stairs should be a piece of cake. As the elevator was going up, I turned around to sprint up the staircase and made it just in time to wait for the elevator to open on the sixth floor. That was pretty good, I thought. But because I was still out of breath, Adm. MC Galwalnadis Diskul, chief aide-de-camp general, sent me right back downstairs to double-check that the arrangement for motorcade on the return trip to the airport was in good order and to make sure that there would be no fiasco like the one in the market. I ran back down the same six flights of stairs to execute the order and back up the same way. (Using elevators was not allowed while the king and queen remained on the hospital premises.)

Altogether I ran eighteen flights of stairs and, on the last flight up, either the air circulation in the hospital wasn't so great or I overestimated my own physical vigor, or both, I felt I was going to pass out, gasping for breath and feeling as though my lung was going to jump out of my chest. Realizing it was inappropriate to faint in the royal presence, I looked for a more appropriate place.

Fortunately soon after, I found a room near the room the royal couple was occupying. I looked inside and found that it was empty. I had a feeling that no one would be showing this room to the royal couple, so I quickly slipped inside and locked the door. But before I could manage to release the belt and unbutton my uniform to ease the breathing, my adrenalin was depleted and then it was darkness.

I woke up again finding myself spread-eagle on my back on the floor in a small, stuffy room but I certainly felt better. Not knowing how much time had passed, I quickly got up and straightened up my uniform and got out of the room just when Their Majesties were right outside. I resumed my duty as if nothing had happened, but to anyone who had eyes I must have appeared like someone who just had a bath with the clothes on, with my open-collared brown uniform totally soaked with sweat.

The incident that day was to me a wake-up call. It was a realization that physical fitness was a critical factor in my work. Anything less than perfect physical condition of the royal security officers could undermine security for Their Majesties. I was lucky that I only fainted and was able to return to duty that day, but what if I had fallen ill and couldn't get up? As the only officer assigned that day to guard the royal couple in the closest proximity at all times, my absence would have meant a compromise in Their Majesties' safety.

From that day on, exercise became an important part of the job for me and other security police officers and the palace guards. We were allowed to join the royal family's evening jog. In Bangkok, the royal couple, together or separately, sometimes joined by the children, jogged inside the Chitralada Palace. For Queen Sirikit, aerobic exercise was also an important exercise regime in addition to jogging. When Dusidalai Hall was finished, Her Majesty moved both the jogging and aerobic exercise sessions there.

The royal couple was disciplined in their exercise program. In Bangkok or upcountry, jogging was always part of the daily routine. In Hua Hin, in addition to usual jogging tracks inside Klai Kangwol Palace, the royal couple had another favorite route, which led outside the village, up the hill to Khao Tao, and then down to Hat Sai Yai Beach, which is now home of His Majesty's agricultural project.

It was hard to find a couple who were more physically fit. The length of the jogging track in Chitralada Palace in Bangkok was about 3 kilometers, but not once did I see either the king or the queen catching breath. This was more than what some of us palace security guards could say for ourselves. The king usually wore a white short-sleeved polo shirt with white exercise pants and a pair of white running shoes. All the palace security guards adopted similar white outfits.

His Majesty had a way of jogging that appeared as though he was floating in the air, with his long steps and each foot touching the ground so ever lightly. Those steps seem deceptively slow. Initially I hung with the latter group of palace guards jogging behind the royal couple, but, finding myself often struggling to keep up, especially when we jogged up the Khao Tao track, I changed strategy to stay with the group in the front. However, even with a 100-meter head start, we in the front group were still passed by the royal couple eventually.

11

Occasionally security was required for the prince and princesses. Jogging with His Royal Highness Prince Vajiralongkorn wasn't much of a challenge when he was young but became increasingly difficult for those of us whose physical stamina was moving in the opposite direction to that of the prince. Eventually, as the boy became a young man with both police and military training, a few other older security officers and I decided to leave the jogging duty with the prince to the younger men. I jogged with the two youngest princesses, HRH Princess Sirindhorn or 'Princess Noi', the second daughter, and HRH Princess Chulabhorn or 'Princess Lek', the youngest daughter. I did not have an opportunity to provide security for the eldest daughter, Princess Ubolratana or 'Princess Ying Yai', because soon after I was assigned to palace security, Princess Ying Yai left for her studies in the United States.

One evening, after returning from a visit to communities in the north I went back to the palace security quarters in Bhubing Palace in Chiang Mai and found that someone had put a beer carton in front of my room. I checked the outside of the carton to see if there might be a bomb inside. As the check was cleared, I opened the carton and instead of beer bottles, I found numerous pairs of eyes staring up at me. I'm not sure whether it might have been less disconcerting to see an explosive instead. I tore the carton wide open. The eyes belonged to *khiad laew*.

Khiad laew was a type of mountain frog, which I had first been introduced to in Mae Hong Son many years before. These *khiad laew*—unfortunately for them—were known for their delicious meat, considered superior to other types of frogs. After locking eyes with these poor, big-eyed, leggy little creatures for a while, I remembered that on my last visit to Mae Hong Son, I had mentioned *khiad laew* to Pol. Col. Sophon Singhaplin, the superintendent of Mae Hong Son provincial police, telling him that I was impressed by their delicious meat. And, as I suspected, the sending address was indeed the Mae Hong Son superintendent.

Apparently, he didn't know that I had done away *panatipati*—taking away life of living things—and that I could no longer send frogs to the executioner in the kitchen and have them returned in *tom yam* soup or fried with garlic and pepper for me to have with ice-cold beer. There was only one obvious thing to do: release the poor frogs.

It was the cool season. Because *khiad laew* were mountain frogs, I thought the best place to release them might be some place on the mountain where there was enough moisture and perhaps pockets of water. So, early the next morning, I asked Princess Sirindhorn to dismiss me from duty in her jogging that morning, It turned out that Princess Sirindhorn wanted to go and release the *khiad laew* together. Princess Sirindhorn, a couple of court security officers and myself went jogging as scheduled and together released nineteen *khiad laew* about one kilometer north of Bhubing Palace (The twentieth *khiad laew* was out of luck and didn't make it). I imagine that today the descendants of those *khiad laew* from Mae Hong Son may still live on around Bhubing Palace.

Two days before the *khiad laew* incident, the north suffered heavy rain-storms and severe flooding. In Tha Pla district, Uttaradit, huge deluge came down the mountains and swept away a number of people's homes. As usual, the palace prepared for a quick visit to the flooding sites. It was late in September 1970. The royal couple got on a plane to Pitsanulok and then on a helicopter to Baan Ngom Sak, Tambon Tha Faek.

As the royal couple and the entourage arrived at the Baan Ngom Sak School where about 150 flood victims from three villages were waiting, it was still pouring. Yet, His Majesty and his queen proceeded directly to the villagers most of whom had all of their homes and belongings wiped out almost in a blink of an eye. The royal couple greeted them with warmth and conversed with them with intimacy, kindness and sympathy. Basic necessities were distributed, from blankets, mosquito nets, T-shirts, men's and women's sarongs and school uniforms to rice grains, salt, vegetable seeds, and other basic assistance packages from the Rajprachanukraow Foundation and the Sai Jai Thai Foundation.

While the healthy were having an audience with the royal couple, a team of royal doctors and nurses, led by Doctor Danai Sanitwongse Na Ayudhaya, attended to the sick. The team continued to work until after the royal couple left the village.

The royal couple left Baan Ngom Sak just in time to have lunch at Sirikit Dam and then after 3.00 p.m. continued on to more flood sites in Wat Bod district and Phrom Phiram district in Pitsanulok. The day finally ended after 7.00 p.m. in Chitralada Palace.

One cannot imagine the sense of great loss, the loss of everything one owns in a flood, but it is difficult to forget the look of great hope and joy in the eyes and the smiles of the villagers that day, when they were looking up at their king and queen, who came to console them in a time of crisis.

Flooding disasters were not limited to the north. People in Isan, in the northeast, also fell victims to the ravaging flood. About five weeks later, at the end of October, the royal couple was off to visit flood victims and provided flood relief in Udon Thani and Nong Khai.

In the many successful royal flights, I must commend the pilots from the Royal Thai Air Force, the Army and the police force for their professionalism. More often than not, the return flights were taken in the night. The pilots as well as the airport navigators on the ground always did their job with great care and superb skill.

Initially I was quite uncomfortable with the royal couple taking night flights. Eventually, however, I grew accustomed to the fact that night flights were a part of life of the people I vowed to protect. So, I adapted and adopted a habit of traveling with new necessities such as a flashlight and emergency light signal when going on duty.

A few months later, in January 1971, I accompanied the royal couple for the first time as a royal court police officer to hill tribe villages in the north. A royal member entrusted with looking after the welfare of the hill tribe villagers was MC Bhisatej Rajani , a younger brother of Thanying Vibhavadi. As a rule, officials from the Royal Guards Division and the police officers and soldiers who provided court security would coordinate each visit under the consultation of MC Bhisatej, or 'Than Bhi' as we called him. The atmosphere in the consultation for each visit wasn't always smooth.

Than Bhi, who was a staunch supporter and a de facto representative of the hill tribe people, always argued for the most intimate and longest possible of royal visit, whereas the royal household and security officials put Their Majesties' safety first. So, often there were disagreements, which occasionally turned into heated arguments. However, eventually a compromise would be reached and both sides were satisfied.

Usually, after a travel program was agreed upon, Than Bhi would take the officials on an agreed route to the real locations as a trial run before the actual visit took place. On the travel day, one group of officials would have already traveled to the destination and the other would travel with the royal couple and the entourage.

12

A young monk in a village (the only monk in the village) in the northernmost district of Chiang Mai had invited the royal couple to the vegetable garden on the temple ground. On 4 January 1971 the royal couple paid a visit to the temple in Baan Muang Ngam in Mae Ai (which was then a subdistrict) on the Thai-Burmese (Myanmar) border. His Majesty gave some suggestions about vegetable growing and left with an old Buddha statue in mediation position of about five-inch base—a gift from the young monk.

His Majesty gave me the Buddha statue to hold during the walk back to the helicopter. Later I returned the Buddha statue to His Majesty.

That evening during dinner at Bhubing His Majesty was in good humor chatting with people around the dinner table about the day—I was sitting on HM's right—and at one point said that 'Vasit had a good karma today. He got to carry Buddha.' I added that the Buddha statue from the young monk had characteristics of a 'good' Buddha statue because it seemed to be an old statue, probably made in Chiang Saen era by a Laotian artist. To this the king responded: 'Old or new, all Buddha statues are good statues.'

Afterwards I had some time to ponder His Majesty's remark and came to agree with him that it didn't really matter in what era and by whom a Buddha statue was made, every maker had the same intention: to make a material representation of the Buddha to remind people his teachings. To believe that only old and ancient Buddha statues were 'good' statues was a form of attachment.

Three days later, the king and Prince Vajiralongkorn visited Mien (Yao) hill tribe villagers in Chiang Rai. This Mien village, called Baan Pha Mee, was off Highway 110 in Tambon Muad, Mae Sai district, near the Thai-Burmese border. A hike to the village was a challenge. We climbed up a steep mountain that from a distance looked like a giant bear—probably how the village got its name Pha Mee, or 'Bear Cliff'. The mountain was so steep that traveling to the village by helicopter or car was out of the question.

Three donkeys were arranged for the king, the prince and the royal secretary, while rest of the entourage were to walk with the villagers. Hiking that morning proved a lot less painful than the first time I hiked up Doi Pui in Chiang Mai, thanks to the newly adopted regime of exercise and my saying no to alcohol.

That visit to the Bear Cliff would be the beginning of an enduring relationship between His Majesty and the Mien people. Many years later, a Mien villager came all the way from his home in the Bear Cliff in the northernmost place in Thailand to call on His Majesty in Hua Hin and brought with him some goats to sell to people in the lowland. On the other side of the 'Bear' mountain lived another hill tribe community—I'm not quite sure if they were Lahu (Muser) or Karen. His Majesty had also visited the community and brought them some animals.

The person who gave me the first, brief and most perfect introduction to the hill tribes in Thailand was a fellow police officer, Pol. Lt-Gen. Serm Yakasem, BPP commander. He was then a lieutenant colonel and the superintendent of the BPP 5th Subdivision when he took me to a *kin wor*, the Hmong New Year celebration on Doi Pui in Chiang Mai, before Bhubing Palace was built on the mountain. We parked our car on the side of Suthep-Doi Pui Road and walked up to the village. The celebration started as soon as we got there and a package of necessities was presented as a gift to the village head who promptly served us the local high-octane corn whisky.

Dinner that night was largely pork. My companion had already warned me about eating pork in the village, saying that the villagers raised free-range pigs that foraged freely in the woods, which also served as the villagers' bathroom. Because the pigs' freedom of movement and free spirit, both the villagers and the guests had to take a long stick to fend off the free-moving pigs when they went on their nature's morning call.

Even compromised by the strong corn whisky, I could tell that the pieces of pork on my plate weren't totally cooked. I came up with a quick solution and asked the host if I could show them a western-style cooking called 'pork flambé'. As all a crowd of children and adults gathered around the table, I proceeded to pour down the entire cup of my corn whisky on the pork, lit a match and threw it on the plate. The plate went up in flames. I waited until I was sure that the pork was quite well done, and then added soy sauce and pepper. I ate the pork—still with some qualms.

The next morning, Col. Serm and I bid farewell to the host and walked (climbed) our way back to the car. It was not entirely a pleasant hike. I was breathing through both my nose and my mouth and would have breathed through seven more passageways in my body, if they had existed. My fellow officer's breathing was also labored but he kept his long, slow pace until we reached the car we left by the road the night before. As for me, as soon as I saw the car, it seemed that my knees just gave in. Even crawling was out of the question. I simply flopped down by the roadside and waited a while before picking up myself and staggering to the car. I knew then that I had a special allergy to mountain climbing. Still, throughout my career I would have to hike and climb a lot of mountains but the mother of all mountain climbing was to Baan Mae Sa in Mae Rim district, Chiang Mai. Mae Sa was also a Hmong village in which the primary means of livelihood was then still opium growing.

As the helicopter decreased altitude in preparation for landing at the foot of the mountain, the view from above gave a pretty clear indication that the most challenging mountain climbing was awaiting us. I proceeded ahead of His Majesty with two permanent royal aide-de-camp officers,

Col. Damrong Sikkamontala and Col. Teanchai Janmookda, (both of whom later achieved the rank of full general and became chief and deputy chief aide-de-camp general, respectively).

Ahead of us was a lieutenant colonel from the BPP in the area. We kept climbing up and periodically turned around to check on His Majesty. It didn't take long before everyone started to give an image of a hen trying to deliver her eggs—red-faced and open-mouthed—only with the chicken sound turned off. Meanwhile, His Majesty kept a steady pace and gradually closing in on us, closely followed by Than Bhisatej. About halfway up the mountain, as I was about to collapse, ahead was the young BPP lieutenant colonel looking like a rooster making a morning call. What came out wasn't a beautiful morning call of a rooster, but the young officer's breakfast.

I turned back to signal Col. Damrong that he could pass me but he responded with a headshake and turned back to give the same signal to Col. Teanchai, who also gave a sign that he could go no further. He had no one else to signal. The next person down the line was the king himself. Meanwhile, His Majesty calmly passed over with Than Bhisatej, giving a side-glance to what must have appeared a very pathetic image of his three royal security guards bending over with their hands on their knees, gasping for breath.

After a while the two colonels and I mustered enough strength to push ourselves up the mountain and finally caught up with His Majesty, Than Bhisatej and other officials. As we caught up, I heard the king saying something to Col. Teanchai but heard no response from the colonel. At the moment, Khun Cholchan Salaksna, a royal page standing nearby, handed the colonel a handkerchief. The colonel unconsciously wiped his mouth. The king said compassionately, 'I see, still not up to royal speak, eh.'

The appallingly embarrassing job performance that day convinced us, court policemen and soldiers, of the need to step up our physical fitness and to do away with any unhealthy habits such as drinking. I learned soon after joining the court security force that the officers of both higher and lower ranks in the force did not drink at all and that many meditated.

13

Prior to the departure on an official royal or personal travel a security survey was required. From the original location to the final
destination, officials from various agencies coordinated their efforts to
make sure that each leg of the itinerary was safe. Even when there were
programs for traveling palace security officers would conduct security
surveys in various locations in preparation for possible visits. From this,
I learned a great deal about the country's topography and got to know
a great number of individuals.

I worked a great deal with two colleagues in security surveys: Col.
Teanchai Janmookda, who was assigned to court security when he was
chief of VIP Protection Branch, a unit under the Supreme Command
Security Center, and Pol. Lt-Gen. Thep Supasamit, former assistant to
director-general of the Royal Thai Police Department.

Occasionally the survey team encountered unexpected situations that
were surprising or humorous. Once, during the royal family's stay in
Bhubing Palace, the team was conducting a land survey in Chiang Dao
district, Chiang Mai. I was with the two usual suspects, Col. Teanchai
and Pol. Lt-Gen. Thep, and Gen. Nual Chantree, former chief aide-
de-camp general. Because all of these gentlemen were serious Buddhist
practitioners, traveling with them always felt like going on a pilgrimage.
Topics of discussion rarely strayed far from Buddhism and spirituality.

The topic of discussion as we were surveying that morning was death.
For most people, talking about death was a bad omen, but for us it was
just another natural topic of conversation. As we reached Chiang Dao,
we decided to stop for a visit to a local temple situated on a foothill, Wat

Tham Pha Plong because we were certain that the king would definitely want to call on the abbot, Ajarn Sim Buddhajaro.

We found, as we entered the temple area, that Ajarn Sim was busily overseeing construction. We greeted and paid respect to the abbot and introduced ourselves and then asked him for a sermon. (I came prepared with an audio tape recorder.) Ajarn Sim quickly scanned around the construction site and pulled a canvas chair, saying, 'Okay, let's do it here.' He then started the sermon. As he uttered the first words, all members of the survey team looked at each other in astonishment. The abbot gave a very brief sermon on death: one needed to live without recklessness because one never knew when and where death would come. We should remind ourselves of the uncertainty of death by quietly saying a Pali prayer: '*Moranang ne bhavisati*'.

Another time the survey team made a trip by car to Wat Hin Hmak Peng, Sri Chiang Mai district, Nong Kai. Before we headed out, one in the team had an idea to test the knowledge of the others and asked what was the content of *patchim owadhi*—the last sermon by Buddha. It wasn't a difficult question for serious Buddhist students and practitioners like us. So, someone in the group gave the answer right away. In his last sermon, the Buddha said to his disciples, 'All *sankhara* is by nature impermanent, one should always be prepared with mindfulness'.

Wat Hin Hmak Peng was situated on the bank of the Mekong River, home of Ajarn Tesq Tesrangsi, a highly accomplished *vipassana* master. As we entered Ajarn Tesq's *kuti*—living quarters, or abode of a Buddhist monk or novice—we asked him to give us a sermon and my tape recorder was again doing its duty. Ajarn Tesq said he was not well and had a sore throat, so he was going to give us a very short sermon—on mindfulness.

On my birthday (14 November), I don't remember what year, the king was staying at Bhuban Palace in Sakon Nakhon in the Northeast. I usually don't care for big celebrations for my birthday, so as usual, that morning I was preparing to make a simple offering of food and necessity items to a monk. The day before Privy Councilor Dr. Shaowana Na Seelawant had told me about a good elderly monk named Luang Puu Kinnaree at Wat Kanta Seelawas in That Phanom district, Nakhon Phanom, not far from the palace.

I asked a fellow security police officer to come along, Khun Rangsi Inthakosai, who later retired as a lieutenant general and deputy chief permanent royal court security police officer. We stopped at a local market to buy food and a few necessities. It was getting quite cold in the cool season there, so I bought some blankets as well. After the shopping errand we set out on our way to the temple. On the way, Khun Rangsi and I discussed many things about work. We had long been close colleagues, even before joining the court security force. I shared with Khun Rangsi my frustrations and mentioned not entirely in jest that I wanted to quit and go into monkhood.

We made it to the temple just before eight o'clock in the morning. Luang Puu Kinnaree just came back from his morning begging alms. I told a novice to inform him that I would like to make an offering to him. Shortly thereafter, Luang Puu Kinnaree came out in full robe and seated himself in front of his quarters. The morning sun was gentle. Khun Rangsi and I moved forward on our knees and made the offering. As soon as the elderly monk received the offering, he uttered in a clear northeastern dialect, 'Don't you want to be become a monk? If you wish, I can ordain you here. There are enough robes'.

I was certainly taken by surprise and at a loss for words. So he continued, 'Can't do it yet, can you? If you can't make up your mind, you should continue what you're doing'. Then, he proceeded to give us a lengthy sermon and ended with his thanks for the offering and his blessings.

Another monk I knew through the king was Ajarn Ngoan Sorayo. I met Ajarn Ngoan for the first time during the king's visit to Kampaengpetch province, if I remember correctly, for an opening ceremony of a national museum there in March 1971. I had gone ahead to make necessary arrangements. The governor, Khun Kaj Raksamanee, introduced me to Ajarn Ngoan. I arranged for Ajarn Ngoan an audience with the king because he wished to present to the king with a few Buddha relics.

I had met Ajarn Ngoan on several occasions after that visit, when he came down to Bangkok, and when I went to visit him at his monastery, Wat Phra Buddhabath Khao Ruak, Taphan Hin district, Phichit. Ajarn Ngoan lived in a small hut on a small hill behind the monastery, which was once a cemetery. Whenever I visited him, I always stayed in a small

hut, a little higher than his. Ajarn Ngoan said that only he and I could
live in those huts.

A strange thing about that place was the flock of ravens that lived in
a big old tree inside the temple compound. The ravens were friendly
to no one but Ajarn Ngoan. They would fly down to stand on his head
or his shoulders or climb up and down his lap. They would also take
whatever belonged to him as they wished.

Once while I was visiting with Ajarn Ngoan, a raven came down,
unzipped a wallet with its beak and carried away the small stash of
banknotes offered to the monk by a layperson. It took the banknotes to
its nest, simply ignoring the novices who were yelling and howling in
protest. The next morning I said to Ajarn Ngoan that it was a pity the
raven had taken his money, but he said it was all right that the raven had
returned the money to him.

Ajarn Ngoan was said to have magical powers, but because I had
little interest in magic and he apparently was aware my views (that
use of magical powers did not lead to the path of salvation) he and I
never discussed anything about magic. Although our discussion mostly
concerned dharma and meditation practice on which Ajarn Ngoan had
abundant knowledge and expertise, I was exposed to other things as
well. One of them was about the King Taksin statue.

In 1981, after I had left my position in the palace, Ajarn Ngoan had asked
to see me. He said, the 'inner knowledge' of his and a few other monks
indicated that the political situation was in turmoil because the soul of
King Taksin was dispossessed, not having found a peaceful resting place.
Ajarn Ngoan would like to build King Taksin statue and place it in an
appropriate location. The statue would not be dressed in kingly attire
but a monk's robe. The king of Thon Buri who died a tragic death had
once been a monk. But because this was going to a be a statue of an
historical king, Ajarn Ngoan thought it appropriate that this project be
approved by or, better yet, done under the patronage of King Bhumibol.
He asked me to deliver his intent to the king adding that he would be
responsible for the design and pay for all the costs.

I was of two minds about bringing up the matter to the king. On
the one hand, the idea seemed supernatural and rather nonsensical. I

wasn't sure how the king was going to take it. But, on the other hand, it came out of good faith and was going to be done under the auspices of Buddhism. The king was himself a serious Buddhist and had also once been a monk. I decided to contact a senior official in the royal household and ask him to bring up the matter with the king. As it turned out, in addition to giving an approval, the king contributed some money for the costs.

14

Ajarn Ngoan was both a painter and a sculptor, trained in Italy. I had seen his sculpting skill in an exceptionally beautiful Buddha image in nibbana position and the statue of King Chulalongkorn (Rama V). Ajarn Ngoan started working on the King Taksin statue as soon as the royal approval was received. The statue would be in a monk's robe sitting in a meditative posture.

I was invited to witness the casting process in a factory that specialized in casting and founding Buddha images in an area in Bangkok that was once Thon Buri. After the work was done, I took a statuette of King Taksin (only five inches high) to Chitralada Palace to receive the king's blessing. The king blessed the statuette along with a number of Buddha images and amulets that would bear the king's initials Bhor. Por. Ror. These amulets would be sold to laypeople and the proceeds contributed toward the construction of Wat Pathum Wanaram.

With the king's blessings, there was a question where to place the life-size statue of King Taksin. Ajarn Ngoan had wanted the king returned to his rightful place—in his old palace. The problem was that the old palace was now the naval headquarters. I suggested that any temple in Thon Buri, the old capital of the kingdom, would be appropriate. Eventually, a home was found for King Taksin, in Wat Phavana Phirataram near Khlong Bangkok Noi canal in Bangkhunnon district.

I had known Luang Puu Kamphandha before he became a *luang puu*. Let me indulge myself with a little bit of complaining here. Nowadays the pronouns used for and by monks are not only incorrect but also don't reflect reality. Before, one would call a monk *luang phor* if he was the same generation as one's parents, or *luang puu* if he was roughly the same as one's grandparents. Today, many monks as young as one's younger brothers are called *luang puu* and *luang phor*. Even the monks started calling themselves by what laypeople called them, instead of using the proper word *attamaphap* or *attama*—the equivalent of 'I' for monks. Some monks even used *khrap* or even the casual word *ha* for positive acknowledgement. It's a changing world indeed.

Returning to my story about Luang Puu Khamphandha Kosapanyo, I was introduced to him at the time I was involved in People's Assistance Teams, training civilian volunteers in self-defense skills in efforts to fight communist insurgencies in the late 1960s, before I was appointed to court security. Then Phra Khamphandha was the abbot of Wat Kosakaram, or Wat Mahachai, as the locals in Baan Mahachai, Pla Pak district, Nakhon Phanom, know it.

The situation in Pla Pak during that time was grave. There were constant attacks by communist insurgents. It was guerilla warfare. The local police station was set on fire and a policeman was killed in a street ambush by a bomb explosion in broad daylight. Traveling in and out of the district was done with great caution. The chance of ambush was high.

When the group of village defense volunteers finished their training course in Prachuab Khiri Khan, they returned to their home districts, divided into different operation units. One such unit set up a camp near Wat Mahachai. A younger brother of the abbot was among the volunteers.

At the time Wat Mahachai had only a *sala*, a temple hall for giving religious instruction to novices, and *kuti*, living quarters for monks and novices. The abbot wanted to build a proper place for Buddhist ceremonies. I had mentioned to Luang Puu Khamphandha then that the villagers were still poor and the situation volatile, and that these needed to be considered. It would be unwise to build a new, fancy structure because it would provide ammunition to the communists' public relations campaign in order to win the villagers to their side. It was not difficult to see that an attack by the communists against the monks for living beyond the villagers' means. The abbot was a rural monk of great intellect and understood the complexity of psychological warfare.

❖

After I took my position in the royal court, the king kindly granted me permission to visit the villagers I had trained who were now working in various People's Assistance Teams in the northeast. I made regular visits to Sakon Nakhon, Nakhon Phanom and Ubon Ratchathani, often with care packages—clothes, basic necessities—from the king. I regularly visited Luang Puu Khamphandha and during those visits saw that faith and respect that the villagers bestowed in the abbot had resulted in a beautiful new temple for Wat Mahachai.

Around 1974 I visited the abbot again and found that a small pagoda was being built on the temple grounds. The abbot had acquired Buddha relics from Laos. When I told the king about this, he would like to offer some relics to be enshrined in the pagoda as well.

Now that there was royal involvement, building the pagoda was no longer a small matter. I quickly contacted Khun Pisal Moolsartsathorn, the deputy governor of Nakhon Phanom, who happened to be a classmate of mine from Chulalongkorn University. Thanks to Khun Pisal's public relations skills, more people were interested in contributing to the building of the pagoda. As it turned out, the pagoda, initially conceived as modest in size, became a rather large and elaborate pagoda. About a year later, the royal couple visited the temple on Visakha Bucha Day and brought the Buddha relics to be enshrined in the new pagoda.

The king's involvement in local affairs, especially in religious activities, was very much prized and sought after by the local people. Even mere royal blessings gave a whole new meaning to a simple activity. I learned this after joining the court security force. Temple gables bearing the king's initials were in great demand of temples around the country. On each of these gables was a Pali verse with a Thai translation: 'Thais can preserve their sovereignty through unity.'

This specially coined verse clearly reflects the king's intent to remind his subjects of the importance of living in harmony and the sovereignty of the nation.

15

The work of palace security police officer sometimes included duties outside providing security to the royal family members, but a duty I did not expect to be given was secretarial support.

On 9 November 1970 the king was invited by the Thai Rotary Club to give a speech at a gala dinner at Dusit Thani Hotel. The speech was to be in English because there would be a number of foreigners there. English is the operational language of Rotary International. I was put to work on typing the speech along with MR Kukrit Pramoj. As most Thai people know, MR Kukrit was a well-rounded scholar and an Oxford graduate. His foreign language skills were unsurpassed. I, with a master's degree from New York University, was not exactly a well-rounded liberal arts student. Nor did I have good foreign language skills. But it was His Majesty's command.

MR Kukrit and I set up a temporary workshop in the royal guards' office, with Khun Phoemphun Krairirk, then secretary of the royal household, making sure we were well fed that afternoon. As the king continued to send down a series of handwritten drafts to the workshop, painstakingly I typed the notes—with two fingers—of the draft on 3x5 index cards on the electric typewriter. The cards were continually collected and sent back up to the king by a royal page.

Touch typing was beyond my ability, although I had begun to learn to type in English while studying in the United States—one finger at a time. By the time I had to type my thesis I managed to use as many as five to six fingers. Typographical errors were my close friends. I knew my skills (or lack thereof), so the more I anxiously wanted to do better, the more mistakes I made on the index cards. Several times, after the typed index cards were brought up, the king would radio down to give corrections.

I was so painfully slow that by the time the king had left Chitralada Palace for Dusit Thani Hotel and MR Kukrit had gone home, I was still going at it on the typewriter. My anxiety was beyond description. I tried to focus on getting the typing done and sacrificed accuracy for speed. I figured, once the king arrived at the hotel, dinner would start and by the time coffee was served after dinner, the king would have to go up the podium to deliver his speech. But *I* had the index cards.

I hopped on a police car that belonged to the Crime Suppression Division and went straight to the hotel, instructing the driver to use both the emergency light and the siren. After a short half-hour ride (short by Bangkok standards), which felt like hours, I was dropped off at the hotel. I ran up to the Naphalai Room where the gala dinner was being held. I tipped a hotel clerk to pull out ML Thaweesanti Ladawal, the king's private secretary. ML Thaweesanti took the stack of index cards to the king. I noticed as I was leaving the hall that the king seemed rather unruffled, smiling and conversing cordially with the two foreigners seated on each side of him, as if there were nothing to worry about.

By the time I got back to Chitralada Palace I started to feel like I was coming down with something, with body aches and some temperature. I contemplated the fact that my career in the palace was not going as well as it should and might even be coming to an end. Even if the king's private secretary managed to deliver the speech notes to the king in time, the notes would be so ridden with mistakes that the king's speech would not be smooth.

I lay down and listened to the radio broadcast of the event with huge qualms. Until the king returned to the palace and few minutes later a royal guard knocked on my door and said the king wanted to see me. As the saying goes in Thailand, my heart fell down to my ankles, imagining the king furious with the many mistakes and that I had caused him embarrassment. I entered the palace, my heart thumping.

The king was with Queen Sirikit and several other people on the first floor. He was in a joyous mood and said to me, 'Thank you, Vasit.' Miraculously, I suddenly stopped feeling ill—literally the situation in which the Thais describe as *'tee ton pai kon khai'* or an unnecessary feeling of dread that something serious terrible was about to happen. I realized then how silly and paranoid I was to have thought that the king would be so troubled by my ineptitude. Inconvenient to not have had a well-typed speech perhaps, but the king was a calm person by nature and always in control of the situation. I wasn't sure if the king had trusted me to finish typing the notes in time but even if I had not finished, he would have gone on to deliver his speech as he had planned without much fuss. After all, the king had drafted his own speech.

I was introduced to King Bhumibol's solid and calm character—never angry or reactive in times of crisis. I would come to see the king's calm composure in many more crises to come, most a lot worse than poorly typed speech notes.

The next morning all the papers reported positively about the king's speech and the English-language papers printed it in full. In the speech, the king reported the work with hill tribe minorities in the north. The previous year, the king had given a speech to the same rotary club and received over 300,000 baht, which became the starting fund for a welfare project under royal patronage for the hill tribes in the north.

The king told the audience about the background, the work, and the obstacles in working with the northern hill tribes. He used a dry humor—unusual in royal speeches in those days. He told the story of local police reporting that a group of Lahu (known by Thais as Muser) villagers ate the pigs, instead of raising them. 'I felt quite uneasy', said the king, as the project was not intended as merely a 'gastronomical' relief for the villagers. However, after some careful investigation, it was revealed that the villagers did not eat all the pigs, but only those that had an 'extra finger' (that is, hoof). Pigs with too many fingers were said to bring bad luck for the Lahu villagers. To avoid angering the ghosts, the pigs had to be sacrificed. From then on, the king related to the audience, the hooves of all pigs had to be counted before the pigs were sent out to the villages. The accounting from that point onwards seemed to have indicated that the number of sacrificed pigs went down substantially.

One important point the king made about the hill tribe people was that they were no different from us. They were ordinary human beings, no more and no less greedy or angry than other Thais. Their standards of behavior and social norms were no less intricate than elsewhere. Like everyone else, when the personal and cultural barriers, suspicions and fears were undone, capacity for understanding, empathy, and logic remained. For this reason, the hill tribe people were entitled to acceptance and participation in mainstream society and the right to develop their own communities.

The king's speeches are often filled with ideas and lessons to ponder: nutritious food for thoughts. Every year Thai people enjoy his speeches and look forward to their beloved king's birthday speech, which is of course delivered in Thai.

In my job, I was also fortunate to have a few opportunities to serve important royal guests. In February 1972, Queen Elizabeth II of England, her husband the Duke of Edinburgh and their daughter Princess Anne visited the country as guests of the royal couple.

Naturally the British royal family came with their own security team, so I had no duty to provide security to them during their stay. But in the afternoon of their second day of the visit, I provided security for the procession of the two royal families to Muang Boran—Ancient City—in Samut Prakarn. The Ancient City is basically a miniature city of Thailand's major historical sites and monuments. The model structures and artifacts have been built with great attention to details and superb skills. Situated near Bangkok, it is a popular destination for visitors who do not have enough time to visit actual sites, a good substitute.

I had taken my family to the place several times before, but hadn't seen it so spectacularly decorated as this time. Each model structure was enhanced with multicolor lighting, apparently much enjoyed by the royal guests. The way back to Bangkok wasn't smooth, however. Queen Elizabeth's limousine had some mechanical problems, halting the procession in the Sukhumvit area. But, after a quick substitute with an alternate limousine for Queen Elizabeth, the procession was again on its way.

During that visit, the British royal family was also invited to Bhubing Palace in Chiang Mai, where they enjoyed a number of activities, from an elephant show in Mae Sa waterfall to a visit to McKean Hospital, the local rehabilitation center for people with leprosy. Again, there, in the north, the experience of the British royal guests was less than perfect. *Time Magazine* published a series of photos of the Queen of England looking uncomfortable in various positions riding on an elephant during the elephant show. I guess the awkward rattan chair on the queen's elephant was the culprit. Presumably no one but the *Time* reporter with a good telephoto lens noticed at the time.

On the fifth day, the royal guests were scheduled to visit McKean Hospital and to have afternoon tea at the British Consulate on Charoen Prathet Road and Ping River. (The British Consulate in Chiang Mai has been long closed and a private company now owns the building.)

I recall that we left the hospital for the consulate at about half past four in the afternoon. Shortly after we left, I was informed by radio that the tea that was prepared by staff at Bhubing Palace was not yet ready. I was asked to stall the procession in reaching the consulate. I radioed the police escorts to reduce speed, causing the procession to crawl. Not long after, Queen Elizabeth's security officers radioed the police escorts to speed up. Obviously the slowing down without apparent reason must have caused some discomfort for the queen's guards, who were using a different frequency for their radio communication and did not hear the order to slow down.

It was a dilemma. I realized that I couldn't stall any longer. Well-wishers waved at the procession from the sides of the road. I stuck my head out the window and waved at them. Sure enough, a number of them flocked to the side of the royal limousine, which had to come to a halt. I got out the window of the car to stop people from coming too close and instructed other police escorts to do the same. It was several minutes before the procession was able to get on its way and as we were about to reach the consulate, I got a radio message that tea was now ready.

16

On 22 February 1972 King Bhumibol and Queen Sirikit attended the funeral of a revered monk, Phraya Noraratana Rajamanit at Wat Thepsirin Tharawat. Known to laypeople as Chao Khun Nor. Phraya Noraratana Rajamanit was an official in King Mongkut's court. When King Mongkut passed on, Phraya Noraratana Rajamanit went into permanent monkhood and became highly respected. All the Buddha amulets made under his patronage were usually in great demand and became valuable collectibles.

Before his death at the age of more than eighty, Chao Khun Nor was ill with cancer. The cancerous wound at the back of his neck was clearly visible. It was said that the revered monk sought no medical treatment because he believed that the cancer living inside him was a living being. Chao Khun Nor was fierce in his religious piety and devotion to the royal family. King Bhumibol and Queen Sirikit had great respect for him and visited him regularly. Whenever he knew that the royal couple were coming to the temple, Chao Khun Nor always came down with other monks to receive the royal couple, though, being quite ill, he could have waited in his room.

❖

It was in a hot month of April 1972. I was in the jungle with Thanying Vibhavadi somewhere in Surat Thani. A coded radio message came from Gen. Teanchai Janmookda: 'Congratulations for receiving a Cherry Pink.' I was clueless as to what this meant until Thanying Vibha took pity on me and translated the code: I was being honored with a royal decoration, The Most Illustrious Order of Chula Chom Klao.

Royal decorations are generally a given for civil servants in Thailand. It doesn't matter whether one wants them or not. They come at given times, often at promotions. I remember after I had served in the border areas for quite a while, I noticed that many of my colleagues were given royal medals for border service. I wondered why I wasn't. I went to the Special Branch administrative office to inquire and was further surprised when the admin officer on duty there asked me, 'Didn't you ask for one for yourself?'

Apparently, although most royal decorations are given automatically, some have to be specifically requested. The automatic ones are such as those in the Crown of Thailand (*Mongkut Thai*) and the White Elephant (*Chang Phueak*) orders. For me and my fellow officers in the Royal Thai Police, we were first granted the Member (Fifth Class) of the Most Noble Order of the Crown of Thailand (*Benjamaporn Mongkut Thai*) once our salary reached a certain level. The next one in the same class is the Member (Fifth Class) of the Most Exalted Order of the White Elephant (*Benjamaporn Chang Phueak*). These two royal decorations, as the names indicate—*benja* means five—are in the Fifth (lowest) Class of royal decorations. Up the next level are the Member (Fourth Class) of the Most Noble Order of the Crown of Thailand (*Jaturathaporn Mongkut Thai*) and the Member (Fourth Class) of the Most Exalted Order of the White Elephant (*Jaturathaporn Chang Phueak*). In each class of decorations, one must first get the Crown of Thailand decorations before one is entitled to a White Elephant. For Thai civil servants, the Knight Grand Cross (First Class) of the Most Noble Order of the Crown of Thailand (*Pathommaporn Mongkut Thai*) is considered the ultimate royal accolade of all.

The family of those who have received the royal sash is entitled upon their demise to a royal mortuary urn. Some do not want their family to use that entitlement and make it clear to the family—before their death, naturally—that they do not want to end up in a mortuary urn, presumably out of fear of being put in a sitting position in the urn. I wonder why one would be afraid of having one's arms and legs contorted into the sitting position. After all, one is already dead.

Beside the Crown of Thailand and the White Elephant orders, there are other royal decorations. Among the important is the Chula Chom

Klao. The Most Illustrious Order of Chula Chom Klao was created in BE 2416 or AD 1873 during the reign of King Chula Chom Klao (known in the west as King Chulalongkorn or Rama V). King Chulalongkorn was enthroned in 1868 when he was only fifteen years old. Somdej Chao Phraya Borom Maha Srisuriyawongse (Chuang Bunnag) was the regent until the king reached the age of twenty. After having spent the remaining years of his teens travelling in foreign countries, King Chulalongkorn went into monkhood for fifteen days. When he reached twenty years old, he assumed his duties as king.

The story has it that King Chulalongkorn wanted to show his appreciation for the peace and tranquility that transpired during the first ninety-year reign of the Chakri Dynasty and the loyalty of royal relatives and civil servants. The king ordered the creation of Chula Chom Klao decorations, which were granted to a number of relatives and civil servants. The decorations, which would be inherited from one generation to the next in the family, were—as was written on them—'keepsakes for those who have preserved our motherland in the past and those who are preserving it today.'

Knowing its history, I was very excited about the Chula Chom Klao Order of decoration and proceeded to learn as much as possible about it. The Chula Chom Klao pendant is a gold circular disc, with the enameled portrait of King Chulalongkorn at the center, surrounded by a blue enameled circlet, engraved with the motto: 'I shall maintain my lineage'. Inside the disc and surrounding the portrait of King Chulalongkorn are eight rays of a star, enameled in pink, backed by a cogwheel of gold. The points of the star are linked to a separate wreath of gold leaves, enameled in green. This is topped with a gold crown of enameled work in green, red, blue and white and a golden starburst.

The backside of the medal contained almost identical details to those on the front, except for that in the center was the Airavata elephant bearing the Trident, enameled in white. The central disc is surrounded by a blue enameled circlet with golden letters 'Year of Rooster, Era 1235.' Around the edge of the disc was the chakra enameled in white on red background.

There has been quite a bit of misunderstanding about the motto on the Chula Chom Klao medal. Many people have understood the lineage in 'I shall maintain my lineage' to mean the Chakri Dynasty, but in fact it referred to the lineage of the holder of the medal that King Chulalongkorn intended to bless.

The (male) court officials who were rewarded with Chula Chom Klao decorations were first given the Grand Companion (Third Class, higher grade) of the Most Illustrious Order of Chula Chom Klao (*Tatiya Chula Chom Klao Wiset*) and then the Knight Commander (Second Class, lower grade) of the Most Illustrious Order of Chula Chom Klao (*Thutiya Chula Chom Klao*), the Knight Commander (Second Class, higher grade) of the Most Illustrious Order of Chula Chom Klao (*Thutiya Chula Chom Klao Wiset*), the Knight Grand Cross (First Class) of the Most Illustrious Order of Chula Chom Klao (*Pathom Chula Chom Klao*), and the Knight Grand Cordon (Special Class) of the Most Illustrious Order of Chula Chom Klao (*Pathom Chula Chom Klao Wiset*) respectively.

The Chula Chom Klao royal decorations were rare and much desired by civil servants. The medal I received on 5 May 1972 at Dusit Palace was the Grand Companion of the Most Illustrious Order of Chula Chom Klao. Hanging on a pink silk strip, the medal was pinned on the chest of my uniform. Pink was the color of King Chulalongkorn's birthday.

The award ceremony for the Chula Chom Klao royal decorations was held every year on the Chatra Mongkol Day, which falls on 5 May. On the afternoon of the ceremony in 1972 in Dusit Palace, both past and present awardees in official attires were waiting for an audience with King Bhumibol and Queen Sirikit. Awardees stepped forward to kneel in front of HM the King and to receive the medal as their name was announced.

The award ceremony required a rehearsal because the kneeling in front of the king was different from the normal day-to-day kneeling. To receive an object from the king (and other major royalties), one approaches, stops, first gives a salute (for men) or a curtsey (for women) in front of the king, then steps forward with one's right foot and kneels only on the left knee. This right foot-left knee business is particularly important for soldiers and police officers because of the sword on the left side of the full official uniforms. In the kneeling position with the right knee up and the left knee down on the floor, the most practical thing to do with the sword is to shift it toward the back. This way the sword will fall nicely down on the floor. Stepping forward with the wrong foot could cause the awardee to look foolish with his sword sticking upright and refusing to let the awardee kneel down in front of the king in a dignified manner.

Another funny thing that happened often enough is that the awardees kneeled down so far below where the king was sitting that the king had to stretch to reach forward to give the medal, or that some stopped to kneel too far away and had to move forward in the kneeling position toward the king. Still others kneeled so close that the king had to lean back to give the medal.

Even after having received the medal, retreating from the audience with the king could also prove tricky, if not done mindfully. At the back of the room was a table with many precious royal decoration items. In the old days, a medal was given with other things such as a golden-footed tray, but nowadays these items are only symbolically displayed in the ceremony. A clumsy retreat might result in knocking down the table, and all the precious items along with it. It has happened.

Many may see this type of court tradition rather silly and dated, but the Thai people have had a monarchy for several hundred years. Court rules have long been practiced and have become a time-honored tradition, symbolic to our national identity. Without it, another meaning of being Thai may be lost. Those who have played an important, albeit little recognized, role in preserving this tradition are the civil servants (regular and political) who enjoy the opportunities to have royal audience the most.

I have heard civil servants such as district chiefs quite embarrassingly use common terms like *phom* (for I) and *khrap* in speaking with the king. I think that district chiefs should learn how to use the royal vocabulary properly.

Those who have received Chula Chom Klao decorations are entitled to wear an ornament corresponding to the medal, a special button in the shape of a silk flower in pink with King Chulalongkorn's initials Jor.Jor. Jor on the button. For the Most Illustrious Order of Chula Chom Klao, the button is the same style but with the initials and a silver coronet; for the Knight Commander of the Most Illustrious Order of Chula Chom Klao, the same button has the same initials and a golden coronet; and for the Grand Companion of the Most Illustrious Order of Chula Chom Klao, the button is the same but the initials themselves are golden embroidered without a coronet. These buttons, often (mistakenly) called *jork* or *jork sii chomphoo* (pink button), can be seen attached on the left lapel of men's suit jackets. Although women, who have received these medals, can do the same thing, I have yet to see women wearing these pink silk buttons.

Given that they have been given well over a hundred years since the time of King Chulalongkorn, the Chula Chom Klao decorations have become highly esteemed and even sacred. Anyone fortunate enough to have been given these decorations should appreciate and behave in a way befitting for this ultimate honor and refrain from committing dishonorable deeds from getting drunk to abusing one's power and position. I believe that those who have committed such unbefitting deeds will eventually be repaid by equal misfortune.

One of the king's regular and increasingly demanding affairs is handing out certificates to university graduates. When this task was entrusted to the king fifty years ago, it was quite manageable. There were only three (state) universities in the country: Chulalongkorn University, Thammasat University (then known as Thammasat Karnmuang) and Kasetsart University.

Over the years the number of Thai universities has grown, as has the number of graduates per year. Nowadays, tens of thousands of university students now graduate each year. Commencement ceremonies take far longer time than before, hours or even days for large institutions, causing the king and other royal representatives who give out the certificates to sit for very long hours at a time.

There have been suggestions to change the graduation protocol that requires the king to give out the certificates to the graduates. Once the court officials and those at the Thammasat University agreed on a new protocol to have the queen help in handing out the certificates because she usually accompanied the king to the ceremonies anyhow. Graduates would then form two rows, one to receive the certificates from the king, and the other to receive them from the queen.

There were also other details to debate. Graduates as a rule expect the nicest and clearest picture of themselves receiving the certificate from the king taken from the best position possible. Someone questioned whether having another row of graduates receiving the certificates from the queen would ruin the chance of having the best possible picture, with an extra set of hands sticking out at the same time. After a long debate and negotiation, the new protocol won.

But alas, after all that came the day of the ceremony at Thammasat and the queen was ill. The new protocol didn't have a chance to be tried out. The king had to hand the certificates to the Thammasat graduates one by one—alone.

17

Many who have seen graduation ceremonies wonder how His Majesty can sit that long in the same position. Those who have had an audience with him can also testify that he sits in the same position for a long time on other occasions as well.

Several times I myself have seen the king playing music without changing position from evening till dawn, though other musicians would take occasional bathroom breaks. I have learned that the king has an unusually focused concentration, once he puts his mind into a task. When committed to do a thing, the king puts all of his attention to executing the task and leaves no room for concerns of his body. He is aware of bodily aches and discomfort but let those feelings go, as if detached from them.

On 30 November 1972 the king traveled to Phitsanulok and gave certificates to graduates of the Phitsanulok Education College. I went in advance for security clearance and had a chance to see the rehearsal, where four rectors took turn sitting to hand out certificates. All four complained of fatigue and discomfort. On the day of the ceremony the king came down by himself as usual and sat for over three hours, went back to Chitralada Palace and continued his evening jog routine.

Another memorable event occurred on 18 May 1971. Prince Vajira-longkorn, who at the time had not been given the title of the crown prince, completed a parachute training course from the BPP PARU, or Naresuan Camp, and graduated with excellent scores. I was particularly proud of this event because the teachers of the prince were also my teachers when I took the course. It was not surprising that the royal children were interested in parachuting. The royal family had always had such good relationship with the paratroops, given the many royal visits to remote jungle areas around the country.

The prince was particularly interested in parachuting. After finishing the course at Naresuan Camp, he took another course offered by the Army's Special Warfare Headquarters at Erawan Camp in Lop Buri.

During late 1972 and early 1973, the security situation in the country remained volatile. There was constant fighting between authorities and communist insurgents. Casualties mounted on both sides.

In January 1973, the king and queen visited the government forces, the police, the soldiers, and the highway officials in Nan and Chiang Rai. Because I worked in that area before I knew that security was problematic in the places where the royal couple was going to visit, such as Baan Pa Ka Luang and Baan Tham Wiang Kae in Nan and Baan Mai Rom Yen in Chiang Kam district, Chiang Rai.

The king and queen spent a long time with the villagers in Baan Mai Rom Yen, a large village newly established for several hill tribe minorities who had moved down from the mountain. The king also gave advice on village development to local authorities. They continued their visits in the north later that month to visit injured soldiers in Lomsak Hospital in Phetchabun, a marine corps unit in Baan Pa Yaab and the 9th Infantry Division in Baan Huay Moon in Daan Saay district, Loei.

From a security point of view, the visit to the marine corps was admittedly a very unsettling one because the camp was situated on top of the mountain surrounded by deep jungles on all sides. Although there was no question about the abilities of the marine corps, the king and queen were going into a war zone and there was no telling when the enemy would strike. The 9th Infantry Division was situated in a volatile area as well. However, all went well and only upon my return did I realize how the marines must have been filled with pride that their king and queen made the effort to visit them, if only for a few hours.

18

I had just received notice that the royal family would be going on a five-day boat trip to visit villagers on the western coast, in the Andaman Sea. Water and I have never been close friends, probably because I was born and grew up in Isan, which is known as the land of droughts. Worse, I had once nearly drowned. This would be my first travel on a large ship. The closest I had come to traveling by boat was a ferry trip.

Their Majesties together with Princess Sirindhorn and Princess Chulabhorn flew to Phuket to board the royal ship Jandara. Jandara—the Moon—was a survey ship built in Germany and was at the time thirteen years old. Jandara weighed 996 tons and was 69.85 meters long and 10.5 meters wide. She had two diesel engines, 1,000 horsepower, and a top speed of 13.25 knots. Ninety sailors were on duty. (This information was kindly given by Sub-Lt. Saranya Sasnupatham of the History Department of the Royal Thai Navy.)

The limited space on the ship meant inevitable intimacy. The royal couple's quarters were a remodeled room on the deck, where the captain's room would normally be. The cabins for others in the royal entourage were one level down. The cabins were tightly packed with bunk beds.

The beds on the bottom were more comfortable and gave better access, but given the Thai tradition that one cannot sleep on the higher ground than another more senior, the younger officers slept on the lower beds. There was one drawback to the lower bunk, however, which was the risk of being stepped on by the person sleeping on the top bed during the night—as I later found out, all too personally, being stepped nightly on by Pol. Col. Pranetr, my senior officer, as many times as he had to use the bathroom during each night.

Jandara took us around Phuket Island, and the southern provinces of Trang, Krabi, Phang Nga and Ranong. We stopped by Phuket to visit a pearl farm of the Thai-Swiss Pearl Company on Naga Noi Island. It was my first time to see how pearls were extracted from oyster shells—a delicate art and a top trade secret. The Japanese experts did not allow the Thais to see how the work was done. The Thais' primary work involved only diving to collect the oysters. Premium quality pearls were exported to Japan and other countries, and the lower-grade pearls were distributed locally.

Besides pearls, I also had an opportunity to see how bird nests were collected—not just any bird nests but the kind that were a delicacy, swallow nests. Swallows made their nests on tall cliffs. Nests were collected on Viking Island on the western coast, a more or less extreme trade.

The older nests were beautifully white and clear but the newer ones, built after the first generation had been collected, looked rather muddied. Some experts explained that the nests were made with saliva of the swallows—presumably even swallows could produce only so much saliva, making the latter generations of nests less clear because the saliva became mixed with blood from their throats. True or not, I felt both disgust and deep pity for the swallows and stopped eating swallow nests ever since.

On an island the name of which I forget, which all royal family members used to visit and had a beach with seawater pits, was a kind of animal I rarely saw living, that is, sea slugs. On that day I learned that Dr. Jinda (Pol. Lt-Gen. ML Jinda Sanitwongs) the queen's uncle, who was the king's personal doctor and hated sea slugs. Princess Sirindhorn didn't hate any animal and was happy to catch living sea slugs. I am not certain if anyone ever photographed Dr. Jinda running away from a sea slug that Princess Sirindhorn tried to hand him.

On 15 September 1973, the King Gustaf VI Adolf of Sweden passed away. Although Sweden and Thailand are geographically far away from each other, the monarchs share a close relationship. The king and the queen used to visit Sweden and have a personal relationship with King Gustaf VI Adolf and the Swedish royal family. The king designated Princess Sirindhorn as his representative to attend the Swedish king's funeral.

The king ordered me to assist with the official escort team. There was also a second informal escort team of court officials and a diplomat. Before the trip, I felt some difficulty about the uniform I was to wear in the funeral ceremony. The program for the ceremony required that I appear in full dress uniform. My police uniform consisted of a white jacket with a stiff collar, black trousers with vertical scarlet stripes on both legs, a saber and gloves.

If you wear this uniform in Thailand in the hot season, you will be hot and sweat but if you wear it in a cold country in winter, you won't be protected from the cold. Military officers did not face this problem because they are issued an official full dress for the cold season (as can be seen in a Ratchawallop Day parade in December). But at that time, police didn't have a full dress for the cold weather—no one thought to design even a normal winter coat or jacket uniform for the police. We had to wear whatever was available. A popular choice was a field jacket.

I solved the problem by taking my official police jacket to my tailor, Khun Chaiyong Maekcharoen and asked him to make a wool lining inside the jacket in hopes that this technique would dull the coldness during the ceremony.

Among the police and military officers at the ceremony, I was the only one in full dress in white, the color of the official uniform in the hot season. The other officers wore a dark or black uniform. I felt quite awkward at first but then I figured I probably already looked rather strange in that crowd already. The white jacket probably didn't make me look any more or less peculiar.

I was a little uncomfortable in my job on that occasion. My job was to provide security to Princess Sirindhorn. According to principles governing security and protection, an escort's place was right by the person you are supposed to be protecting. But according to the program, set by the Royal Household Bureau, Captain Sayan Khampheeraphan (who later became a general and deputy chief aide-de-camp general to HM the King) and I were assigned to a different car from Princess Sirindhorn's. The escorts in her car were Thanying Vibhavadi and Pol. Maj-Gen. Chote Klongwicha. Although Khun Chote held a military rank and had been a soldier, at that time, he was the ambassador of Thailand in Stockholm and had no direct responsibility to provide security to the princess.

I imagined that before making a trip, the Royal Household Bureau and our security team, my superiors, should have held a meeting to decide which royal court security soldier or police officer, or both, had responsibility for escorting royal family members. In case of an overseas trip, an invitation should be extended to representatives of the security unit of the host country, requesting a consultation to specify certain security details. Where in a procession our security officers would be positioned, and that our officers should not be assigned to a different car or a car outside the procession is a fine example.

The most important point is that those responsible for escorting members of the royal family be assigned to places where they can effectively carry out their security tasks. It is clearly not possible to provide security if you are in a different car from the person you must protect. In that case, you sit wondering about how you might respond in the event of danger to a royal family member. That was my dilemma in Stockholm that day.

❖

In the past I noticed that foreign representatives visiting Thailand arrived under the escort of a large group of security guards armed with pistols and machine guns. I don't know why Thai government allowed this. But when Thai royal family members visited abroad, we do not demand similar permission. I am not suggesting that we should demand to be fully armed, just to be adequately and reasonably equipped to do our job.

Princess Sirindhorn left Thailand with the escort teams for Stockholm at night on Sunday 23 September 1973. After she had reached Stockholm Airport, she stayed at the Grand Hotel. After that mission, I wrote about my experience in escorting her in *Fah Muang Thai,* a newspaper. Thanying Vibhavadi wrote an article for another newspaper. Given the passage of time and the pre-Internet world we worked in, our writings on this subject are probably not easy to find.

❖

The funeral of King Gustaf VI Adolf took place at the cathedral (called Storkyrkan in Swedish) on 26 September. The new king, King Carl XVI Gustaf, the nephew of the deceased king, invited me to the funeral.

At 9.20 p.m., Princess Sirindhorn with Prince Bhanubanah Yugala and Thanying Vibhavadi visited the royal cathedral in the palace where the late king lay in state.

At 9.30, King Carl XVI Gustaf reached the ceremony with his relatives and officers escorted the casket to the carriage, to which three pairs of black horses were harnessed. The procession began slowly toward the cathedral. The new king walked with heads of state from many countries and his male relatives behind the carriage. After members of the royal family, including Princess Sirindhorn and Thanying Vibhavadi, watched the funeral procession until it had almost reached the cathedral, Princess Sirindhorn left by car to welcome the procession at the cathedral.

I took my place at the seat specified by the invitation card, which was nowhere near Princess Sirindhorn. Before the royal corps reached the cathedral, I received the program for the ceremony, only to find that it had been written in Swedish. The information was almost useless for me. However, after reading it, I guessed that there would be a musical performance, following western tradition, as part of the funeral ceremony. The performance consisted of music by Anton Brukner, an Austrian composer, and Johann Sebastian Bach, a German composer. I knew the names of the musicians and used to listen to some of their works.

Admittedly I had no mind for music that day because my attention was focused on keeping watch on Princess Sirindhorn, who was seated far away from the kings and representatives of other countries.

19

When the body of King Gustaf VI Adolf was moved to the cathedral, a musical performance on large electric organs was followed by an orchestra and a choir. After the performance ended, the head of the church read an announcement as part of the funeral ceremony. The chief of the royal court took a crown from behind the coffin and placed it on a prepared table. The archbishop chanted, allowing soil to spill from his hand onto the coffin, and a cannon fired a salute. The ceremony ended with the choir singing.

Later, the body was moved from the cathedral to the royal cemetery at Haga Park. During this time, only King Carl XVI Gustaf, the new king, some members of the royal family, the prime minister, the minister of foreign affairs, and selected visitors continued to the cemetery.

During the procession, when King Carl XVI Gustaf was taken from the royal cathedral to Storkyrkan and eventually to the royal cemetery, I noticed no particular reaction among the Swedish people watching the procession. Some were even very noisy at a construction site—which seemed disrespectful to me. I was left with the feeling that, in general, the Swedish people felt differently about their king than the Thai people did toward theirs.

As the procession left the cathedral for the royal cemetery, Princess Sirindhorn, along with other visitors, went to the House of Nobility to wait for the return of King Carl XVI Gustaf, who would host lunch. The official duties of Princess Sirindhorn relating to the royal funeral of King Gustaf VI Adolf ended at this point but her trip aboard continued.

❖

On evening of 25 September, Princess Sirindhorn went on to Belgium as a royal guest of King Bodoin of Belgium and then to England for a personal trip. As a result I had the good fortune to visit both Belgium and England.

The trip from Sweden to Belgium was convenient because King Bodoin had a private plane. The princess and her entourage were invited to travel on the same plane along with King Bodoin and Queen Fabiola back to Belgium. The plane arrived at Brussels at night. The most striking thing for me at the airport was the reception for King Bodoin and Queen Fabiola on their return. There were no more than thirty people welcoming them, most of whom seemed to be government officers. This is a stark difference from what one would see in the case of a return of the Thai king and queen or their children from an overseas or an up-country trip. There would be a huge reception by the officials and their subjects at the Bangkok Airport.

King Bodoin accompanied Princess Sirindhorn on visits to various places in Belgium. On each occasion, I couldn't help but notice that Belgian people did not show any particular enthusiasm toward their king or give him any special treatment. There were only a couple of people coming to give him a special welcome and asked for his handshake.

Escorting Princess Sirindhorn, I saw how she used the opportunity to improve her knowledge of all people and countries. She was interested in all places she visited, even when they were merely tourist attractions. The guides that King Bodoin provided on these tours had expertise about the place and related stories about the history of the place. Princess Sirindhorn paid attention to the stories and made detailed notes. She also had a habit of collecting mementos. Apart from receiving various articles from other people, she bought books and souvenirs from the places she visited. Her escorts carried many books and souvenirs back to her residence every time she went outside.

The princess was a guest at Laeken Palace, which is the king's own court, located north of Brussels. Captain Sayan, myself, and the rest of the small entourage were provided accommodation at a hotel; we were again forced by circumstances to provide our security to Princess Sirindhorn from a distance, keeping in communication by means of radio transceiver. I was unhappy that I could not do my job as effectively as required to provide maximum security and protection.

The situation was better for Princess Sirindhorn's outings, however. Because the princess's trip to Belgium was a personal trip, there was no procession as in Sweden. King Bodoin offered a few cars. Apart from Thanying Vibhavadi, I sat in the same car as Princess Sirindhorn. Close escort and security for Princess Sirindhorn was what I had desired but been unable to perform in Sweden.

Her personal vehicle was a limousine with double-side seats and fold-able chairs, which could be pulled down in front of the back seats. The first time I pulled a chair down and jumped into the car to take a seat, I heard Princess Sirindhorn say softly, 'The chair is on my leg.' I knew that I had really disturbed her. Princess Sirindhorn is like her father in that way: she does not make a fuss during a time of crisis but confronts and resolves a problem with cool composure and calmness.

Among the princess's itinerary in Belgium was an important place, an ancient city called Bruges. It is located in the northwest of the country near the North Sea. The name Bruges first appeared in history in 892 AD (BE 1435). Over a thousand years old, Bruges had been an important port and commercial center of Belgium, as well as the residence of many dukes of Burgundy, giving it political importance. The city had many museums, churches, and cathedrals. Because it is located near the sea, there were many man-made canals leading to the nickname the Venice of the North—the north meaning the northern European continent.

King Bodoin and Queen Fabiola had a rather close relationship with Their Majesties King Bhumibol and Queen Sirikit, whom they called 'uncle' and 'aunt' respectively. Thanying Vibhavadi told me that the first time that Princess Sirindhorn visited King Bodoin and Queen Fabiola, she prostrated herself before them according to Thai tradition, which so impressed Queen Fabiola that she wanted to prostrate herself back to Princess Sirindhorn. Fortunately, Princess Sirindhorn was able to stop her from prostrating and explained to Queen Fabiola that the queen was like a senior relative and that the queen was not supposed to return the same greeting to someone of a junior status. The princess also gave a Thai commentary that had the queen prostrated back to her, 'Lice will be on my head.' Thanying Vibhavadi explained this ancient Thai expression to Queen Fabiola (that it is used as either a reprimand or a tongue-in-cheek comment when a Thai is somehow disrespectful to another of a higher social status or did something that seemed to bring someone of a higher status down to one's lower level).

After Belgium, we went on to London, where the entire group stayed in the same hotel—Claridges Hotel. In London, Princess Sirindhorn was able to really be herself because there were no official affairs. The only visit that came close to being official was a visit with Princess Margaret, the younger sister of Queen Elizabeth, at Regent Park. Thanying Vibhavadi was accustomed to life in England and could offer good advice to Princess Sirindhorn for planning her trip.

Princess Sirindhorn visited the Royal Academy of Art to see an exhibition of newly discovered archaeological objects from China. Among the artifacts in the exhibition was a flying horse statuette from Gansu province and a jade dress of a deceased Chinese princess. Princess Sirindhorn also visited the British Museum.

Besides museums, Princess Sirindhorn's favorite places were bookstores. There were many bookstores along the road in front of the museum. Because I knew her taste in books, I was her book scout.

There was a bookstore that sold rare old books. The shopkeeper let Princess Sirindhorn select a great many books. When she went to pay, the shopkeeper said that he would not sell them to her.

Princess Sirindhorn told me that the shopkeeper might have assumed that she was a student and knew the books well, so he allowed us to finish searching for the books only to tell us at the end that the books were not for sale. He may have wanted to keep them to sell at a higher price.

I also accompanied the princess to the opera 'La Traviata' of Verdi, performed by Sadler's Wells at the London Coliseum. I confess that to this day I cannot understand opera. I can appreciate some beautiful music in it but every time the performers engage in a dialogue by singing to each other, the performance became the antithesis of entertainment for me. That night I struggled to keep my eyes open until the opera ended.

The entertainment for the next evening was a stage play 'Crown Matrimonial' at Theatre Royal Haymarket. This was something I could understand and be entertained by. It helped greatly that the play was in English. The play was a satire of the English royal family.

There was one thing I had not expected to see in the play. Sitting in the row behind Princess Sirindhorn and Thanying Vibhavadi, I swooped my foot on the floor—something of a personal, uncontrollable tick that I sometimes do—and found a cushy object under the chair in front of me. I turned on my flashlight to look at it and discovered a dead mouse (believed to have English nationality) and it might just have died then, because it did not smell.

I considered the situation. Princess Sirindhorn and Thanying Vibhavadi were in front of me and also other ladies in waiting. I suspect none of them would have liked to see a dead mouse, especially while enjoying a play. The dead English mouse therefore went unmentioned and without introduction to the ladies.

After returning to Thailand from my escorting mission, on 9 October 1973, I went upcountry. I was still occasionally assigned to see to the delivery of goods under the royal patronage to various government offices and people upcountry. Sometimes, certain complaints sent to the king needed to be investigated. In some cases, I conducted the duties alone, but in other cases went with other court officers from Royal Pages Division or Office of the Secretary of the Queen.

Upon returning to Bangkok on 11 October, I found that the political situation was in a crisis. The police had arrested and detained thirteen individuals suspected of communist action. Among those detained, apart from two well-known politicians—Khun Khaisaeng Sooksai and Khun Veera Musikaphong, were university students and student leaders.

The action that was ostensibly communist was in fact calling for a permanent constitution. At that time there wasn't a constitution. Instead Thailand had the Constitution of the Kingdom of Thailand BE 2515 (1972 AD), which had been prescribed after the coup d'etat in 1971. The arrests of the constitution activists outraged the students and caused massive, protracted protests, especially around Thammasat University.

This was the first political crisis in my royal court security police career. Royal court security officers had a consultation and agreed to study the situation more closely because political crises always affected the king. Besides, we realized how the king was always concerned about the well-being of the Thai citizens in all areas, be they economic, social, or political.

In the night of 12 October, the situation still did not seem to have improved. A large number of people were at Thammasat University and more continued to join the demonstration. Together with a few court soldiers and court police officers, I decided to go to Thammasat to assess the situation up close. In plain clothes, we parked the car outside the campus and walked among the sea of other people onto the university grounds.

The situation we witnessed was very unsettling. The speech of the student leaders at Thammasat University was heated and violent. The emotions were running so high among the audience, smoldering, that it seemed it could burst any moment. The University Student Center distributed leaflets, giving the government an ultimatum to release those who had been arrested within twenty-four hours. Otherwise, 'serious measures' would be taken.

The largest demonstration in Thailand's political history was looking to be increasingly volatile when the crowd of over 100,000 people led by university students moved from Thammasat University to assemble at the Democracy Monument on Rachadamnoen Klang Avenue. When the huge crowd moved from the Democracy Monument farther to the Royal Plaza in front of Anantasamakhom Throne Hall, only a few hundred meters from Chitralada Palace, I felt that the situation was reaching a critical point for the government and Thailand itself. At that time, all royal court soldiers and police as well as officials with court security duties were on duty inside Chitralada Palace.

In the afternoon of the next day, Saturday 13 October, at around 4 p.m., the king invited nine university student representatives to have an audience with him at Dusidalai Hall at Chitralada Palace. The student representatives heard from the king that the government would release all the thirteen people arrested and a new constitution was promised within a year and a half. The king told the students that now that the government accepted their demand, the situation should return to normal.

When the student representatives left Chitralada Palace on that night, no one expected that the following day—Sunday, 14 October 1973—would become the saddest day for the Thai people, *Wan Maha Wippayoke* or the Day of Great Sorrow.

I have written extensively on the Day of Great Sorrow in a series in *Siam Rath* newspaper under the title 'The Events of Krung Rattanakosin'. The account was also published as a pocket book and ran into many editions. Therefore, I do not go into details of the event here, where I give only a few appropriate reference points (and even if I had gone into details of the event again here, I would not have done justice to it as I did in the *Siam Rath* series).

20

The crisis of the Day of Great Sorrow in October 1973 made me realize for the first time that people's suffering is the king's own suffering. From the beginning of the demonstrations at Thammasat University until matters escalated into a full- blown riot at dawn on 14 October 1973, the king had not taken a rest.

No matter how late it was at night, we could always hear the king's voice via radio and on the telephone. Although I did not attend to him personally, it was well-known among royal court staffs and those working close to him that he was closely watching the situation and keeping himself informed about the unrest and its severity.

When the crowd moved from the Royal Plaza toward Phra Warunyujane Entrance of Chitralada Palace on the side of Rama V Road, opposite to Dusit Zoo, the king was keenly aware of the seriousness and severity of the situation. It was this time that the king ordered the royal guards and police officers inside and around Chitralada Palace to remove live rounds from all firearms to ensure that military and police officers in the service of the king were also in the service of his people and would not harm them.

It was regretful and sad that the government at that time did not understand (or was not in the position to understand) the situation. Instead of allowing people who had stopped assembling in front of Chitralada Palace to return home freely, they ordered a handful of police forces from Special Branch to block the road to the Dusit District Office, which happened to be the way to Suan Ruenruedee, where Internal Security Operation Command (ISOC) was located.

That order resulted in a confrontation between the demonstrators and the police. In only a few minutes, the confrontation escalated into a riot throughout Bangkok and other provinces. And this made that Sunday, 14 October 1973 to be known as the Day of Great Sorrow for the Thai people.

Fortunately for Thailand, peace quickly returned after the government leaders resigned and left the country, because the student leaders and the Thai people did not want to see any prolonged conflicts and bloodshed among their countrymen.

The king's work after the sad event reflected hardship as well as his capacity in finding peaceful solutions. His first important task promptly carried out was to appoint Sanya Dharmasakti as the interim prime minister, who was at the time the rector of Thammasat University and a privy councilor.

I had a chance to meet Ajarn Sanya Dharmasakti and heard him say that he did not want to be the prime minister but accepted the appointment because it was the king's wish. His government was the thirty-third of Thailand and consisted of nineteen civilians, two military officers, and three police officers.

When the new cabinet took their oaths of allegiance before assuming their official positions, the king gave a speech, which in part, I reproduce:

A government has difficult tasks and special burdens to pursue with honesty, diligence, patience, courage and thoughtfulness. . . . It must restore what has been damaged and develop people to be thoughtful and honest. It must repair the hearts and minds that have been destroyed by the event. . . .

On 10 December 1973, all the members of the legislature previously appointed during the government of Field Marshal Thanom Kittikhachorn resigned. The resignations were followed by the king's command to establish a National Convention of 2,346 members representing

people from various professions and walks of life. I was one of the members.

The National Convention's major responsibility was to elect 299 individuals to become members of the National Legislative Assembly. Establishing the 1973 National Convention to elect the National Legislative Assembly showed the king's political acumen as well as the fact he was not in favor of the previous tradition of appointments. The king selected the 2,346 members himself from the list of individuals gathered by many groups of officials. He also asked me to suggest names of people I viewed appropriate.

The National Convention took place on 18 December 1973 at the Royal Turf Club, the Nanglerng Horse Racing Stadium. Nanglerng Horse Racing Stadium was selected as the venue for the conference because, apart from its spaciousness for the members and officers, it had a horse gambling machine, which could be used as a vote counting machine. This was why people later called this National Convention as *Sapha Sanam Ma* (the 'Horse Racing Stadium Convention').

The election result showed that I was one of the 299 elected members of the new legislature. I never really liked politics or had any aspiration to be a politician of any kind. The only duty that I deemed most important for me at the time was to provide security to the royal family.

However, after some reflection, I accepted my accidental involvement in politics. More important, I saw it that the king had appointed me as a member of the National Convention, so this might have signaled his desire for me to be involved in politics. I felt it was another way to serve the king and my duty to accept the position.

Another special task I was given after the Day of Great Sorrow was to coordinate between the prime minister and the university student leaders. I felt that although the students were happy with their victory, they were not so enamored of this achievement that they ignored listening to other opinions. The 'coordination' went smoothly with only a few small conflicts that were easily resolved with objective reasoning and mutual understanding. My being an alumnus of Chulalongkorn University and a royal court police officer sent by the king may have helped making the job easier than would otherwise have been the case.

After the new cabinet was set up and in operation, the king resumed his normal work. First, on 17 and 18 October 1973, the king visited those injured during the Day of Great Sorrow at Chulalongkorn Hospital, Vachira Hospital, Ramathibodi Hospital, Police General Hospital and Women's Hospital (which is now Rajavithi Hospital).

❖

On 27 October 1973, the king, the queen and Princess Sirindhorn presided over a Buddhist blessing ceremony at the Emerald Buddha Temple. Monks from all over the country joined this ceremony for national blessing.

That was not the end of the bad news. On 30 October 1973, Their Majesties and Princess Sirindhorn went on a mission for an opening ceremony of a rural school called Romklao in Baan Nong Kaen, Dong Luang district, Nakhon Phanom province. This was yet another school under the royal patronage in remote area, difficult to get to, and susceptible to communist insurgency.

On that day, after the school opening ceremony and giving a flag to a class of village scouts, the royal mission continued by helicopter to Bhuban Noi to visit an infantry battalion, 23rd Regimental Combat Team.

I was in another helicopter of the Royal Thai Air Force, farther ahead and nearer the destination, to prepare for the arrival of the king's helicopter. As my helicopter was about to land, right before my eyes, a white Royal Thai Police Department helicopter was taking off, apparently after dropping some passengers to pick up another group, and directly collided with a green Royal Thai Army helicopter coming in for a landing. The crash happened near the landing point assigned for my helicopter. Given the proximity, our captain lifted the helicopter right back up. I immediately radioed the officers in the king's helicopter.

This was the first time I had witnessed an air collision close up. I saw a military officer in uniform running out of the helicopter after the crash run back to the helicopter and go through the flame to help passengers stuck inside. Then I saw another man run out of the helicopter covered with blazing flames. The person fell down on the ground before someone ran to extinguish the fire. That man was the governor of Nakhon

Phanom province, Sunan Khan-asa, who later died as a result of the toxemia from the burns.

While our helicopter hovered above the accident waiting for landing, I smelled something terrible in the smoke from burning wreckage of the two helicopters and I suddenly knew that the smell was that of burned human bodies.

The head of the police aviators, who died along with a newspaper journalist in the accident, was Pol. Cap. Preecha Khlaaylee. I had been his passenger when insurgents in Nakhon Thai district, Pitsanulok province, ambushed the helicopter he captained.

Nine people were injured in the accident that day. The royal doctors in attendance provided primary medical attention and the helicopters in the royal mission helped transport the injured to the hospital.

Their Majesties spent the king's birthday that year (5 December 1973) at Vachiralongkorn Dam, Tha Muang district, Kanchanaburi province. The king held the celebration at Wat Sangkharam in the capital district of Kanchanaburi. HRH Prince Pittayalappruetiyakorn, president of the Privy Council, presided over the royal ceremonies in Bangkok, as the king's representative. After returning from Kanchanaburi on 8 December, the king attended the funeral of the Supreme Patriarch Pun Punyasiri.

The political situation was again in turmoil as prices soared. Day in and day out were protests and rallies by one group or another. People were driving provincial governors and district chiefs out of office. There were calls to bring down the price of rice. During this time, in the midst of fuel price hikes, the government was forced to raise the bus fare (from 50 satang to 75 satang). Workers around the country went on strike to demand higher wages. During November and December 1973, it was estimated that there were as many as eighty-eight strikes per day.

In such a situation, the king and the queen always showed their awareness of the seriousness of the problems and sympathy for the people. They consoled people and called for reason and understanding.

At dawn of the last day of 1973, the king, Princess Sirindhorn and Princess Chulabhorn offered alms to monks on New Year's Day at

Sanam Luang. An excerpt from the king's New Year speech on that occasion is as follows:

> The present task that everyone has to undertake is to respond to the crises with strength and equanimity. Full awareness, solidarity and peaceful cooperation will lead us away from disturbances and alleviate the current strife. All parties need to exercise mutual understanding, empathy and sympathy, and to let go of self-interests. Focus on collective interests. Support one another as we have always done. When we unite, there will be great power that will extinguish all the obstacles we face.

Six days into the new year, on 6 January 1974, the king and the queen moved to Bhubing Palace in Chiang Mai, as was their custom every year. His schedule in Chiang Mai at that time was not much different from that in the previous years. That is, he visited hill tribe villages near and far, as well as villages on the plains.

That year was the first year I accompanied the king to Wang Nam-khang Tangerine Orchard. The owner of orchard was Khun Phanlert Buranasilapin, who later became a deputy minister of agriculture and cooperatives. The orchard was located in Tambon Bankad, Sanpatong district, Chiang Mai. Whenever the king wished to visit this tangerine orchard, he preferred to drive there himself from Bhubing Palace. When he arrived, the owner and his relatives would offer him refreshments, after which the king and the queen would walk around the orchard for a long period.

During the first visit at this orchard, Khun Phanlert told the king and the queen of his special technique: playing soft music (through an amplifier) for his tangerines. Khun Phanlert testified that tangerines near the amplifier grew bigger and more beautiful than the ones further away, which were also near the traffic on dusty roads.

Khun Phanlert's theory reminded me of an experiment of Dr. Aat-ong Chumsai Na Ayutthaya. In his experiment Ajarn Aat-ong asked several of his students to focus their attention through telepathy on one plant and ignore the other. It turned out that the plant that received the students' attention grew better than the other one, which was of the same kind and the same age.

I thought about a Buddhist precept: monks shall not destroy plants. I guessed that Lord Buddha knew the truth, and that Khun Phanlert and Ajarn Aat-ong might know that plants have not only life but also a soul. If all this can be called wisdom, it can be said to have come from being with the king.

21

The royal trip to Bhubing Palace in early January 1974 made me appreciate something important—the king did not allow the political crisis in late 1973 to stop him from continuing his regular work. What many saw as a crisis, the king saw as just another problem to be solved. Also, not all problems need to be solved with the king in Bangkok.

As I began to understand His Majesty's way of working, it became clear to me that royal residences upcountry were effectively an extension of the royal offices. The king was not limited to living in Bangkok and was able to operate more efficiently from different provincial residences, whether in Chiang Mai, Sakon Nakhon, or Narathiwat. Facilities and security were as available at these provincial residences as they were at Chitralada Palace in Bangkok.

Early 1974 was a time of crisis for the Sanya Dharmasakti government, which just had begun administration in October the year before. Student demonstrations and mass protests were daily occurrences.

Students of political science would understand that Thailand had been under a series of military dictatorships for a number of years. The rights and freedom of citizens were merely words in the constitution, which the powers that be wrote (and tore up), and were restricted in reality. After the unexpected demise of a military dictatorship, it was only natural to find the citizens in frenzy, excited by the prospect of enjoying genuine rights and freedom. The Sanya Dharmasakti government had a difficult task of creating understanding among the populace that was thirsting to exercise their rights and freedom.

There were pressures on the government from all sides. Some demanded resignations of a number of ministers for various reasons. The economic minister was criticized for failure to solve the country's economic problems. The education minister was alleged to have supported the rector of Ramkhamhaeng University (who was in disfavor of a group of students). Finally, under pressure, Than Ajarn Sanya Dharmasakti and the cabinet resigned en masse on 20 May 1974.

On 22 May 1974, amidst uncertainty and chaos of finding a new prime minister, the king left Bangkok for Nakhon Si Thammarat. Normally, the royal journey to Nakhon Si Thammarat was by plane from Bangkok Airport to Nakhon Si Thammarat Airport, which at that time was a military airport, not a commercial one, as it is now. The aircraft used was normally a C-123, adapted with passenger seats, provided by the Royal Thai Air Force. However, for that trip the king elected to go by train. The reason for this was the hike in the fuel price. OPEC controlled the world fuel sources and the oil price was set even higher than before.

The staff responsible for preparing the king's travel might have considered that using a plane would use substantially more fuel than by going by train and told this to the king, who decided that it was better to travel by train.

Escorting the king at that time was especially important for me because it affected some personal changes, which can be said to have caused a revolution in myself. I was warned that a train trip would be extremely time consuming. This was not only because a train goes slowly than a plane but also because at each station along the railway, there would be many people and government officers waiting to welcome and see off the royal family. When the royal court soldiers and police officers were not on duty, they would have a lot of free time on the train journey.

Someone suggested that I take along items as a diversion to kill time on the train. The only diversion I could think of was a book. I hurried to get an English paperback book. The reason why I chose an English book was not to show off but they had much smaller print than a Thai novel of the same size. I chose an especially thick adventure novel, one of my favorite type of book, in anticipation that it would get me through the trip. On the day of our departure, Their Majesties, Crown Prince Vajiralongkorn, Princess Sirindhorn and Princess Chulabhorn left Chitralada Palace and boarded the train at Chitralada Train Station, opposite to the palace along the side of Sawankhalok Road.

❖

Chitralada Train Station had been built for royal trips during the reign of King Mongkut. In the past, leaving Chitralada Palace for Chitralada Train Station was easier because there was an eastern gate to exit. The gate was named In-yoochom (Indra in Attendance). It is now closed and has been fenced.

The train left Chitralada Palace after 4 p.m. Even before the train had crossed the Chao Phraya River, I realized that the journey would really be a long one. There were people waving the Thai national flag along both sides of the railway, waiting for a glimpse of the royal family. At many stops, people prepared altar tables to show their respect. As the train approached each group of waiting crowds, the train engineer slowed the speed to allow people to have a clearer view of the family, who sat near the windows, waving at the people who had come to greet them.

Moreover, when the train passed through major train stations located in a district or a provincial city, provincial government officers in white uniform were waiting to have an audience with the king. The king would then ask to stop the train to allow time for an audience with the local officers. In some provinces the time for audience was even more extended because the governors performed an ancient tradition of offering the king with a royal sword, which was always returned before the king left the station. Some local people also presented the royal family with gifts. It wasn't until 8 p.m. that the mission was able to leave Nakhon Pathom.

The royal guards and the court police alternated their shifts as set by the Royal Aide-de-Camp Department. I spent my free time reading the novel, which I finished even before we reached the southern province of Chumphon. The two royal guards, my shift mates, did not have any books with them. They killed time by sitting with their eyes closed. They were meditating—a popular practice among royal court staffs and servants.

Both men were permanent royal guards: Col. Nual Chantree and Capt. Sayan Khampheeraphan (both of whom were promoted to general in the later years of their career, with the former appointed chief aide-de-camp general to HM the King and the latter the deputy chief). At first, I was both amused by and curious about their meditating. Amused because I thought there must be other, more productive ways to pass the time, and curious about the technique.

I had read about mediation, especially Buddhadhasa Bhikkhu's work, and understood the basic concept of *anapanasati*. Buddhadhasa Bhikkhu's and other masters' writings on meditation had intrigued me. I thought that if these two senior guards were doing it, perhaps I could as well. I felt the urge to try.

I sat up right in my chair and opened the palms of my hands on my lap, with the right palm over the left. I closed my eyes and started becoming familiarized with my breath as I breathed in and breathed out. My thought became focused on just my breathing. 'Anapanasati' means awareness of the breathing in and the breathing out.

Not long after sitting in that meditative position, I started experiencing a new phenomenon. My eyes were still closed, but instead of complete darkness, I started seeing many colorful illuminations—green, red, yellow, orange, violet and blue. The illuminations were not static but moved across a horizon as if someone had been putting them on display for me.

I remembered from books that these colorful illuminations were called *nimitta*, which means images in the mind of those sitting in mediation or *kammatthana* (meditation exercise). I knew that *nimitta* is a sign showing that the mind of the meditator is becoming peaceful. I also remembered teaching of mediation masters about not attaching importance to this *nimitta* no matter how beautiful or ugly the experience. One was supposed to only acknowledge that it occurs and in the meantime effortlessly hold one's feeling of calmness. My feeling of calmness and peace at that time was simply breathing in and out.

I might have sat looking at the colorful illuminations for only about ten minutes. After I opened my eyes, I realized that I could achieve *samadhi* (calm peaceful mind). From that moment on I decided to continue practicing meditation as an important part of my life.

The realization that I could enter into the state of *samadhi* gave me an incredibly wonderful sense of encouragement. Since then, I have practiced mediation at all places and occasions. I have also come to realize that *samadh*i is only one among the three things that I should practice at the same time, the other two being *sila* (precepts) and *panya* (wisdom).

I began with observing the five basic *sila* immediately, because I knew that I could not observe all of many other precepts. On holy days, I observe additional three precepts. To express compassion to all living beings I eat only one meal a day and abstain from eating meat on Buddhist days.

At the time, I was unaware of the revolution in my mind had already started and that my knowledge of mediation would allow me to teach meditation to other people over the next twenty years.

On 25 May 1974, Ajarn Sanya Dharmasakti was once again appointed as prime minister by royal command. During that time, the political role of MR Kukrit Pramoj became increasingly prominent. He was elected as the president of National Legislature. Apart from myself, there were also other political science alumni of Chulalongkorn University in the National Legislature, taking part in drafting many laws and the new constitution.

My fellow political science alumni and I had been regular guests of MR Kukrit's house at Soi Suan Plu since we were students. The visits became more frequent once we were all involved in politics. During one of those meetings, MR Kukrit discussed with us the domestic situation. He said that once the draft of the new constitution was completed, the National Legislature would be annulled and a new election of members of House of Representatives would be held under the new constitution. He asked us what he should do. I recommended to him that because he was one of the founders of the new constitution he should continue in public life and form a political party.

I had no part in the founding of his Social Action Party. However, when the constitution of the Social Action Party was finished, he sent it to me for review and comment. I gave it a quick read and kept it for many days. I had not yet given him any comments. Finally, I decided to tell MR Kukrit that I was a member of the court police and that my major responsibility was providing security and serving the king. It was time to limit my political involvement. Since then, I had no involvement with Social Action Party, though I was still a regular guest at his Soi Suan Plu residence.

Around the middle of 1974, the political situation was still filled with chaos. The most violent event was a riot at Plabplachai Metropolitan Police Station on 4 July 1974. It began when a taxi driver who parked in a no-parking zone resisted arrest by police. In the attempt of the police to arrest the man, he shouted police brutality to the crowd just coming out the cinema.

This incident escalated when the crowd attacked the police station, destroyed property, and assaulted police officers in the station. The police officers fired their weapons, resulting in several deaths and a number of injuries. The fighting spread around Plabplachai area and the government had to announce state of emergency. The situation then calmed and the government lifted the curfew five days later.

The new constitution drafted by the National Legislature went into effect on 7 October 1974, following persistent calls for constitutional amendments by students and the people.

22

In August 1974, Their Majesties changed place of residence to Thaksin Palace in the south. The Thaksin Palace is located on Tan Yong Mountain, on the seaside in Muang district, Narathiwat.

The king's choice of Narathiwat as the location of his southern residence might have disappointed people in the other southern provinces because everyone would like a royal residence to be located in their province. However, when considering the geography and situations in the south, Narathiwat is a suitable choice for a royal residence.

Among the four southernmost provinces—Narathiwat, Pattani, Yala and Songkhla (Satun is also along the southern border but on the west, on the Andaman Sea), all except Yala are on the South China Sea. All four had problems of separatist insurgency fighting for independence from the Thai state. Especially in Yala, Chinese communist insurgents affiliated to Malaya Communist Party were also operating in some parts of Bannang Sata and Betong districts deep into Malaysia. Economically, Narathiwat was the most impoverished.

I have noticed that in selecting a base for a royal residence the king usually selected provinces that were not so prosperous and had security problems. One such choice is Sakon Nakhon in the northeast where Bhuban Palace is located.

Tan Yong Mountain, where Thaksin Palace was built, is not a high mountain. It is only 100 feet in height and located on the coast. At the bottom of the foothills is a beach. The sea there was not suitable for swimming because it was deep and had strong currents. Not far from the beach, the shore is steep. Several careless swimmers had been rescued from being swept away into the sea because they could not fight the strong current.

Around the residence, on the shore near the royal palace was a Muslim cemetery, quite an important one for the local people. This is unusual because a place of residence would not normally have been built near a cemetery (due to traditional beliefs that the living and the dead should not mix). In this case, however, the king did not mind the location and Muslim people there were willing to have the royal residence located near the cemetery. This makes Thaksin Palace the only royal residence in Thailand (and perhaps the world) located in the same area as a Muslim cemetery. The local Muslims can still pass through what is now a royal property to perform religious rites for the dead buried in the cemetery anytime they wish.

The flower *fueang fah* (bougainvillea) was the cemetery's landmark. When *fueang fah* bloomed it covered the entire cemetery, making the grounds so beautiful that they did not seem a cemetery.

I had some connections with the south in my youth. I was in lower secondary school in Yala, and later became chief of the Southern Special Branch field office in 1963, stationed in Songkhla. So every time I escorted the king to Thaksin Palace, I felt as if I were returning home.

As in all other royal visits upcountry, I spent my free time traveling by car to become better accustomed to the topography and population of the south. Roads in the four border provinces were good. Most were asphalt and there were many of them, allowing for many alternative routes to travel to other provinces.

My regular companions in surveying topography of the provinces in Thailand were Pol. Lt-Gen. Thep Supasamit, former assistant director-general of the Royal Thai Police Department (who is very seriously ill while I am writing this book), and Gen. Teanchai Janmookda, who was then a colonel and held the position of chief of VIP Protection Branch attached to the Royal Aide-de-Camp Department (who is now deputy chief aide-de-camp general to the king).

Our regular driver was Khun Atthawatya Khongsuwan, a highway police officer (who is now a police senior sergeant major of the Immigration Bureau stationed at Samui Immigration Checkpoint in Phuket). Khun Atthawatya is a native southerner and fluent in Malay as well as Thai. Being well accustomed to the customs and topography of the region, he was an important guide in making contacts with the local people who did not speak Thai.

Phi Thep and Phi Teanchai had a few things in common. They were both interested in nature and dharma practice. Neither man drank nor smoked, both had a calm disposition, and both could bear my sense of humor. They were and remain my true friends and compatible companions, providing me with new things to learn.

Another characteristic they shared was affection for animals. Once while we were walking to survey a province in Isan, we stopped for lunch at a temple. We brought our lunch, which had been prepared for us by staff at the palace. While we were eating, a temple dog strayed nearby as if asking to share our lunch. Phi Thep placed the rest of his food on the ground. At the time, the wind was so strong that the lunch paper wrapper flapped back and forth, covering the food. That dog tried to use its mouth to open it. Impatient with the dog's clumsiness, I snapped at the dog: 'Imbecile! Why don't you know to use your feet?' The dog coincidentally used its front paw to step on the paper and used its mouth to open it. Finally, he ate the food. I was (unduly) praised for my ability to communicate with a dog. In fact, I think the dog should be given the credit for being able to understand human language.

During our survey in Tak Bai district, Narathiwat, Phi Thep and I traveled by Land Rover to a village where we saw two or three bamboo poles on the roof of a house. There was rigging between the poles. Phi Thep was very excited because he understood that the bamboo poles with rigging might be used for illegal radio communication. After considering this possibility, we probed the villagers about the use of the rigging on the poles. As it turned out it was nothing to do with radio communication at all, but a bat trap. The villagers had erected the poles to stretch ropes hung with hooks to catch the bats that were flying by.

Phi Thep had great observation skills as well as an excellent memory. He is well rounded. Although he was a native of Taphan Hin, he had been a government official stationed in the northern provinces for a long time and had acquired considerable knowledge about northern Thailand. I learned a great deal from him about the northern region.

When talking about Narathiwat, it is inevitable for the discussion to turn to Pru Bajoh. On a royal trip to Narathiwat (before there was Banthorn Airport in Narathiwat), royal trips were taken by plane to Pattani Airport and then by a helicopter from Pattani to Narathiwat.

In the first trip to Narathiwat, the king asked the senior government officials about a swamp he saw from the helicopter as they passed Bajoh district. The king asked where the water came from and if the water remained in the area throughout the year.

The officials said that what the king had seen was called Pru Bajoh (*pru* or *po-ra*, as pronounced in southern Thai dialect, means a lowland area filled with stagnant water, like a marsh or a swamp). This marsh was located in Baan Shuwo in Bajoh and was wet throughout the year and the area was thus not useful or productive. The king said that if the water in the *pru* had been drained, the areas for agricultural use would increase by about 100,000 *rai* (about 395 acres).

To me His Majesty's interest in the matter showed his genuine concerns about the lives of his people. Any number of people had flown over this marsh countless times, but not one had the idea of draining it. Most people thought of this marsh as a marsh, but the king saw the potential of arable land. The king not only talked about it. He followed up with a feasibility study, asking the Royal Irrigation Department to consider measures to drain the water from Pru Bajoh. Two years later, Pru Bajoh was no more. The canal dug by the Royal Irrigation Department drained water from Pru Bajoh and returned it to the sea. The dry *pru* became a plain with an arable area of about 60,000 *rai*.

Throughout the period when the Royal Irrigation Department was digging the canal, His Majesty made frequent visits to Narathiwat to observe the progress of the project and advise the officials. He also presumed that there would be some complexities regarding entitlement to the new land, so he gave special advice to concerned government offices such as the Land Development Department about the terms of allocating the reclaimed land so that the people would receive fair treatment.

Today, if you visit Bajoh and ask about Pru Bajoh, many may not know the history. Old people who remember the marsh may point to the plantations and asphalt roads cut into a piece of land that once was a *pru* and think about the time of the past when all of that land had been wet and useless.

❖

From Bajoh district in Narathiwat, I followed His Majesty's footsteps to Tak Bai district in the deeper south that bordered Malaysia.

A vast piece of land above Khlong Kolok or Kolok River (southern Thai people call a river *khlong,* which means canal in standard Thai; the Malay term is *su-ngai*) was surrounded by Ra Ngae district in the northwest, Tak Bai district in the east, and Sungai Padi and Sungai Kolok districts in the south. Sungai Padi and Sungai Kolok had vast marsh areas as well. During the monsoon season (eight months of the year) the districts would flood up to the roofline. The land was not good for agriculture.

In 1974, Malaysia constructed a long dike on the bank of Khlong Kolok from the area opposite Sungai Kolok to Kotabaru on the east coast opposite Tak Bai. Malaysia probably used the dike to block water from Khlong Kolok to prevent flooding in Malaysia, but the consequence was more floodwater on Thailand's side.

The king did not easily surrender to Mother Nature and did not accept there wasn't a solution to the flooding problem in this area. He went to the area to find a solution, traveling there by car, boat and on foot. He covered all: Tak Bai, Ra Ngae, Sungai Padi and Sungai Kolok.

Once, while I was escorting him as he walked near a marsh in Sungai Padi, I asked him why he had not ordered the Royal Irrigation Department to construct the dike on Thailand's side. The king replied that if this had been done, there would have been a war of dikes between the two countries. I told him that a canal could be dug to draw the water into the sea as done in Pru Bajoh. The king smiled and said that if this had been done as in Pru Bajoh, areas around the *pru*, especially Sungai Padi, would sink and collapse like the ancient city of Sakon Nakhon, which became the marsh of Nong Harn.

He explained that the soil around the *pru* in Sungai Padi was not firm as in Bajoh. Therefore it required a different solution. Instead of draining the water, the water volume and level needed to be adjusted by digging several canals to control the waterway. The Royal Irrigation Department dug many canals around the *pru* according to His Majesty's advice and a few years later, the water level decreased. I remembered that a dike was also constructed, making the area dry enough to allow of crops even in the wet season.

23

Another example that demonstrates His Majesty's expertise in water and soil management in Thailand happened one day in the afternoon as I followed the king along the fringe of a marsh in Ra Ngae district. His Majesty was walking along a brook. As we neared a grove, the king stopped and asked an irrigation officer where the water in the brook was flowing. The officer replied that the water did not flow from the brook but gathered at the end of the swamp forest.

Smiling, the king explained that the flow from the brook did not stop at the end of the swamp forest but surely must pass through and beyond the *pru* on the eastside into Tak Bai. The king pointed at the brook's line on a map.

Those familiar with the history of the king know that he had initially studied science. When he became the ninth king of the Chakri Dynasty, he changed to the study of political sciences. However, he knew that livelihood of most Thai people was based on agriculture, and that their success depended on water and soil. His Majesty therefore made personal efforts to educate himself about water and soil and had developed an expertise in water and soil management that rivaled the experts in this field. Accordingly, most of his suggestions for water and soil solutions were practical and had helped government officials to develop water and soil sources that were beneficial for a large number of people in all regions of Thailand.

The king always used a map during the course of a trip. A map can be said to be his additional regalia. There are five items in a set of royal regalia for the king: Great Crown of Victory, Sword of Victory, Royal Staff, Royal Fan and Fly Whisk and Royal Slippers.

The map carried by the king had been adapted by himself. When he visited an area, he always folded the map to expose the targeted location so that he could easily see or point to when talking with villagers. When he wanted to identify an area, he marked it with a pencil.

When he made a personal trip in casual wear, a small row of sharpened pencils were usually tugged inside his shirt pocket. He preferred to do things himself. Sharpening pencils was one of them. Another indispensable item for the king and a candidate for additional royal regalia was a radio receiver.

Normally, His Majesty stayed in Bangkok and attended his birthday ceremony at the Grand Palace. But in 1974 he decided to stay in Bang Pa-In Palace in Phra Nakhon Si Ayutthaya province and made his birthday merits at Wat Suwandararam. Queen Rambhaibharni, of King Prajadipok (Rama VII), performed the formal birthday ceremony in his place in Bangkok.

Bang Pa-In Palace may be the oldest royal residence. Although it was built in 1872, during the reign of King Rama V, the grounds had previously been used as a royal court since the reign of King Prasartthong in the Ayutthaya period. During construction of Bang Pa-In Palace, the workers digging the pond found 120 poles and the top of a castle buried in the ground. The site was believed to contain the ruins of the throne hall of King Prasartthong that had been built in 1632. King Rama V named the traditional Thai-style throne hall in the middle of the pond Isawan Thippaya Assana Throne Hall in honor of the ancient throne.

I had visited Bang Pa-In Palace several times but never imagined that I would one day visit as a member of the royal staff. Even though the residence for court security staff was located in the south quite distant from the throne hall, it was hard not to appreciate the place, an ancient treasure rich with history. Bang Pa-In Palace had been the resort of many kings since the Ayutthaya period. Before going to bed, I prayed and dedicated my merit and compassion to all past Thai kings and their courtiers.

Central Thailand is the region about which I had the least knowledge. This was probably because I was from upcountry and most tourist attractions were in other regions, except for ancient palaces in Ayutthaya and Lop Buri. This was a chance for me to learn more about the region.

During their stay in Bang Pa-In Palace, Their Majesties visited a number of temples in many provinces near the palace, both by car and by boat. On 7 December, they visited Wat Bang Nom Kho and Wat Sam Kor in Tambon Sam Kor, Sena district, Ayutthaya, using the Iyarapot Barge. Wat Bang Nom Kho was the temple where Luang Phor Paan, the teacher of Praratchapromayarn (Veera Dhavaro) who was commonly known as the Black Monkey Ascetic. Both have since passed away.

Two days later Their Majesties went by car to Wat Wiset Chai Chan and Wat Si Roi in Wiset Chai Chan district, Ang Thong province. The Wiset Chai Chan people were descendants of warriors who fought against the Burmese when Ayutthaya was the capital of the country. During that trip I learned that Wat Si Roi (the Temple of the Four Hundred) was given that name because it was intended to be a place for commemoration to the 400 fighters who united in the battle against the Burmese.

Before Their Majesties moved to Bhubing Palace at the end of that year, on 16 December His Majesty performed a royal ceremony bestowing the official rank of general to soldier and police officers. I was among the newly appointed police major generals of that year.

The ceremony took place in a hall on the second floor of Chitralada Palace. Before the ceremony, the officers waited for the king to descend into the hall, dressed in white uniform, their official swords at their waists and gloves hanging in their left hands.

As part of the ceremony, when the king in his dress as commander-in-chief entered the hall, the most senior of the soldiers gave a short address and called out the names of the soldiers who were to receive their *sanyabat* (royal commission) and decoration. Then the police officers were called.

The ceremony itself was not long or complicated, but the atmosphere was one of excitement because to be appointed by the head of state was one of the most important moments in a lifetime.

When the superior (in my case, the director-general of the Royal Thai Police Department) called out the name of an officer, he would bow and then walk toward the king and kneel. In receiving anything from the king, one had to bend one's left knee while holding the right knee straight. Both hands were held straight beside the body, then the king would touch both of epaulets on the left and the right shoulders with a baton (in case of police officers, their epaulets with his Sword of Victory) and then give them their commission. Each showed his respect before he received it, then stood up, stepped backwards in a good distance, and finally bowed again and returned to the line. All the while, the officer was to hold the commission above chest level, but this was often forgotten.

At the end of the ceremony, the king gave a small speech, which was always a short reminder for the newly appointed to remember their duties and responsibilities in their work and for their country.

Toward the end of 1974, political unrest persisted. There were still many demonstrations and strikes by workers and farmers. In September, assemblies of the students, who had an important role in the political changes of the previous year, continued to demand changes in the constitution being drafted by the National Legislature.

Amid the unrest, the king continued his tasks uninterrupted and on 17 December moved to Bhubing Palace in Chiang Mai, as he has always done in the cool season. While there, as always, Their Majesties visited the hill tribe communities in their villages on the northern mountain range, as well as people living on the plains.

One of the local trips was a visit to Luang Puu Waen Sujinno in Phrao district. This widely revered monk lived in Wat Doi Mae Pang. As usual, along with the royal aides and the officials from office of the king's private secretary, we went on our advance survey of the area. This was my first time to visit Luang Puu Waen.

There were two alternative routes to reach Luang Puu Waen's temple, located on the mountain with the same name, Doi Mae Pang: from the south, by Highway Route 1001 from San Sai district through Baan Mae Malai and Mae Hor Phra, or from the north, by Chiang Mai-Fang Highway Route 107 through Chiang Dao district and further to Route 1150 to join Route 1001 in Phrao district. But whether one took the southern or the northern route, the travel was rough. Except for Route 107, the road conditions in those days were unpaved and rugged.

When we reached the temple in the afternoon, I was responsible for informing Luang Puu Waen of the king's visit to Phrao district and his wish to visit the revered monk. Luang Puu Waen was silent until I finished what I had to say and then he asked me in only one sentence, 'Is that all?' I replied, 'Yes, that is all.' Then I paid obeisance to Luang Puu Waen before leaving his quarters.

During our return trip, I was harassed by my colleagues and traveling companions for not asking for any talismans from the revered monk while I had a chance. My failure to ask meant that others would also not get one.

I did not give any explanation or make an excuse for my not asking for the talismans. Even now, I think I did the right thing. Luang Puu Waen's question, 'Is that all?' suggested that he no longer had any other matters to discuss and indicated that we should go back. And it was clear that at that time, apart from being old, he was also ill. Those having love and respect for him should not disturb him but instead let him rest. Moreover, I think asking for talismans at that time might have even brought us ill fortune instead.

The king drove the queen and the crown prince to Doi Mae Pang on 23 December. They arrived in the afternoon. Their Majesties and the prince went directly to the temple and paid homage to the Triple Gem—the Buddha, his teachings and his disciples. The king then offered blankets and talked with Luang Puu Waen and the abbot.

After the visit, ten monks chanted a prayer. Their Majesties and the crown prince came out of the temple to meet a large group of local villagers waiting for an audience in the temple's area.

After a half an hour at the temple, the royal mission went on to Tambon Mae Waen in Phrao to meet with members of the Phrao Settlement Cooperative and officials from the Department of Cooperative Promotion. His Majesty discussed agricultural activities and advised the cooperative to grow the type of rice suitable to the climate there. The king also gave some lychees and mangoes to the director-general of the Department of Cooperative Promotion and asked him to distribute them to the members of the cooperative. After another visit with the local people, Their Majesties and the prince had lunch arranged for them near the river.

In His Majesty's Footsteps

The king always visited people in the late morning, after 10 a.m., and had his lunch in the afternoon, often in the late afternoon. As was often the case, the royal lunch was a simple bagged meal prepared from the palace for all royal staff and the entourage. Because lunches were often late during royal missions, Her Majesty the Queen suggested that the royal staff and entourage bring snacks in case anyone felt hungry. Many times snacks were delivered by the ladies-in-waiting.

24

In 1974, the roads from Doi Mae Pang to Phrao and from Phrao to Baan Ping Khong were in poor repair. The vehicles on the roads were in no better condition. The picture of the king driving on these dusty and rugged roads was beyond the imagination of the villagers living along the side of the roads. Delight showed on in their faces and eyes. Neither the king nor the queen was in a rush. They always stopped to meet the villagers.

On the same day of the royal visit to the Phrao Settlement Cooperative in Tambon Mae Waen, they drove farther to Tambon Pa Toom to meet members of the local chapter of the Phrao Cooperative there as well. They first listened to the president of cooperative report about the business, then visited the house of a member, Khun Sao Supharak, to see his vegetable garden, fish farm and chicken coop.

The king had a talk with Khun Sao. He suggested that all members of the cooperative cooperate with the government in constructing a dike and dam to create a reserve of water and to dredge canals for irrigation to the fields. The king also suggested that trees be planted on the mountain to secure the source of water and to prevent the soil from collapsing into the canal.

It wasn't until 5 p.m. that the royal mission left Phrao. There were still many groups of villagers waiting on the roadside on the way back. The mission stopped along the way to allow people to give gifts to the royal family. By 6.30 p.m., the mission entered Mae Talai Farm in Tambon In Ching, Mae Taeng district, to receive 300 mango seedlings from Khun Wanit Chantara. That day trip ended at 8.00 p.m. when the mission arrived back at Bhubing Palace.

I have been asked if the king uses everything given him by the people. I had wondered about this myself. Finally I asked a person in the royal court and received an answer. If the gift was edible, it was sent to the royal kitchen and used to make food for the royal family. If it were in a large quantity, the king would give the surplus to various nearby governmental offices and organizations whose staff provide services to the royal court.

As for other items, he might select some for himself and give the rest to a public charity. For example, he gave the things to the queen's shop on Red Cross Day or to schools, hospitals and government offices that were in his view deserving.

One visit that I would not forget was a visit to Doi Inthanon National Park. The royal family, as usual, was visiting some villagers there.

On Monday, 3 December 1974 the royal couple left Bhubing Palace at 10.20 a.m. His Majesty drove his car as usual and I was in one of the preceding cars of Special Branch, and ahead of us were several Highway Police cars.

Special Branch officers were responsible for surveying the route, checking and reporting on the conditions and traffic. In case, for example, there were an obstruction or a need to stop the procession, the king and drivers of other cars would be aware of the problem and stop their cars to avoid the danger.

Traveling by car from Bhubing Palace to Doi Inthanon seemed pretty easy on the map. But in fact, it was quite a way. The distance between Bhubing Palace and the foot of Doi Suthep was about seventeen kilometers, and from Doi Suthep down south to Doi Inthanon exit on Chiang Mai-Chom Thong highway was another sixty kilometers. Then, it was another forty-seven kilometers to the west to Doi Inthanon. The road up the mountain was steep and with frequent switchbacks.

Doi Inthanon is the highest mountain in Thailand measuring 8,000 feet or 2,667 meters above sea level. The climate at the top remains cold all year. The procession arrived at Doi Inthanon at half past noon. Their Majesties went to see a stupa that contains the relic of Chao Inthawichayanon, the local royal and past ruler of Chiang Mai, then had lunch.

The royal couple had a small tour, examining trees and plants on the mountain after lunch. Then after 2 p.m., they went on to visit a village, Baan Khun Klang, Tambon Baan Luang in the Chom Thong district area on Doi Inthanon and stayed until almost 3 p.m.

The word *'khun'* in the name of the village means a water source of the river. Khun Klang means a water source at the middle of the mountain that flows down to the foot of the mountain and became a waterfall called 'Mae Klang', Chom Thong's famous waterfall. The villagers of Baan Khun Klang are from the Hmong tribe (Thai people like to call them Maew, which is actually pejorative, but having been called that for such a long time, they have somewhat become used to it and grudgingly accepted the name.)

Before the king visited Baan Khun Klang, the royal medical unit had gone to village to examine the villagers and then continued on to treat people living in nearby villages. It should be known that when the king goes on trips such as the one to Baan Khun Klang, royal doctors from Chitralada Palace follow the king and attend to people in the villages who require medical attention. During that time, the director of the Royal of Chitralada Palace was Dr. Pramot Sophak. This was a customary practice: unless the royal mission is arranged with any urgency, normally a royal medical team from Chitralada Palace was always at the mission. In my time, the director of the Chitralada Medical Department was Dr. Pramot Sophak.

After arrival at the village, the royal couple observed the medical team at work in the temporary marquee. After all the medical examinations were done, His Majesty gave a breed of chicken called Bar Plymouth Rock to the village headman to cross-breed with the local breeds of chicken.

Another favorite breed given by the king to the villagers was Road Ireland Red. I don't remember exactly what the strengths of these two favorite breeds were, but as I recall when these two breeds are bred with the local stock, they produced offspring that were even stronger than their purebred parents. Besides chicken, blankets were distributed because winter on Doi Inthanon at the time was chilling.

Then, as the royal mission was taking a walking tour and having an audience with the villagers in the center of the village, some villagers asked the king for wood to repair their houses. The king then asked Khun Preeda Kanasutra, permanent secretary of the Ministry of Agriculture and Cooperatives who was present to provide four timbers from the Department of Forestry to the people.

Some of the things that the villagers asked for during royal missions could be a little strange or unexpected. For example, later that day, some villagers asked for a vasectomy. The king asked the officials from a royal project on hill tribe people development to later take the villagers to have the procedure in the hospital as patients under the royal patronage. Becoming a patient under the royal patronage means that the patient will have medical care, paid for by the royal household. However, not all patients can be cured, so in case of death, costs for the funeral would also be under royal patronage.

After the visit at Baan Khun Klang, just before 4 p.m. the royal couple drove ten-minute to Baan Ang-ka Noi. The mission got out of the cars and hiked for three kilometers on the mountain path to Baan Ang-ka Noi. There, the royal couple had a visit with the local Karen villagers and gave them a Road Ireland Red chicken breeders and blankets and then walked another two kilometers to Baan Tha Fang, which was also occupied by the Karen, to give them the same gifts.

I thought that the trip would end at Baan Tha Fang, but what happened next was unexpected. MC Bhisatej Rajani , the royal mission manager, asked the royal couple to walk another kilometer to see the Karen's coffee field. That afternoon Their Majesties had already walked six kilometers. I was not yet an old man (fourty-four years old) at the time and did not mind long hikes but what made me quite upset was that that once we reached the coffee field, there was only *one* coffee tree planted in the field.

If the king had not been close by, I might have criticized MC Bhisatej for asking the king to walk an extra kilometer to see a solitary coffee tree. I felt this extra walk had exhausted the king and for little apparent purpose. However, I tried to calm myself, but couldn't help let it out to my colleagues on the way back to Bhubing Palace.

I had, in my view, a good reason to be upset. After the hike to see a single coffee tree, the royal couple had to walk back to the car that was parked at the entrance of Baan Ang-ka Noi. It was another six kilometer hike back and the king had to drive back to Bhubing Palace as well.

Somebody told the king that I was angry with MC Bhisatej. The king asked to see me. He asked if it was true that I was angry with MC Bhisatej. And I said yes, I was. The king then further asked me if I knew what crops the Karen people had previously grown and I told him that they had grown poppies for opium.

The king then explained to me so gently and kindly, with no hint of blame whatsoever, that the Karen had previously grown poppies. 'I' had persuaded them to abandon poppy growing to try coffee growing. The Karen had no experience growing coffee, so having at least one surviving coffee tree left was evidence of progress in changing crops. His Majesty continued that he had to see the field so that he could give them suggestions on how they could keep more than one coffee tree alive.

His Majesty opened my eyes and I understood both His Majesty and MC Bhisatej. I was reminded again of His Majesty's policy is not one of 'rushing development' but letting people learn by themselves at their own speed.

I must report that in the following year, the Karen on Doi Inthanon grew beautiful coffee trees all over their fields and a coffee company in Bangkok bought their coffee at 1 baht per kilo. The Karen earned more per *rai* selling coffee than they had previously from growing poppies.

HM the King started 1975 by visiting the hill tribe people as he had done in the previous years. And because it was the New Year's holiday, some villagers offered him their traditional food, or performed for him their traditional dance.

On Sunday, 5 January 1975, His Majesty had a personal trip with Princess Sirindhorn and Princess Chulabhorn to Wang Namkhang Tangerine Orchard of Khun Phanlert Buranasilapin, a former agriculture minister.

I had accompanied HM the King to this orchard before, but for this trip there was a conflict between MC Bhisatej and the security staff (including me). The weather forecast predicted rain and the king was having a cold. The security staff did not want the king to walk long distance at Wang Namkhang Tangerine Orchard because the possibility of rain and the staff recommended that the king should stay in the car. However, MC Bhisatej insisted the king should follow his plan. What made me angry was what MC Bhisatej said: 'the king is not sugar so that he will melt under the rain.'

Finally, the king went to the orchard and it rained. The king and Princess Sirindhorn and Princess Chulabhorn had to walk in the rain. In fact, this was not the first or the only time that the king and the princesses were exposed to the rain. It did not rain heavily, however, and each had an umbrella. The event passed smoothly as in previous times and no one thought that there would be adverse consequences.

HM the King continued making visits to various villages. On Thursday, 9 January that year, the royal couple presided over a graduation ceremony at Chiang Mai University, handing out certificates to graduates. The couple returned to the university again the next day for a tea session with the graduates. Apart from having an audience with the graduates, His Majesty joined in a session with traditional Thai and Western music bands of Chiang Mai University Students Association until late in the evening. It was 10.30 p.m. by the time the royal couple got back to Bhubing Palace.

On 15 January 1975, the king drove Princess Sirindhorn and Princess Chulabhorn for lunch by a lake in Doi Tao in Hot district. The lunch was organized by the Department of Highways. About 4 p.m., the king and the princesses went on to Wat Baan Pang in Tambon Mae Tuen, Li district, Lamphun province. This temple is significant. It was a temple where one of Chiang Mai's most revered monks, Kruba Srivichai, was ordained as a novice.

25

On 17 February 1975 about 10.30 a.m., Their Majesties traveled by a helicopter from Bhubing Palace to Baan Khum, Tambon Mon Pin, Chiang Mai's Fang district. The helicopter ride took an hour.

Baan Khum was situated on the east ridge of a continuous mountain range called Ang Khang. When viewed from the sky, the mountain appears as a huge circle or a giant bowl and this is the origin of the name (*'ang'* means 'bowl' or 'tub' in Thai). Ang Khang's edge connects Thailand to Myanmar (Burma).

I am not sure about the meaning of the word *'khang'* in the northern Thai dialect but in northeastern Thai (which is similar to northern), it means a kind of metal that is smelted from mineral found on the surface of pebbles, which is hard and not rusty. People in the northeast call a pan made from the kind of metal 'Mo Khang'. The word *'khang'* in northeastern Thai dialect also means to heat or broil.

Villagers at Baan Khum were from the Lahu ethnic hill tribe (Muser). Lahu ethnic group are divided into many sub-groups such as Lahu Daeng (Red Lahu), Lahu Dam (Black Lahu), Lahu Lueang (Yellow Lahu), Lahu Khao (White Lahu) and Lahu Che-le. The reason their tribal names are based on colors is not clear but what is clear is that the color in the names does not necessarily correspond to the color of the subgroup's clothing. The villagers at Baan Khum were Lahu Che-le, wore black, and were rather poor.

The village head of Baan Khum was Ja-lu Saen-nor. Ja-lu Saen-nor liked to take the villagers, some of whom were his relatives to welcome the royal couple at the helicopter landing point whenever the king and the queen went to Baan Khum. After the royal couple got off the helicopter, the villagers would present flowers to the royal couple and perform their traditional dances. Sometimes, the princesses and female royal staff would join the dances.

That day, after the dances, HM the King visited the Animal Husbandry Research Station of the Hill Tribe Development Project under royal patronage, and gave the village head Ja-lu a number of blankets, winter jackets, whetstone and snacks for children for distribution to the villagers. The king also gave blankets, winter jackets, shoes and medical supplies to Khun Winai Pansiri, the head of Ang Khang Agricultural Research Station to distribute to officials working in the station as well as forestry officials in the area. Khun Winai and the Ang Khang officials had worked there for so long that they almost became another native hill tribe.

I remember that Khun Winai's office-cum-residence was like a large barn, roofed with grass, similar to the villagers' houses, only bigger. It had inadequate protection against the cold season. The inhabitants had to depend on the warmth from the fires they made inside the house.

The lives of officials working in the Ang Khang Agricultural Research Station and the Forestry Department were not so different from those of the police officers and soldiers stationed on the mountain. The only difference was that Ang Khang and the forestry officials did not carry weapons.

After handing out the goods to the people, Their Majesties walked over to the nursery of the Forestry Department at Ang Khang and down a narrow passage between the valley and mountain ridge to a place built by officials of the Royal Irrigation Department for agricultural purposes.

When the king saw the water source, he asked the Royal Irrigation Department officials to survey the streams around Ang Khang and to build a pond to store and drain water. He asked the Forestry Department officials to grow various species of plants on the mountain near to conserve the water source.

The visit was special because the guests accompanying the king included members of diplomatic corps and their wives representing sixteen countries. HM the King led a walking tour of the diplomatic corps to see various crops and fruits. Those such as apple and peach would be sold to the hill tribes to plant on their land.

Strawberries were among the crops introduced to the hill tribe villagers on Doi Ang Khang. I had strawberries when I studied abroad but I had never seen how they were planted. When I had a chance to see the strawberry patch, I understood why they are called strawberries: farmers cover them with straw. I wondered why Thai people did not call them *'mak fang'* (*'mak'* in the old time means fruit and *'fang'* means straw) because it is much easier to pronounce for Thai people than strawberry.

The walking tour lasted over an hour. The mission then stopped for lunch at the Bear Cliff, where there were some poppies still to be seen.

At this point, I should mention something about HM the King's policy about opium eradication. His policy was linked to development, which is to inform the hill tribe villagers about the benefits from growing other crops that could be sold at higher market prices than poppies. The various royal agricultural research stations on mountains in northern Thailand conducted agricultural experiments to select the best and most suitable crops for the land occupied by the hill tribe villagers.

Apart from this, the king also had a canned fruit factory built in a village on the east side at the foot of Doi Ang Khang. The factory bought fruit from the hill tribe farmers and canned the fruit for resale, allowing for a complete cycle of substitute agricultural business for the villagers.

If you visit Ang Khang now you see an asphalt road from the plains below going to Ang Khang. The drive from Chiang Mai to Ang Khang takes only a few hours. Some may not realize that when the king visited the hill tribe people in those days, there were no roads, but only walking tracks to the villages.

The king did not suggest building an asphalt road to Ang Khang. His concern was to find a way for local people to use mules or horses to transport their harvest to sell on the plains. This is another example of how the king does not support the idea of 'accelerated development' but instead to help people help themselves. The Lahu Che-le in Baan Khum village once asked the king for tractors to cultivate their fields. Soon enough, a Royal Thai Air force helicopter delivered six buffalo to the villagers so that they could learn how to use buffalos to plough rice fields for the first time. I don't know if today the Lahu Che-le at Doi Ang Khang has changed over to using tractors to plough their field.

After lunch at the Bear Cliff, the king led the tour, passing plant nursery, to a little sheep farm, where both local sheep and a breed known as Merino sheep were being raised. The Merino sheep, known for its soft wool suitable for weaving, were reared for breeding purposes. The specimens were sent for breeding in other parts of the country.

Around 4.00 p.m., the royal mission traveled by helicopter to Baan Doi Pa Kha, Tambon Mon Pin in the same district, Fang. It was a fifteen-minute helicopter ride to Doi Pa Kha. The villagers there were also Lahu Che-le—relatives of those in Baan Khum. The headman of the village at Doi Pa Kha was Ja-mo Saen-tako. The welcome was no different from that in the village of their relatives. As soon as the royal guests got off the helicopter, Ja-mo and his villagers started their welcoming dances. After the gift giving ceremony, the royal couple walked into the village and visited Ja-mo's house.

The visit was long. This was not the first time that the royal couple visited inside a hill tribe villager's house. They had done so many times. And every time I felt a little anxious when the hosts offered homemade spirit to the king, which he would take and drink. I could not help but worry about the safety of the spirit itself and the sanitation condition of the bottles and cups, although I knew that the hosts must have chosen their best to offer to the king.

The king always graciously took whatever was offered by the hosts, of whichever tribes that showed their utmost delight in having the king visit their house and drink their spirit.

On that day, the royal mission returned to Bhubing Palace after 6 p.m.

I don't know exactly what day that the king became ill. But I remember that on 20 January 1975, the queen with Princess Sirindhorn and Princess Chulabhorn left Chiang Mai for Nan to visit villagers and officers without the king. This was unusual because normally the king and the queen always went together to visit places in crisis. Furthermore security in Nan was anything but stable at the time. Fighting against communist insurgents resulted in many deaths and injuries among authorities and villagers.

On Wednesday, 22 January 1975, the queen left the palace on her own by car to Baan Chang Khian, Tambon Suthep, Chiang Mai's Muang district to visit the Huay Mai Nai Highland Agricultural Research Station and Baan Hmong Chang Khian. This caused some to wonder why the queen went out alone.

Later it became known that the king was ill from scrub typhus, which was not malaria. I knew nothing about the disease at first but later was told that scrub typhus is a communicable disease, the symptoms of which include high fever, extreme tiredness, and purple spots on the body. It was worrying to see many doctors coming from Bangkok to Bhubing Palace. Some doctors told me that the king had a high fever of 40 Celsius for a week.

One evening, I saw a female doctor walking down from the palace, crying. I knew then that the king was not merely ill but was in serious condition. The atmosphere at Bhubing Palace was quiet and sorrowful. All officers were in low spirits. The queen stopped all her missions and did not leave the palace. Royal representatives were asked to perform important tasks on the king's behalf.

The court servants and officers went to the temple each day. Several soldiers and police officers, sat in meditation for many hours each day. I did as well. We dedicated our merits from calming our bodies, speech and minds to the king. I formed the intention that, if the king recovered, I would ordain as a monk to dedicate merit to him.

Then we received good news. The king was better and his fever had fallen. He remained weak, however. The team of doctors requested that the king stop working for thirty days. The clouds were lifted and laughter returned after many long days.

On Saturday, 1 February 1975, I sat reading and listening to the radio in my room in the Royal Aide-de-Camp residence near Bhubing Palace. Normally, I checked in on many radio frequencies but mostly police networks to keep up with current events and to prepare myself for any case of emergency.

While tuning, I noticed something rather strange. The BPP 5th Subdivision station at Dara Rasmee Camp in Mae Rim district, Chiang Mai, the master station of the Border Patrol Police in Northern Thailand, had called for a police helicopter periodically but hadn't received a response.

About 10 p.m., I heard a hoarse and trembling voice calling to the Dara Rasmee Camp radio station with the news that the helicopter that Dara Rasmee Camp had been trying to contact since the morning had landed at a village in Mae Hong Son province. I realized before the caller finished his sentence that it was the king.

I was so excited and so delighted that I could not hold back my tears. I had not heard his voice for many days, since he had fallen ill. But as soon as I began to feel the sense of delight, it turned to one of acute dissatisfaction because the king was not resting, as the doctors had advised, but instead was working, listening and talking on the radio.

I could not think of anything other than protesting to him. I then sat at my desk and immediately wrote a letter to the king. The letter might be called a petition because it was something of a complaint. In that petition, I told him that he might not have realized how much his people suffered along with him in his illness and prayed for him to make a full recovery. I told him also that I had the intention, after he recovered, of seeking his permission to allow me to be ordained and dedicate merit to him.

I revealed a lot of emotion in the letter. At the end, I asked him to stop working, as advised by the doctors, and explained that if he needed to talk with anyone, he did not need to get up to talk by radio receiver himself, but could write a note. I took the letter to a high-ranking court officer I knew to give to the king. I did not expect any reply. The next day when Princess Sirindhorn handed me a letter from the king, I almost fainted.

His reply was typewritten, a page long, and signed 'Sirindhorn', without any title.

พระราชกรณียกิจ
พระบาทสมเด็จพระเจ้าอยู่หัว เสด็จฯ ทอด
พระเนตรงานโครงการเกษตรหลวงโครงการหลวง
ป่าไม้ป่าแป่ อ.แม่แตง จ.เชียงใหม่ เมื่อ 18 กพ.
ในการทรงเยี่ยมราษฎรที่มาเฝ้ารับเสด็จฯ

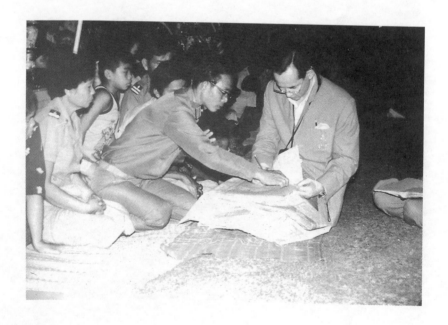

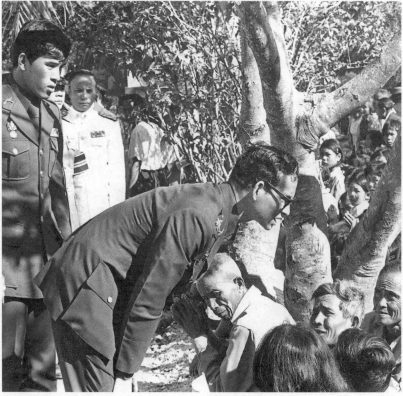

พระ บาทสมเด็จพระเจ้าอยู่หัว พร้อมด้วย
สมเด็จพระ เจ้าลูกเธอทั้ง 2 พระ องค์ เสด็จฯ
ทรงเยี่ยมพสกนิกร หมู่บ้าน หุบกะพง แดง ทอด
พระเนตรการร้อยตะกร้อ อ.เมือง เพชรบุรี
ที่ หมู่พระ อ.ชะอำ เพชรบุรี เมื่อเวลา ๑๓.๓๐ น.

26

I don't remember everything that I said in my letter to the king but his reply was arranged by item. The first must have been a response to my complaint of his work on the radio and to my suggestion that he write instead of speaking on the radio.

1. *If it were to write, it would have been difficult to read. My hands would be unsteady and tired and that would slow me down. This is why I spoke instead.*

As for my pouring my heart out that I would die for him, he said:

2. A. *Will die for me? Who will die? I am tough and I won't die easily. If I am not dead, I need you to work, and you can't just go off to find personal comfort in the monkhood.*
   B. *If I die you are permitted to be ordained in my funeral (but I am not dead).*

All his responses reflect his personality and clearly show his kindness and his style of working.

3. *If something needs to be done, there will be an order. You must follow the orders, otherwise you are worthless. Don't do things just according to your own wishes but work as part of a team (I have been doing this for a long time).*
4. *I have said before: routine work must be carried out. Even though you are not told to do the work, you nevertheless must do it. There is no need to repeat an order for routine work. Whether or not I am ill, the work needs to be done according to the set policy. Don't be a traitor and don't be foolish.*

5. *I agree that everybody needs to look out for his own interest. But if that looking out for self-interest is done with a pure heart, the country will survive (we mustn't have bias).*

The last item must have been in response to the style of my letter.

6. *The form of the letter is very old-fashioned.*

I have kept this reply in a high place along with other royal articles such as royal decorations. Once in along while I take it out to read to remind myself of his words, especially, 'Don't do things just according to your own wishes but work as part of a team.' and 'Even though you are not told to do the work, you nevertheless must do it.'

The king's condition gradually improved. On Saturday, 15 February 1975, the king was fit enough to leave Bhubing Palace. He granted an audience to the speaker of Parliament (Khun Prasit Kanchanawat and the secretary-general of Parliament (Khun Prasit Srisuchart), seeking royal approval for the appointment of MR Seni Pramoj as prime minister (this proved to a shortlived administration lasting one month, though MR Seni would again in 1976 serve as prime minister following his younger brother MR Kukrit Pramoj's adminstration which lasted about ten months).

On 14 March 1975, MR Kukrit Pramoj was appointed prime minister of Thailand by royal command. Three days later, a new cabinet was formed. After that audience, the king continued to recuperate following the doctors' advice. The queen went on a number of missions to visit villagers and local officials as his representative. The missions taken by the queen were no different from those taken by the king.

On Monday, 24 February 1975 around 12.30 p.m., the queen, Princess Sirindhorn and Princess Chulabhorn visited the base of Special Warfare Task Force in Baan Kaeng Lat, Tambon Baan Yaeng, Nakhon Thai district, Pitsanulok. Afterwards, about 2.30 p.m., they visited the

Provincial Police Special Operation Division at Baan Mak Khaeng, Tambon Koksato, Dan Saay district, Loei.

These bases were critical from security point of view at that time. The queen and the royal mission were briefed on the situation, observed activities in both bases, and provided medical supplies to the commander of each base, vegetable seedlings to village heads for distribution to villagers, as well as sport equipment, stationery and textbooks for teachers and students. HM the Queen visited with the villagers coming to have an audience with her at both bases. It wasn't until 3 p.m. that they had lunch at the base of Baan Mak Khaeng that day.

As the king's representative, the queen started attending a graduation ceremony to give swords and certificates to military graduates at Army Cadet Academy of Phrachulachomklao, Naval Academy and RTAF Academy. The ceremony was held on the field in the hall of the Ministry of Defense on Thursday, 27 February 1975.

Then on Tuesday, 8 April 1975, the queen went again as the king's representative to the graduation ceremony at Police Cadet Academy in Sam Phran district, Nakhon Pathom. This was the first time that new police officers received the ceremonial sword from the queen.

In 1975, the king stayed at Bhubing Palace until 4 March. After his return to Bangkok, he granted occasional audiences to some people but did not take long trips to remote areas. The queen continued working on his behalf. The king resumed his work after moving to stay at Thaksin Palace in Narathiwat in late April. He started by driving to visit royal projects in Narathiwat.

The duration from the onset of the king's illness until he recovered was about three months. During the period that he was ill, the political situation in Thailand was still volatile. The government of MR Seni Pramoj lasted only one year because it suffered a no-confidence motion in the House of Representatives.

Although I had been appointed a royal court security police officer and mainly worked at the royal court, there weren't any vacant permanent royal court police officer positions at the time. This meant that all non-permanent royal court police officers (myself included) had to have a separate affiliation to another posting in the Royal Thai Police Department. I was a police major general but I had an attachment to the post of the BPP commander.

By the end of 1974, the Royal Thai Police Department set a new regulation that eliminated the permanent positions in royal court security police force and required all court police officers to be affiliated with one of the units in the Royal Thai Police Department.

I wasn't familiar with the politics in the Royal Thai Police Department and naively assumed that when the department launched this new policy, the superiors would decide upon the unit that I would command. Little did I know there would be no one to look out for me, except one person, when the assistant director-general of the Royal Thai Police Department, Pol. Lt-Gen. Witoon Ya-sawasdi, nicknamed 'Phi Thep', asked to see me and asked where I would like to be the commander.

He said that many positions would become vacant. When he mentioned the post of the commander of the BPP Tactical Training Division, I could see myself in that position. I had been a lecturer for the Border Patrol Police and had been involved in setting up the Marigadayavan Training Center, which became the Tactical Training Division. In addition, I thought that the duties attached to this position would not interfere with my work as royal court security police officer. I explained these advantages to Phi Thep.

While I was sitting in his office, Phi Thep called the BPP commander (Pol. Lt-Gen. Suraphon Chulaphram, who later became a police general and director-general of the Royal Thai Police Department) to request that I should be appointed to this position. It appeared that the BPP commander was unwilling to appoint me to that post but, instead, suggested that we ask the assistant director-general of the Royal Thai Police Department to find me a position in the Police Educational Bureau.

I heard Phi Thep explain on the telephone, 'Vasit is a Border Patrol Police true blood.' And when the BPP commander gave his approval, a royal command was issued soon after, appointing me as the commander of BPP Tactical Training Division.

More work ensued from this new position. I was handling two jobs at once, performing my usual duties as a royal court security police officer and working as the commander of BPP Tactical Training Division. My office in Bangkok was located at Border Patrol Police Bureau on Phahon Yothin Road. But I had to supervise five offices for Tactical Training Division around the country. To perform both duties well, I delegated supervision to the vice-commander and tried to coordinate my court security work with my duties at the Tactical Training Division.

I took an opportunity to visit those provincial tactical training offices whenever my security job took me near them. When the king moved his base to Bhubing Palace, for example, I took a chance to Tactical Training Division 5 facilities in Mae Taeng district.

In my past experience with the BPP, I had had a chance to work closely with the trainers and had formed a special attachment to them. In my new assignment I proposed a training review course for the BPP trainers. My proposal was approved. The first batch of students to attend the course started in May 1975 at Subdivision II of the Tactical Training Division, located at Tambon Phang La, Na Thawi district in Songkhla province.

During the training course, I was stationed in Na Thawi for closer supervision. As in the past, I gave lectures in training on history and communism. It was important to help the participants in this training of trainers to understand why it was important to combat communism. The BPP tactical trainers were an important force for the security of country. Their job was to train other police officers, especially the BPP officers who confronted considerable danger that menaced all regions of Thailand. Previous generations of trainers and their students had sacrificed themselves on duty. This new generation of trainers would follow the path of those who had come before them in facing the dangers that they knew were waiting. As a result, I sought to uplift their spirit and give them as much encouragement as possible.

I realized that Their Majesties always had concerns about the well-being of police and military officers on duty in the line of fire all over the country. They regularly visited the police officers and soldiers on duty. Knowing this, I decided to request for an audience for the BPP trainers with His Majesty. I believed that the opportunity to have an audience and to listen to the king's speech would encourage them a great deal.

My request was granted, so the BPP commander Pol. Lt-Gen. Suraphon Chulaphram, the subdivision II superintendent Pol. Col. Chertchamrat Chitkarunrat and myself took the BPP trainers to have an audience with the king at Klai Kangwol Palace on Wednesday, 21 May 1975.

Before the audience, I took the tactical training participants to Malaysia to observe the training of the Malaysian Police Field Force in Kotabaru. The mission of Police Field Force was similar to that of Thailand's BPP and both forces had enjoyed a rather close collaboration, particularly in the southern Thai provinces, which shared the problem of insurgency launched by the communists based in Malaysia.

We traveled in a large bus from Songkhla to Kotabaru. During the trip, the commander of Malaysia's Police Field Force complimented the Thai Border Patrol Police as being very well-disciplined. He also asked me how I managed to get them to have such short crew cuts. I am not sure that he would say the same about the Border Patrol Police today.

On the day the BPP trainers visited Klai Kangwol Palace, Their Majesties received them in Sala Roeng. His Majesty gave a short speech to all 129 BPP trainers, emphasizing the importance of their mission and wishing them success and safety in performing their duties.

I did not know what other people felt hearing this speech but I was delighted. The king, the commander-in-chief and the monarch of the Thai people giving them encouragement and blessing was one of the greatest honors in my and their lives.

Because of such overwhelming emotions, when the king's speech ended, I did what other people did not expect, that is, prostrated myself in front of His Majesty. I tried to tell him that we all were ready to sacrifice our lives for our monarch and our nation.

27

I spoke a few words and then was so overcome by emotions that my voice trembled. I almost could not continue. I could not even remember what I had said before closing the audience.

This was another time I realized that I should not say something at a formal audience with the king without preparation; otherwise what I wanted to say might come out wrong. Although it is well-known that the king is compassionate and never blames people for misspeaking, this impromptu speech of mine taught me that it was unwise to speak without preparation. Having notes would also be helpful. Some people might consider speaking from notes embarrassing, but to me it's more embarrassing to be speak clumsily and incorrectly or to be speechless in front of the king.

I witnessed again another incident that confirmed the king's and the queen's kindness to the BPP while I was commander of the BPP Tactical Training Division. During 1975, the Americans withdrew the last of their forces from Vietnam. Prior to that time the United States decided not only to end their involvement in the Vietnam War but also to change their foreign policy, which included stopping or reducing military aid to many countries. Thailand was one of the countries affected by this change of policy.

Actually the U.S. military aid to Thailand did not suddenly stop. In January 1973, after four countries signed a treaty in Paris to end the Vietnam War, the Americans informed Thailand's top military and police officers that United States would stop providing further military aid. As I recalled, the Thai government of the day either did not understand or failed to grasp the consequence of such a change of policy. It did not seem to pay attention to what Thailand would do in the event the Americans no longer gave aid and support to Thailand. The reaction of the Thai government was not unlike a boxer who has been knocked out, lying on his back and waiting for the referee to count to ten, and gets up clueless as to where his trainer and coach have disappeared.

The Royal Thai Police Department had received substantial aid from the United States, including vehicles and fuel for police operations. They also received arms, guns and ammunition. When the Americans said that they would stop giving aid, we suddenly were aware that we would be in trouble. As the commander of the BPP Tactical Training Division, my view was that our work to combat communist insurgency must continue—with or without aid from the United States or any other country. If there would not be any help from the United States, we had to help ourselves.

I held a meeting with my junior officers and informed them about the situation, and explained to them the need to depend on ourselves and to continue our mission. I mobilized my colleagues to draft a training plan based on a premise we would not receive aid from any country and that we had to be self-sufficient. If this crisis had not happened, we might not have learned how much native intellect and ability the Thai people possess when it comes to self-reliance. This is especially true in the case of the border patrol police, who now had to learn to rely on no one outside the country for help.

This was the first time I truly understood the resourcefulness and the capacity for improvisation of the Thai BPP officers. They made grenades and mines by mixing gunpowder, saltpeter and sugar. A trainer of Subdivision I of the Tactical Training Division, at Marigadayavan Palace brought many kinds of explosives made by the officers and tested them for me. The results were satisfactory.

Meanwhile, I asked my colleagues to look for alternative weapons that might be available locally in the event that our sophisticated weapons and bullets were exhausted. We trained the police to use crossbows, relying on our close relationship with the Sagai, a native tribe of the Betong district, Yala. The Sagai were invited to demonstrate to our officers how they made and used darts. The Sagai also taught us the technique of using poisoned darts.

I felt that the BPP's self-reliance and resourcefulness should be brought to the attention of the king, who immediately expressed his wish to see a demonstration of the BPP-made arms and explosives.

Once we learned of the king's interest, we quickly started preparing the demonstration of our improvised weapons and explosives. One member of the preparation team was Sgt-Maj. Third Class (his rank at that time) On Maithaothong, a trainer in explosives and a specialist of Subdivision I of the Tactical Training Division (at that time called Marigadayavan Camp and later renamed Rama VI Camp).

On Sunday, 1 June 1975 around 2 p.m., the king and the queen, Crown Prince Vajiralongkorn, Princess Sirindhorn and Princess Chulabhorn went to the football field of Klai Kangwol Palace to village scout banners to the village scouts who came from Prachuap Khiri Khan, Phetchaburi and Samut Songkhram. At 6.30 p.m. the royal family left for the demonstration of explosives at Marigadayavan Camp.

Sgt-Maj. Third Class On Maithaothong, also known as Khru On, made explosives by mixing gunpowder, saltpeter and sugar and loading them in sheaths of rifle bullets. He blended the three ingredients with a small stick about the size of a toothpick. Although he was very careful, an accident happened. The explosive device blew up in his hand, causing him to lose the tip of his finger. Khru On in effect was one police officer who presented his fingertip to the king and the queen even before meeting them.

The royal family was asked to watch the demonstration from behind a bunker of sand sacks. We gave the demonstration our full effort and it was clear that the king was satisfied with what he saw. After the demonstration, the king left the bunker to talk with the officers. The conversations lasted until 8.30 p.m. Before returning to the palace, the king gave some money to Khru On for medical expenses.

On the queen's birthday, 12 August, that year, the royal family again moved their base to Thaksin Palace in Narathiwat. In the afternoon of the following day, the king drove the queen, Princess Sirindhorn and Princess Chulabhorn to visit several royal projects in Narathiwat as usual.

On Friday, 15 August, all royal family members joined a dinner at the field in front of Thaksin Palace and attended a play, 'Pathom Chakri'. The play was based on a story written by Princess Sirindhorn. There were also other performances organized to celebrate the queen's birthday.

On 9 August there was an incident at the Border Patrol Police Company 2 of BPP 8th Subdivision, located at Baan Sai La, Tambon Chawang in Nakhon Si Thammarat's Chawang district. Late that night, a group of communist insurgents slipped past the security guards and attacked the company base, causing several deaths and injuries. Luckily, some officers managed to reach two parked armored cars before the insurgents were able to seize them (the two armored cars were equipped with heavy arms) or the loss of life might have been greater. The insurgents finally drew back.

The attack at the BPP company was brazen and affected the morale of the officers as well as the villagers in the area, some of whom also witnessed the attack. On Tuesday, 17 August, the king and the queen with Princess Sirindhorn traveled on a C-123 from Banthorn Airport in Muang district, Narathiwat to Nakhon Si Thammarat, to visit the BPP company in Baan Sai La.

After Pol. Col. Prem Chanarat (his rank at that time), superintendent of the BPP 8th Subdivision read a brief report of the situation, Their Majesties and HRH Princess Sirindhorn observed the damage from the attack, especially that at the Border Patrol Police Platoon No. 812—Armored Car Platoon. The king talked with the officers and gave them his good wishes. He was there until after 2 p.m. and then went to a cement factory at Thung Song district and had lunch there.

Then, at 4.10 p.m., Their Majesties and the princess went on to Nakhon Si Thammarat Hospital. Before the hospital, they stopped by Wat Mahathat, a sacred place in southern Thailand. The king gave the officers flowers, incense and candles to worship the Buddha relics inside the pagoda. At the hospital, the royal couple and the princess visited nine BPP officers who had suffered injuries from the Baan Sai La attack. They gave money to the officers and then visited the families and the relatives of the officers who were killed and injured. The royal visit lasted until 6 p.m.

Traveling with the possibility of grave dangers in remote and risk areas was normal for the king and queen. Some roads on which they traveled to visit the people were at risk from ambushes and mines planted by the insurgents. One such road linked Ra Ngae and Rue-Sor districts. Another was Highway 4207, which linked Sukhirin district and Baan To Mo in Narathiwat.

Baan To Mo was the southernmost village of Thailand. Like Betong district in Yala, the village is surrounded by the Malaysian territories. There was once a gold mine in Baan To Mo but it is no longer in business.

Their Majesties, together with Princess Sirindhorn and Princess Chulabhorn, traveled to Baan To Mo on Thursday, 18 September 1975. The king drove his car from Thaksin Palace and arrived at the Waeng District Office around 11.50 a.m. There were a number of villagers gathering for an audience. The king stopped the car to visit and chat with the people for about ten minutes before he continued on to other destinations on the itinerary that day. The first stop was the I Bajoh Farmers Evacuation Project. The official report of the situation at the project was worrying. The officials reported that there were regular bombings by either the Malaysian or the Chinese communist insurgents in the project area.

The road from the I Bocho Farmers Evacuation Project to Baan To Mo was rough traveling. Because there wasn't much time left, the travel to Baan To Mo had to be done by helicopter. The royal mission arrived at the BPP PARU operation base in Baan To Mo around 1.45 p.m..

Their Majesties and Princess Sirindhorn had lunch at the base. They visited and gave gifts and medical supplies to the police paratroopers, and then went to see the weapons seized from the insurgents. Afterwards they walked about one kilometer on the road under construction to observe the area. It was drizzling and the road was muddied and it became difficult to walk. Finally, the officials provided an armored car for the royal family.

That was the first and only time that I saw Their Majesties and Princess Sirindhorn in an armored car—a war car—on a battlefield.

28

I was born in Udon Thani but grew up in Khon Kaen. I have always had a special attachment to Sakon Nakhon because of my involvement in the People's Assistance Teams Project under the CSOC (becoming the head of the training division in 1967). The first volunteers to come for village defense training came from Sakon Nakhon. The later generations came from Nakhon Phanom, especially Pla Pak district.

After the volunteers finished their training, they returned to their provinces. At least once a year I would take a team of trainers to visit those volunteers, to give them support and to evaluate their operations.

Even after I joined the royal court police and was no longer with the CSOC, His Majesty the King still allowed me to continue my visits every year. He also allowed an official from the Royal Guards Division to accompany me, and gave supplies, including clothes, dry food and other necessities, to be distributed to the villagers. That Royal Guard official was Khun Somchai Satachutha, presently director of Pra Dabot School, a school under royal patronage.

During a visit to the People's Assistance Teams in Sakon Nakhon's Muang district in 1967, a group of insurgents had encircled a nearby village and demanded food and provisions from the villagers. This kind of extortion was common at that time. The district chief of Sakon Nakhon's Muang district (Khun Suep Rotprasert, who later became governor of Chon Buri province before retiring) and I led the People's Assistance Team in the area and a team of police officers from the Tao Nguay Police Station in a mission to ambush the perpetrating insurgents. The ambush lasted for only a few moments before the insurgents withdrew. The details about the attack aren't important for my story here. I mention it in the context of the events in Sakon Nakhon that made me feel a close attachment to the province.

Amid security crises in northeastern Thailand, Their Majesties continued to visit the region. Often times, they visited the areas where fighting between authorities and the insurgents had just occurred. Whenever the king went to Sakon Nakhon, I felt as though I were returning home.

Incidentally, the king had chosen Sakon Nakhon as his base of operations in the northeast. Before Bhuban Palace was built, the king's northeastern residence was Nam Un Dam Irrigation Project in Sakon Nakhon's Waritchaphum district.

Aside from being known as a hotbed of communist activities, especially in the Bhuban mountain range, Sakon Nakhon was also the birth place and residence of many revered monk, such as Phra Ajarn Man Phurithatto, a senior monk in the Vipassanadhura meditation tradition, a native of Sakon Nakhon. His temple was Wat Pa Phurithattawat in Baan Nong Phue, Tambon Na Nai in Phanna Nikhom district. His *kuti* (living quarters) at Wat Pa Phurithattawat, registered by the Department of Fine Arts, is still in perfect condition. It lies off Highway 22 Udon Thani-Nakhon Phanom.

Phra Ajarn Man passed away at Wat Pa Sutthawat in Sakon Nakhon's Muang district. This temple, which was the place of his funeral, also houses a museum where his relics and eight necessities (for Buddhist monks) are kept. One among the other well-known monks was Phra Ajarn Wan Uttamo, the abbot of Wat Aphai Damrongtham in Song Dao district (which at that time was only Tambon Song Dao, under the jurisdiction of Sawang Dan Din district).

On 13 October 1975, Their Majesties, Princess Sirindhorn and Princess Chulabhorn moved their stay to the Nam Un Dam residence in Sakon Nakhon. They flew from Don Muang Airport to Udon Thani province and transferred to a helicopter for the balance of the journey to Nam Un Dam.

The royal family visited Wat Aphai Damrongtham, located on Bhuban Mountain. Of significant interest offered by this wat was a Buddha image displayed at Wiharn Tham Phong, a place where Phra Ajarn Man Phurithatto and Phra Ajarn Sao Kantasilo performed monastic observances. The Buddha image was built with donations from monks, merchants, government officers and lay people in memory of the two monks.

After arrival, the royal family paid homage to the Buddha image. The king also visited Phra Ajarn Wan and gave contributions to several ongoing construction projects at the temple, including the building of Buddha images and halls in which to house them, study halls, and a school for underprivileged children. Phra Ajarn Wan also presented the king with a relic believed to have belonged to one of Buddha's disciples.

Phra Ajarn Wan was a tall, big, elegant man. His appearance seemed imposing but he was very compassionate. I had previously visited him and knew him to be reserved in terms of action and speech, a monk of few words. To me, his sermon suggested that he was a monk in the tradition of Phra Ajarn Man, which was concise, to the point, and easy to understand.

There were a large number of people from Sawang Dan Din and neighboring districts who arrived to greet the royal family. There were also several former students of mine from the People's Assistance Teams training courses. The people were happy to have an audience with the royal family and to see me again. The royal family members generously spent time visiting with the villagers. They spent about two hours there and left the temple around 6 p.m. to return to Nam Un Dam.

The next day, Tuesday, 14 October 1975, the royal family left before noon by helicopter for an opening ceremony of Romklao School in Baan Khok, Tambon Tong Khob in Sakon Nakhon's Muang district.

There are actually many schools named Romklao. Romklao schools are schools under royal patronage that were jointly built by the government (usually the army of the region) and the local people. These schools allow students in remote areas to study in the secondary school level. In the case of Romklao School in Baan Khok, this was the second built by the Second Army Area Command and the local people. The Second

Army commander at the time was then Lt-Gen. Prem Tinsulanonda, current president of the Privy Council.

After the opening ceremony of Romklao School, the royal family visited with a large group of people waiting to have an audience. Village scouts from Sakon Nakhon also gave a performance on the occasion.

After 2 p.m., the family continued by helicopter to Tat Tone Waterfall in Tambon Huay Yang. Tat Tone Waterfall was situated in Kham Hom Park in Bhuban National Park. The name of the waterfall was originally not Kham Hom 'fragrant gold' as it is now pronounced, but Kham Hom, encircled by gold. The family had lunch and rested there before going to the location near the waterfall where Bhuban Palace would be erected.

After the site survey, the king said he would like to go to Wat Pa Udom Somporn, which was in Phanna Nikhom district down the mountain. The king wanted to visit Phra Ajarn Fan Ajaro, the abbot of the temple.

This was a spontaneous visit, but still security officers had to survey the place beforehand. They quickly discovered that there was only one tiny spot where a helicopter could land, on a field in front of Ba Thong School near Wat Pa Udom Somporn. The landing zone was narrow and large enough for only one helicopter. This meant that each helicopter had to land, drop off its passengers, and lift off before the next helicopter could land and unload passengers.

The helicopters did drop off the passengers one by one. The last to be dropped off were the royal family. As I have indicated, this was a spontaneous visit. However, when I climbed down from the helicopter and stood on the field in front of Bathong School, Phra Ajarn Fan Ajaro was already waiting, walking with a cane in his hand. He had seen or foreseen our arrival.

There was another transportation problem to be resolved before the king and other royal family members arrived at the field. Because the visit was not planned, there were no previously arranged cars to take the royal family to the final destination. However, this problem was solved quickly by a number of people offering their personal vehicles to the royal family members and other escorts. I remember that a green Volvo owned by a businessman from Sakon Nakhon was chosen as the car to transport members of the royal family. The Volvo was driven by police officer.

Northeastern Thai or Isan people called the *ubosot* of Wat Pa Udom Somporn 'Sim', which in Isan dialect means that the temple was located in the middle of the water. The family visited Phra Ajarn Fan Ajaro at the ubosot and later came out to meet a group of waiting villagers outside the temple. At 7 p.m., the family returned to Nam Un Dam in the borrowed Volvo.

I know the car's owner but have forgotten his name. I remembered his great delight when he had a chance to offer his car for use by members of the royal family. This was twenty-five years ago and I would not be surprised if he still has the car.

In December 1975, an event worthy of record was Crown Prince Vajiralongkorn's graduation from the Royal Military College, Duntroon in Canberra, Australia. The queen also went to attend his graduation ceremony.

Before she went, she asked the Australian Embassy not to provide a special welcome because her intention was to attend as the mother of an army cadet graduate, not as the queen of the kingdom of Thailand. The Australian government obliged and did not hold a welcoming ceremony but provided other appropriate facilities.

The queen left Thailand on Sunday, 7 December. And three days later on Wednesday, 10 December, the queen and the crown prince returned to Thailand. One week after he returned to Thailand, the crown prince performed his own official duties as a representative of the king and the queen. On Tuesday 16 December, he was the king's representative to attend the opening ceremony of the Eighth Southeast Asian Games, or SEA Games, at the Subhachalasai National Stadium.

On the morning of the following day, the crown prince followed in the king's footsteps by driving from Chitralada Palace to visit soldiers, police and villagers in Aranyaprathet and Ta Phraya districts in Prachin Buri (both districts are now in Srakaew province).

Crown Prince Vajiralongkorn left Prachin Buri around 4 p.m. and arrived back at Chitralada Palace at about 7.25 p.m.

29

In December 1975 the royal family did not stay at Bhubing Palace in Chiang Mai as customary in the cool season. On 29 December, Their Majesties together with Crown Prince Vajiralongkorn, Princess Sirindhorn and Princess Chulabhorn went instead to Bang Pa-In Palace in Bang Pa-In district of Ayutthaya.

During their stay in Bang Pa-In that year many provinces in Thailand were flooded. Farmlands were damaged. Their Majesties visited the flood victims almost everyday. The king normally drove out in the afternoon and came back to Bang Pa-In Palace in the evening.

On Friday, 2 January 1975, the king, with the prince and princesses, went to Baan Kwang, Tambon Baan Kwang, Ayutthaya's Maharat district to visit the flood victims and check on damaged rice fields of the local farmers.

The Ayutthaya governor at the time, Khun Witthaya Kesornsaowaphak, and the director of the Eighth Irrigation Office, Khun Chop Cholakate, were also on the visit. They reported that the flood was seasonal and happened because the dike of the conveyance canal had been damaged.

The king advised that the problem be solved promptly and that the authorities and the local people cooperate on the repair of the damaged dike and irrigation system. His Majesty also suggested that substitution crops be provided to the farmers for temporary plantation in the areas not flooded. Village scouts were advised to act as the representatives of the local people; they should report problems to relevant authorities and assist the Royal Irrigation Department when available.

In addition to solutions to the immediate flooding problems, the king also advised the local villagers to form a cooperative and set up a village rice bank and a rice mill. Vegetable seedlings were then given to the head of the Provincial Agricultural Extension Office to distribute to villagers affected by the flood in Ayutthaya's Maharat and Bang Ban districts.

What the king said to the village scouts that day reflected his view on their role. The king had faith in the training of village scouts. He had given village scout banners to many groups of village scouts all over the country. He envisioned that village scouts were not merely a group of people to sing songs as a show of unity but a group that would give tangible benefits to society, including acting as the representatives of local people and bringing problems to the attention of the relevant government authorities.

After leaving Baan Kwang, the king and his children visited Baan Kum in Bang Baan district in the same province. The rice fields in Baan Kum were also flooded. The *kamnan* of Tambon Baan Kum (Khun Charat Niranthawi) reported that some dikes were not strong enough to prevent floodwater from entering and damaging the rice fields. To further complicate matters, usually in the planting season there was a shortage of water.

Upon hearing the report, the king advised the Royal Irrigation Department to deal with the problem promptly by strengthening the dikes, enlarging conveyance canals, and providing sufficient water.

The picture of a *kamnan,* or head of *tambon*, the lowest ranking local administrator, having an audience with the king and reporting on the difficulties of his villagers' well-being is a picture I saw many times on my royal escort duty.

After the visits to the flooded areas, the royal mission went into village of Baan Kum to see how the local people supplemented their income with temporary work in brick making and production of incense sticks. This was the first time for me to see how incense sticks were made. The villagers told the king that these temporary jobs earned them enough money to substitute for the loss of their rice crops in the flood.

The royal family stayed at Bang Pa-In Palace until 6 January 1976. But even after they returned to Bangkok, the visits to central Thailand continued. Four days later, on Saturday, 10 January at about 10.20 a.m., they went to Chainat Dam to inspect a sluice gate on the Chainat-Ayutthaya Canal in

Tambon Bang Luang, Chinat's Sapphaya district, had lunch at a guesthouse near the Chao Phraya Dam, and then around 2.10 p.m. went farther to inspect the irrigation system in Maharat Irrigation Project (Lop Buri River) in Tambon Muang Moo, Muang district, Sing Buri province.

His Majesty followed up on the progress at other irrigation projects he had earlier advised on in Maharat district. After the Maharat Irrigation Project, he continued to Baan Bang Khan. On the way, he watched as a tractor of the Royal Irrigation Department repaired a dike in Tambon Bang Khan.

Around 5 p.m., the king visited Wat Kai Fah (or the Temple of the Celestial Bird, which the villagers call 'Wat Kai', or the Temple of the Chicken) in Tambon Hansang, Bang Pahan district, Ayutthaya. The king visited with the abbot, provided medical supplies to the monks and the villagers, and then went in to pay homage to the Buddha image at the *ubosot*. Finally, he gave time to the villagers waiting around the temple ground for an audience with him.

The king left Wat Kai at 6 p.m. and returned to Baan Kum, which he had visited on Friday, 2 January. This time, the king informed Khun Charat Niranthawi, the *kamnan* of Tambon Baan Kum, and Khun Riang Phuanglap, Bang Baan district chief, that the Royal Irrigation Department was correcting the problem of inadequate water supplies. He suggested that people form a group to make decisions in case they experienced trouble and needed further assistance from the government. He also recommended that the farmers conserve soil by using organic fertilizer, which was cheaper than chemical fertilizer.

His speech was no different than the one in which he solved the water problem of the villagers in Baan Bang Kum. The king and the rest of the mission returned to Chitralada Palace at eight thirty that evening.

The king made a point of returning to meet the same people at their villages and the same set of officials. During the early stage of my work as a royal escort, I had not fully appreciated why he did so and felt bored by it. Only later did I come to understand that it is his intention and policy to keep in close touch with the same set of people and problems so that he could follow up with them. He was neither bored nor ever abandoned what he had set in motion and took the time to review and reflect on the ways to improve their lives.

❖

In 1976, the royal family's move to Bhubing Palace in the north happened on 17 January. During their stay there, Their Majesties visited the hill tribe villagers as usual.

Escorting the king in the northern Thailand was a yearly test of physical fitness for all of the security officers. That included me. Because I was forty years old I developed a slipped disc condition. The disc pressed against the nerve and occasionally caused pain to shoot through my upper right leg. The condition, when severe, effectively made it impossible for me to move. The treatment for my condition in those days was for the doctor to pull the hip to move the disc to its normal position. This relieved the constant pressure against the nerve. Luckily, I had never suffered such a serious condition on my escort duty that I was unable to do my work. Later, I found someone, a highly skilled masseur, who could whisk away my pain with a one-hour massage using both hands and feet, and that was the end of the hip pulling. Even now I still visit the masseur on occasions. (For those who may be tempted to ask for the name of this masseur, I am not permitted to divulge his name because he is not a masseur by profession. He only helps me as charity, free of charge.)

Having mentioned physical fitness, I should note that at Bhubing Palace all the royal family members always maintained a program of exercise. The king and the queen exercised in the evening or at night. As for the prince and princesses, they usually exercised in the morning, but sometimes also in the evening along with Their Majesties. Royal security officers divided our tasks to escort different members of the family.

Apart from jogging around Pha Mon (Pillow Cliff) in front of Bhubing Palace, the king sometimes ran outside the palace along a two-kilometer stretch of a road to Doi Suthep. It was easy to run from the palace because the run was down the mountain, but running up the steep road back to the palace was hard work, especially directly in front of the Police Guard of the palace.

The king had another form of exercise—walking from the top of Doi Pui to Baan Khun Mae Nai, located at the foot of the hill and back to the palace. I had to lead the security team, comprised of royal aides-de-camp, royal court police officers and other security officers, during His Majesty the King's walking exercises. His Majesty used his wristwatch to measure the time. If the walk took more than thirty-five minutes, HM would say that the walk was slow. His record was 33.5 minutes, up and down the mountain!

Despite all the advance survey and coordination we usually conducted before each royal visit to the hill tribe villages on the mountain, we sometimes still faced some obstacles, one of which was that the helicopters lost their way and could not find the landing.

On Sunday, 1 February 1976, Their Majesties and Prince Sirindhorn had a visit in Sukhothai province. Two places were on the agenda. Before they left at about 8.45 that morning, a group of security officers, royal guards, and I went in advance in a Royal Thai Army helicopter. A Royal Thai Police helicopter took doctors and nurses from a royal medical unit to provide services to the villagers in both destinations ahead of the royal arrival.

Around 9.30 a.m., the Royal Thai Army helicopter arrived at Baan Mae Saan in Tambon Mae Sam, Si Satchanalai district, Sukhothai, which was where the royal mission would have lunch. We dropped a group of officers at Baan Mae San and flew on to Sukhothai's Sawankhalok district—the first destination where the king would give village scout banners to local village scouts. Our landing point was an old airport in Tambon Nai Muang, Sawankhalok.

However, we discovered as we left Baan Mae Saan that the pilot of the Royal Thai Army helicopter had lost his way and had to land at a Baan Dan School. We did not know in which *tambon* and district the school was located. Our flight resumed and we reached Sawankhalok after 10 a.m.

Getting lost that time was better than when we were trying to find two villages in Chiang Mai's Doi Inthanon on Monday, 19 January. Their Majesties and the crown prince were going to visit Baan Pui, Tambon Baan Thap, Mae Chaem district and Baan Mae Tho, Tambon Bor Salee, Hot district on Doi Inthanon. As usual, I, along with other officers, had gone in advance by Royal Thai Army helicopter at 10.25 a.m. The pilot had a difficult time finding the place. We arrived at Baan Mae Tho almost an hour later, twenty minutes late and only five minutes before the royal helicopter arrived.

30

Most of the aircraft used as transport for the royal staff and security officers were those operated by the Royal Thai Air Force, the Royal Thai Army, or the Royal Thai Police. They were not necessarily new and flights could at times prove rather exciting for the passengers.

A Royal Thai Air Force C-123, carrying officers and royal staff to Chiang Mai in advance of the king's move to Bhubing Palace, once prepared to land in Chiang Mai Airport, but could not open the landing gear. The pilot was forced to circle the field many times before the landing gear finally opened and the plane could land.

As for the helicopters used in royal transport, they also belonged to the Royal Air Force, Army and Police. Many of the pilots were on duty in the field or on the battlefield to provide services to the royal family whenever air transport was needed.

During such transport, ladies-in-waiting and court ladies often asked me if the aircraft in which they were passengers had ever been attacked in combat. Generally, out of consideration for their sensibilities yet not wishing to lie, I often I said it might be better to reword their question. Which plane had never been fired at? I did not want to tell them that the patches on the plane's floor were repairs of the damage from the incoming fire or that the brown stains were blood that had not been completely washed away.

It should be noted that the king did not like to keep idle the planes and helicopters that the Royal Thai Air Force and the Royal Thai police had assigned as exclusive royal aircraft. He gave permission for them to be used for other official duties when they were not used in royal transport. As far as I know, however, they were only sparingly used for other functions. It seems that Thai people still felt inhibited to share things used by their monarch.

I remember that after the king and the queen visited MR Kukrit Pramoj at his house on Doi Khun Taan in Lamphun/Lampang on the border of the two provinces, MR Kukrit had his toilet bowl that the king had used during his visit destroyed. As for his chair on which the king sat, he pasted gold leaves on it, kept it in a high place, and did not permit anyone to sit on it.

❖

Political and social strife lingered into 1976. Demonstrations and strikes, which had begun after the Day of Great Sorrow in October 1973, persisted. In January, a new cabinet was formed and MR Kukrit continued as prime minister. But the new cabinet would not last. Under heavy pressure from the members of the House of Representatives, the government dissolved parliament on 12 January 1976.

On Wednesday, 21 January 1976 at 11.30 a.m., Princess Sirindhorn as the king's representative welcomed Queen Ingrid, the mother of Queen Margrethe II of Denmark, at Chiang Mai Airport. She had a close relationship with our king and queen. The queen was later welcomed as a royal quest at Bhubing Palace.

Normally royal court security police officers are not directly responsible for welcoming and providing security for royal guests except when especially assigned to do so. On that day, after I accompanied Princess Sirindhorn to Chiang Mai Airport, I had no further duty; however, I had the time to observe that one of Queen Ingrid's Danish escorts was Count Gregers. I remembered his name without difficulty. Another escort was a lady by the name of Countess Nonni Ahlefeldt Laurvit Bille. There was no way I could remember that without writing it down.

Queen Ingrid stayed at Bhubing Palace until Friday, 23 January. Despite the visit being short, she had a chance to go with the king and the queen to the Highland Agricultural Research Station of Khun Huay Mai Nai, under the Hill Tribe Development Project under royal patronage in Mae Rim district, Chiang Mai.

The night before the Danish royal guests' departure, the mother of Queen Margrethe and other foreign dignitaries were invited to dinner in the main hall in Bhubing Palace. Traditional Thai music and dances were performed for the guests. Queen Ingrid might have been surprised to see the crown prince sing the famous traditional Thai song 'Lao Duang Duean' and to hear Princess Sirindhorn play a Thai fiddle and sing traditional Thai songs as well.

❖

On Sunday, 25 January 1976, a special event was held that had not been on the list of the king's official duties. On that day, a representative of a foreign arms manufacturing company requested an audience with the king at Bhubing Palace. The representative wished to present the king with a pistol, which was regarded as a new product in Thailand at that time, as well as ten flak jackets.

Before the representative had a royal audience, he contacted me through a senior police officer to ask for the king's permission to present the pistol. I considered that there was nothing to worry about and I said so to the king, but could not help feeling a little cautious and emphasized to the senior police officer that offering the gun was a personal affair and there would be no public mention of that event or no advertisement for commercial benefits.

On midday of Sunday, 25 January, the representative arrived at Bhubing Place, with the police officer. Another man came along as well, Khun Amnuay Kohphet, the owner of the gun shop Amnuay and president of the Gun Trader Association (he has since passed away). The king came down to meet the group at 12.45 p.m., received the pistol and the flak jackets and returned to his quarters.

The next morning, an English newspaper in Thailand reported a fanciful ceremony of the pistol presentation to the king. There was a picture of an automatic pistol inscribed with the king's initials. It was apparent that the advertisement was prepared even before an audience with the king took place.

❖

Sunday, 15 February 1976 was a Makha Bucha Day, a Buddhist holy day of worship on a full moon day of the third lunar month in commemoration of the Great Assembly of Disciples. Their Majesties together with Princess Sirindhorn and Princess Chulabhorn left Bhubing Palace by helicopter for Phrathat (Pagoda) Chom Kitti in Chiang Rai's Chiang Saen district, where they would perform a ceremony of lifting the tiered umbrella of the pagoda.

Chiang Saen is an ancient city located by the Khong River, which flows north of Chiang Rai. Built in 1328, it had been deserted for a long period. Today, ruins of ancient remains and shrines are scattered throughout the city. I saw Chiang Saen for the first time in 1962, when I posted as chief of Special Branch field office in Chiang Rai. I have developed attachment to Chiang Saen and ever since always tried to visit it whenever I had a chance.

In northern Thai dialect *chom* means a hilltop and *that*, as in Isan dialect, means stupa or pagoda, and contains relics of the Buddha or his disciples. According to a legend, Phrathat Chom Kitti was built in 940 AD during the reign of King Phangkharat. It has been restored many times since. At present, the pagoda is thirteen meters high and eight meters wide.

On Sunday, 15 February, the ceremony of lifting the tiered umbrella of the pagoda was presided over by Somdej Phra Yannasangvorn. At that time, he had not been appointed as supreme patriarch. He arrived at the place of ceremony early in the morning. Along with other officers, I arrived at the foot of pagoda just before the monks' daily mealtime (11.00 a.m.) and had a chance to pay my respects to him while he was having his meal. It was the first time that I saw Somdej Phra Yannasangvorn eating from his alms bow. I later learned that this was one of the Buddhist ascetic practices.

Although the place where he had his meal was in the shade, the weather was burning hot under an unforgiving sun. I was kneeling beside him, observing him with amazement and admiration how he was eating with ease and calm, as though he was not in the least bothered by the heat of the sun.

Generally the security staff was informed of the royal travel itinerary, and this was the practice even for personal trips. On occasions, however, security officers were not given notice until a radio message was received after the king had already started his journey.

Tuesday, 9 March 1976 was one such occasion. On that day, we were informed only that the king was going out but the final destination was not yet known. The order was merely that we had to provide the king a car and listen to his order over the radio. At 3.10 p.m., the king drove the queen outside Bhubing Palace. I was in a preceding escort motorcade and heard from the king's order on the radio to take the motorcade down Doi Suthep.

I was nearly forty-seven years old that spring. Albeit fit and in good health, I was becoming aware of my mortality. One of the changes that began that year was that, for the first time, I started experiencing carsickness, which usually happened during the journeys up and down to Bhubing Palace. And when this happened, the only effective cure for me was meditation. I asked a fellow police officer to take over for me, and, then, I closed my eyes. Instead inhaling and exhaling according to *anapanasati* meditation approach, I used my sensation of carsickness as the focus—the dizziness and the loss of balance.

I must have closed my eyes for about five minutes, and with my eyes still closed, I had a vision—not the luminous light as I had experienced before, but a large Buddha image entirely made from gold, enshrined in an *ubosot* or a *vihara*. And in front of the Buddha image was a busy crowd walking about. When I stopped the mediation and the carsickness had disappeared, I was secretly delighted I had such a good vision—a Buddha image, the symbol of Lord Buddha.

When the procession passed the foot of Doi Suthep along Huay Kaew Road to Chaeng Hua Rin and reached Boon Rueang Rit Intersection, the king ordered a left turn. I guessed that he would take Highway 108. This road, which connected Chiang Mai to Mae Hong Son's Mae Sariang district, was 188 kilometers long. He might want to stop anywhere along the way. It was probably a fruitless exercise to guess where he might wish to go. The best thing for me to do was to focus on my order at hand and wait for the next order.

When the procession reached San Patong Intersection, the order was to take a right. I couldn't help guessing that his plan was to visit Wang Namkhang Tangerine Orchard of Minister Phanlert Buranasilapin. But I was wrong. At 4.15 a.m., we were ordered to stop in Baan Kaat in San Patong, a big village ten kilometers from the intersection.

Only then we learned that Their Majesties came to Baan Kaat to see Sala Ruamjai, a public pavilion that the queen had contributed to the villagers of Baan Kaat. When I saw that there were many people waiting for the royal couple there, I realized that we probably would not be going anywhere else. The king and the queen would be visiting with the villagers until late.

Their Majesties stayed at Sala Ruamjai until nearly dusk. The assistant village headman invited the royal couple to visit Wat Don Pao, the village temple. The king was going alone to the temple. I went in advance as usual. I knew that the king would not immediately meet with the people waiting to see him there but would first go in to pay homage to the main Buddha image in the temple. I walked ahead to the *ubosot* of Wat Don Pao.

When I reached the stairs of the *ubosot*, I looked up, and there, in front of me, was the very Buddha image that I had seen in my vision during my meditation on the way down Doi Suthep. The Buddha was entirely covered with gold leaves. Many people hurried to find a seat for an audience with the king.

That phenomenon made me realize the power of calmness of mind that comes through meditation. Many teachers, including the king, had warned me before not to have any hubris from this manifestation of meditation success. I remember the wise words of my teachers well: be aware of everything that happens during meditation, acknowledge its existence, but do not allow any attachment to it or speculate if and when it would reoccur.

I still try to follow the wisdom of these words.

31

In 1976 Visakha Bucha Day fell on Thursday, 13 May. The king and the queen, with Princess Sirindhorn and Princess Chulabhorn, performed a ceremony to enshrine a Buddhist relic as well as a personal merit-making ceremony at Wat Pho Sri That in Rattanaburi district, Surin province.

By personal merit-making is that the king makes merit formally and officially at Wat Phra Kaew (the Emerald Buddha Temple) in Bangkok. Prince Bhanubandh Yugala was designated as the king's representative to perform the official royal merit-making ceremony at Wat Phra Kaew on the same day.

We left Don Muang Airport by a Royal Thai Air Force C-47 at 9 a.m. and arrived at Ubon Ratchathani Airport around 11 a.m. The C-47 was a transport plane used by the American and British Air Force during World War II, known as Datoka, which is the name of a river in the American West. At the time we were flying in it, our Dakota was about thirty-one years old, no longer young. However, it was still in good condition and the Royal Thai Air Force used it regularly. It was also used as a spooky plane in combat against the communist insurgents.

From Ubon Ratchathani, we transferred to Royal Thai Air Force helicopters to Rattanaburi in Surin, arriving at a landing site in front of Wat Pho Sri That in the afternoon. It was not exactly a smooth helicopter ride because we flew through a rainstorm. I hated flying in bad weather because once in 1968 we had had a close call in a Royal Thai Police helicopter from Chiang Mai to Nan. The helicopter dropped from 8,000 to 2,000 feet, where the pilot fortunately regained control, and we all arrived at Wat Tri Thosathep in one piece. Only a few seconds longer and all five of us might have arrived in coffins at the *wat*. That experience caused me to mediate on the mindfulness of death whenever flying through a rainstorm.

The governor, Khun Suthi Ob-om and other senior government officials of Surin province welcomed the royal family in a pavilion in Wat Pho Sri That just before 3 p.m. The king began the ceremony by lighting the candles and incense sticks in front of the Buddha images. The then head monk chanted the Five Precepts. Afterwards the governor gave a status report on the construction of a *mondhop* (chapel) containing Buddha's relics.

The king went to the table where the Buddha's relics were placed. After he sprinkled the Buddha's relics, he placed them in a casket, and lowered the casket into another casket, which was taken to the *mondhop* by the officials. Then, Their Majesties and the two princesses approached the *mondhop*. The king placed the casket in a pagoda in the *mondhop* and sealed the pagoda, which concluded the ceremony.

With the ceremony ended, the royal party left the *mondhop* for the pavilion and made merit on the occasion of Visakha Bucha Day—the day that Buddha was born, reached enlightenment, and ascended to nirvana. The king lit candles and incense and paid homage to the Buddha's relics. He led the group in chanting in worship of the Triple Gem. Then the royal family led the procession in a ceremonial walking around the *mondhop*, that is, walking clockwise, candles in hand, with the *mondhop* on the walkers' right side.

Normally, such a religious ceremony would be followed by a donation session by the pilgrims. That day was no exception. After the walking ceremony, the king re-entered the pavilion and made offerings to the monks. The monks accepted the offerings and gave the king and the queen the special blessing, called *Adirek*. Then, the governor called the name of each donor to come forward for an audience with the king. The donations were made to the king's charity funds and the Sai Jai Thai Foundation.

The *Adirek* blessing is a special blessing reserved for the king and queen. It is said to have been originated in King Mongkut's reign. King Mongkut was making offerings on his birthday to the monks, one of whom was Phra Udom Pitaka, the abbot of Wat Suntharawat (also known as Wat Son Sa) in Phattalung's Khuan Khanun district. After King Mongkut had given the offerings to Phra Udom Pitaka, with whom he was well acquainted, he asked for a special blessing. Phra Udom Pitaka was caught off guard. He had not prepared any special blessing, but because he had a great deal of knowledge and wit, Phra Udom Pitaka lifted a fan from the monks' rank and gave the king a blessing in Pali, beginning with '*adireka wasatang chiwatu*'. Upon hearing this, King Mongkut was so delighted that he established this blessing as part of royal ceremonies. However, it must be noted that only the king and the queen can receive this *Adirek* blessing. At the end of the blessing, only they can raise their hands in acceptance of the blessing.

The king then went to the temple hall to pay homage to the principal Buddha image. The abbot and monks from the nearby temples presented the king several Buddha amulets. After that, he gave an audience to a number of villagers who had been waiting for him around the temple.

Following the audience with the villagers was a session in which the king presented village scout banners to twelve groups of village scouts from many districts in Surin. After the king had given his speech, the governor presented a group of donors who had made contributions to the village scouts. As in similar ceremonies of presenting village scout banners, the village scouts gave a performance. Afterwards, the king, the queen, and the two princesses chatted warmly with the village scouts and the villagers.

Before the day was concluded, the weather took another turn for the worse. More rainstorms hit the area. It rained heavily and for a long time. Finally, the officers informed the royal mission that it would be too dangerous to return by helicopter. The royal family was then transported by car to Nakhon Ratchasima to board a plane back to Bangkok. The royal procession had to stop at Surin Provincial Army Headquarters to fill the cars with petrol and left the province at 10.30 p.m.

At 1.30 the next morning, the royal family reached Wing 3 in Nakhon Ratchasima, boarded a plane at 2.40 a.m., and arrived at Chitralada Palace at 3.10 a.m. As soon as I sent off the royal family at the airport in Nakhon Ratchasima, I returned in a Special Branch car, which had been

the forward car for the procession. My companion was Pol. Maj-Gen. Thep Supasamit. We drove along Friendship Highway, or Highway 2.

On the return journey, many trucks came from the opposite direction. This was the first time that I saw firsthand the menace of Thailand's trucks. Many truck drivers drove as if they owned the road. They overtook one another freely. Even when our driver flashed the light on the roof of our car—a police car—the truck drivers did not seem to care. At times, the Special Branch cars had to take to the side of the road to avoid an accident.

If I had not directly experienced this, I would not have understood the true risks of highway driving for ordinary people. We reached Bangkok at 6.00 a.m. on Friday, 14 May.

After only two days in Bangkok, His Majesty went on another mission, this time to the guesthouse on the grounds of a factory of the Siam Cement Group in Thung Song district, Nakhon Si Thammarat in the south.

I flew ahead on a Royal Thai Air Force C-123, which was more spacious than the C-47 but more noisy. On the positive side, the drone of the engines meant that the passengers would have to shout to one another. There was therefore no talking and I took the opportunity to meditate, which was what I usually did in flights on a C-123.

The C-123 took us to Trang Airport, where we boarded a Royal Thai Air Force helicopter for Wat Don Sala in Tambon Makok Nua, Khuan Khanun district, Phatthalung. The flight took only twenty minutes. After we arrived, we immediately began preparing the welcoming ceremony.

Their Majesties and the two princesses arrived at Wat Don Sala at 2.50 p.m. After the king finished cutting the boundary marker for the temple by the invitation of Phatthalung Governor Khun Bamrung Sookhabusaya, he visited Phra Ajarn Nam Kaewchan at his *kuti*.

Phra Ajarn Nam was a monk highly respected in the area. His Buddha amulets were highly valued and in great demand. At that time, he was ill. His Majesty the King provided him with medicine and other necessities and also to Phra Khru Kachaat, the abbot of Wat Don Sala. After that, the royal family visited with the local people. Royal doctors had arrived in advance and sent a medical unit to examine and give treatments to villagers at Wat Don Sala School. The doctors found that there were ill people wishing to have an audience with the king and he asked the doctors to admit them as patients under his patronage.

The royal family had an audience with the villagers until 5 p.m., when they left Wat Don Sala to take a helicopter to Siam Cement guesthouse and arrived there at 5.30 p.m.

Whenever the king and the royal family went to the south, it was safe to assume that they would visit several provinces. On the following day, 17 May 1976, the king and the queen, with the princesses, flew in a Royal Thai Air Force helicopter to Tambon Don Sak in Surat Thani's Don Sak district.

The first destination was Wat Khao Suwan Pradit. They arrived there at 11.20 a.m. and immediately entered the sermon hall to pay homage to the temple's principal Buddha image. Then, the king had a visit with the patriarch of the Maha Nikai sect, Chao Phrakhun Thep Rattanakawi, and Phra Khru Suwan Pradit, Choy Thittapoonyo or Luang Phor Choy, a highly respected monk in Surat Thani and southern provinces. Southern Thai people called venerable monks 'Phor Luang' instead of 'Luang Phor'. I had known Luang Phor Choy when I accompanied MC Vibhavadi Rangsit to Samui Island. He was widely revered and it was believed that he had magical power to stop the storm coming in from the sea.

The king made offerings to the temple and provided medicine to the monks and the villagers, and then handed out village scout banners to forty groups of scouts. After having given a speech and watched their performance, the king and other royal members met a large number of village scouts and villagers.

32

The royal visit with the village scouts and the villagers at Wat Khao Suwan Pradit lasted well into the afternoon. The royal family had lunch at the temple around 2.00 p.m. and left Don Sak district at 3.30 p.m. to take a helicopter to Wat Sukhonthawat in Tambon Pru Pri, Baan Na San district, Surat Thani. They arrived at 4 p.m.

Baan Na San was considered a critical area at the time. Communist insurgents were active, especially in Tambon Pru Pri, where confrontations between the insurgents and government forces were constant. Yet this place was like a home base for Thanying Vibha, or MC Vibhavadi Rangsit, whenever she visited Surat Thani. Dr. Sawat Srisakulmekhee, the Baan Na San Public Health head doctor, acted as her trip manager. His assistants were Khun Benchamas (Noi), his wife, and other staff in his office, including Khun Malee Chantharaksa, a dental staff member, who became much like a royal servant of Thanying Vibha.

The royal family visited Wat Sukhonthawat and performed religious ceremonies, gave offerings to the temple, and goods and medicine to the villagers, as they had done earlier in Don Sak. The king also had a visit with the patriarch of the Thammayut Nikai (a sub sect of the Thai Theravada school of Buddhism), Than Chao Phrakhun Phra Thep Sarasuthi, and the abbot, Phrakhru Khanti Thammakhun. Again, the royal medical team examined the sick and admitted them as patients under royal patronage.

A visit to Baan Na San Midwifery Station was also planned that day. Thanying Vibha had gone ahead, waiting for the royal family to arrive at the station. Some wanted the royal family to cancel the visit over fears for their safety. However, His Majesty the King would not hear of it and went ahead to the Midwifery Station. Dr. Sawat was asked to go along in the royal car. The royal mission stayed in Baan Na San until 6 p.m. and took a helicopter back to the guesthouse in Thung Song district.

On the next day, Tuesday, 18 May, I heard that the king had a stomach problem, but he still went with the queen and princesses to present village scout banners to the village scouts and meet with villagers in Nakhon Si Thammarat province before returning to Bangkok the same day.

The royal family moved to Thaksin Palace on 23 August that year (1976), but I did not go along as usual as I had been invited by the Asia Foundation to attend a conference in San Francisco. I left Thailand on Sunday, 1 August.

This conference was an international seminar on independence. The delegates were late middle-age scholars representing many countries. Apart from me, another delegate from Thailand was Dr. Warin Wong-hanchao. As the conference does not directly relate to His Majesty's footsteps I will not go into all of the details. After the conference ended on Sunday, 14 August, I flew to Billings in the State of Montana to give a speech about Thailand. Three days after that I flew to Washington, DC.

While there, I visited the FBI National Academy, my alma mater, in Quantico, Virginia, just outside of Washington DC. I also visited the Secret Service, which is responsible for providing security to the U.S. president and VIPs. The Secret Service has an unusual history. It was originally a unit in the Treasury Department responsible for conduct-ing investigations into counterfeit currency. Later, its jurisdiction was expanded to undertake the responsibility for VIP security.

On Sunday, 22 August, I left Washington, DC to visit Mrs. Betty Dumaine at her house in Holly Crest, Pinehurst, North Carolina. This part of my trip does relate to His Majesty because Mrs. Dumaine was a classmate of Her Royal Highness Somdej Phra Sri Nakarindra (HRH the Princess Mother) during the time both studied nursing. I had known Mrs. Dumaine during her many visits to Thailand. I stayed overnight at her house. The next day, Monday, 23 August, after visiting the Institute of Military Assistance at Fort Bragg, I returned to Washington, DC.

One week later, it was time for New York, which was another old haunt of mine. I went to graduate school and obtained a master's degree there. Apart from visiting old friends and relatives, some of whom had become American citizens, I gave a speech about Thailand to members of the Asia Society and visited the New York City Police Academy, another alma mater.

Another visit unplanned was to the Port of New York Authority. Dr. William J. Ronan, former dean of International Relations of New York University and my old teacher, invited me.

I left John F. Kennedy Airport in New York for England on a Pan Am flight on Tuesday, 31 August. I was invited to observe the training of the UK's Special Air Service. I remained in England until Tuesday, 7 September, when I left for Geneva, Switzerland, and then took a bus to Lausanne.

I went to Lausanne because I wanted to see the place where His Majesty the King had lived and studied during his early years. Before I left Bangkok, I met the king and asked his permission to visit the Princess Mother in Lausanne. I arrived in Lausanne after 5 p.m., and immediately took a taxi to the apartment of Lt-Gen. Thongsuk Butsai, deputy chief aide-de-camp general, who was providing security to the Princess Mother there.

At 7 p.m., Lt-Gen. Thongsuk took me to visit the Princess Mother at her residence and to have dinner there, where I also had a chance to have an audience with Her Royal Highness Princess Galyani Vadhana, the king's older sister. The residence of the Princess Mother was also an apartment large enough for a small family, not a fancy mansion as some might imagine. It was located on 19 L'Avenue de L'Avant Poste.

I was greatly impressed by the simplicity of the dinning room and food. I had heard about the Princess Mother leading a simple life but this was the first time that I experienced it directly.

On the following day, Wednesday, 8 September, after breakfast, Lt-Gen. Thongsuk took me to Lausanne University, where the king had studied. After that, he drove me to Ecole Nouvelle de la Suisse Romande in Chailly-sur-Lausanne, where the king attended secondary school.

We met the school principal, who showed great delight when he learned that we were Thais who wished to see the school where the king had studied. The principal showed us the room in the attic where the king had stayed during the course of his studies. As soon as I saw that room I was struck by how simple it was. It was a clean, small room, simply furnished, with no hint that it once housed a boy who would become the king of Thailand.

In the afternoon, Lt-Gen. Thongsuk took me to find the house that had once been the Villa Wattana, the place where the Princess Mother had lived with her children—King Ananda Mahidol, King Bhumibol and Princess Galyani Vadhana.

We spent some time asking about the house. Fortunately, Lt-Gen. Thongsuk spoke French. Finally, we located the house on 51 Chemin de Chamblandes.

That house was at the foot of the hill and from there we could see Geneva Lake below. At that time, the new owner was repairing the house. The place was therefore rather messy. We took the liberty of entering the property. Once inside, I could not help but compare it with the king's residences in Thailand, most of which are also located on a mountain.

During the visit in Lausanne, we met an old French gentleman who, upon learning that we were Thais, delightedly told us that he was a shoe repairman and had repaired the shoes of both of our kings.

After leaving the house that had once been Villa Wattana, we visited the Princess Mother and accompanied her shopping. Princess Galyani joined us later, and we stopped for tea at Au Pelican, where I tasted the princess's favorite ice cream.

I was invited for dinner again on the second night. The following afternoon around 3 p.m., the Princess Mother and Princess Galyani Vadhana went shopping at a big department store outside of Lausanne—Carrfour, if I remember the name correctly. Lt-Gen. Thongsuk, Khun Sawat who was a royal attendant, Lt-Gen. MR Sangkhadit Diskul the Thai Ambassador of Berne, his wife and myself, were in the company.

I bode farewell to the Princess Mother and Princess Galyani Vadhana after the third dinner with them. On Friday, 10 September, I left Switzerland and returned to Thailand.

Apart from the compassion that I felt of Princess Mother and Princess Galyani Vadhana in Lausanne, one thing that I still remember to this day was the sense of calm and peace during my stay there. The stay in Lausanne felt to me like a quiet stay at a temple. I suppose that this was because the power of their compassion to me.

Three days after my return from Switzerland, on Monday, 13 September, I went to Narathiwat to resume my duties. That afternoon, Their Majesties drove to meet the villagers of the Mai Kaen subdistrict and the Bajoh district in Narathiwat. It was Pru Bajoh, a large area of marsh, that had been turned into agricultural lands on the advice of His Majesty, as discussed earlier.

In Mai Kaen subdistrict, the king discussed with government officials, *Imams* (heads of local mosques), teachers and villagers about cultivation mapping, that is, to make a map for cultivation designating the arid or flooded area and a plan showing the kinds of crops to be cultivated. The map would aid the government authorities in helping the villagers solve their problems.

In Bajoh district, Their Majesties visited Baan Klorae School in Tambon Barae Tai. This was a follow-up visit, to check whether the school still had the flooding problem it had experienced before. The king had suggested digging a canal to discharge water, which seemed to have solved the problem. The king also suggested that the students grow vegetables and different kinds of grass to demonstrate to the villagers how to maintain a vegetable garden for consumption or sale. He also suggested the idea of raising oxen for breeding.

On that trip, I also saw the Pru Bajoh area that had once been a huge marsh and was now agricultural land. The villagers now grew crops and earned a living, thanks to His Majesty's concerns and tireless efforts to improve their livelihood.

33

During the royal family's stay at Thaksin Palace, we, the court officers, liked to spend our free time at the market in downtown Narathiwat. I went to the market at dawn every day to buy food to offer to the monks in their morning alms round. Going to the local market in the morning has become my routine when going upcountry.

After offering food to the monks, we usually looked for breakfast, often in the market, where we also got a chance to buy other things. A popular breakfast in those days was called *mee sua*, which were fine, yellow Chinese noodles (only slightly thinner than Italian angel hair spaghetti) stir-fried with beef meatballs. Another popular dish was pork bone soup called *ba kud-te*.

There was a shop in the Narathiwat market, which did not sell food that I regularly visited. The shopkeeper was Da-O, a Muslim, as the name indicates. His wife was Khun Na. His shop sold birdcages, bird food, and equipment for all kinds of birds. Southern Thai people liked to have zebra doves as pets. People would pay tens or hundreds of thousands of baht for these birds. It was said that a zebra dove with an extraordinary singing voice could cost as much as a million baht.

I don't like keeping animals in cages. The reason I became a regular customer of the shop was that Khun Da-O also sold wild animals. The common ones were *hia* (Bengal monitor), *takuat* (water monitor) and snakes. I usually bought them to release them in the wild. Pol. Gen.

Thep Suphasamit also became a regular customer. Khun Da-O would keep the animals for each of us to buy for release.

The first time, Khun Da-O asked me if I minded taking those animals in my car because Thais consider them a bad omen. Thais become extremely anxious of imminent misfortune if a *hia* enters their house. There are stories about people inviting monks to their house to give a blessing to purge the bad luck of these animals having entered the house.

I told Khun Da-O that because I was going to release them for merit, there would be no reason to fear bad luck. I can testify now that I did not experience any bad luck from my involvement with them. I seem to have done quite well enough in my life and my career. I sincerely recommend that those who haven't been promoted or made good progress in their business ventures might want to buy these captured wild animals for releasing, especially those that are feared by people. The act might yield a quick result.

The location where I released the animals that were thought to bring bad luck (and sometimes also turtles) was in the vicinity of Thaksin Palace. The royal residence was located on Tan Yong Mountain and surrounded by jungle. The point of my story is that I knew that the king and the queen were kind to all kinds of animals and prohibited people from killing or hurting the animals near their palaces.

Klai Kangwol Palace in Hua Hin also had plenty of butterfly lizards that grew to wrist size. No one dared to disturb or eat them because the queen strictly prohibited people from doing so. She had even set fine rates for any abuse of the butterfly lizards—twenty-five baht each. All royal residences are thus safe for animals.

I recall an event during the royal mission to Baan Du Songyor in Ra Ngae district of Narathiwat. As I was surveying the route before the royal arrival, I was informed that a villager would present a python to the king. I looked around for the python but couldn't see one, so I asked the villager where it was. He promptly told me that it was inside a wooden crate, which I had been leaning against. My heart dropped and I hurried away from the crate. After regaining some amount of composure, I turned back to see crate and saw that it was quite large and as tall as my waist. The python inside must have been huge and long.

The king accepted the python and took it to his zoo in Thaksin Palace and gave it a name, Indrathep. It didn't take long for the python to become a problem. He was a big eater. Khun Indrathep's healthy appetite forced his keeper to commit a sin daily by feeding him many live ducks and chicken. Finally, the king decided to let Khun Indrathep be taken back to the wild. The python was released at Bajoh Waterfall in Narathiwat, after being carried there by seven BPP officers.

Sometimes the offering of animals to the king can be difficult to understand. Once, also in Narathiwat, a villager offered the king a water buffalo that had only two legs. When I asked about the purpose of the offering, the villagers usually didn't have an answer. The two-legged water buffalo case was the same. The giver couldn't tell me why he would like the king to keep the buffalo and what the king was to do with it. Anyhow, the king took the buffalo under his patronage just the same, and the two-legged buffalo became a royal buffalo.

Another rare animal given to the king by yet another Narathiwat villager was Sumatran serow, which was the same size as a buffalo but had a goat-like face. It sported a horn and a beard. This animal retained its original name Bang and came to live in the zoo of Thaksin Palace.

Khun Bang was very tame. Anyone could touch and play with her. She was also strong. Early one morning she jumped over the zoo fence and wandered into the camp of the soldiers outside the royal residence. The soldiers were cooking and when Khun Bang saw them, being familiar with humans, she just walked toward them. A soldier, confronted with the disheveled, hairy creature that was Khun Bang emerging from the forest during the night, was frightened, and thinking that Khun Bang was going to hurt him, he hit her with an axe. Khun Bang subsequently died.

The royal family stayed at Thaksin Palace until 29 September in 1976.

❖

The political situation in Thailand at that time became shaky again. Field Marshal Phrapat Charusathien, who had gone into exile following the tragic event in October 1973, returned to Thailand on 15 August. The given reason was that he required medical treatment for his eyes and heart disease. After many groups protested his return and filed complaints to the police, the field marshal was forced to leave the country again for Taipei on 22 August.

Not long after, on 19 September, Field Marshal Thanom came back however, this time ordained as a novice. He later was ordained as a monk at Wat Boworniwet. The return of Field Marshal Thanom stirred up another round of demonstrations. The biggest group gathered at Sanam Luang, led by university students. They later marched to Thammasat University. Meanwhile, another group formed to protest against the students-led group.

Finally, at about 2.50 a.m. on Wednesday, 6 October 1973, the counter demonstrators attempted an invasion into Thammasat University. A confrontation between the two groups soon became a riot. Police entered the scene to take control of the situation. Guns were fired and many were injured or killed.

On the afternoon of 6 October, the police had seized Thammasat University but the counter demonstrators had not stopped their protest. Tens of thousands gathered around the Royal Plaza, marched to Government House and broke the gate in to force the prime minister to appoint individuals of their choice to ministerial posts.

At 6 p.m., the National Governing Reformation Group, led by Admiral Sa-ngat Chaloryu, seized the country in a coup d'etat. The rationale was to 'save the national, religious and royal institutions from the crisis.'

Two days later, on Friday, 8 October, Thailand had a new government with Thanin Kraiwichian as prime minister

Amid the crisis, the king and the royal family continued their affairs as usual. On Wednesday morning, 6 October, while the sound of gunfire could still be heard from Thammasat University, Princess Chulabhorn took her examination at Kasetsart University. On the next day, Thursday, 7 October, Princess Sirindhorn and Princess Chulabhorn visited those injured during the riot and hospitalized in the Police Hospital and Vajira Hospital.

In the afternoon of Friday, 8 October, as the new government was hastily formed, His Majesty the King drove his family on a mission to Ayutthaya and Ang Thong provinces. On the mission villagers told the king about their problem of water shortage on the hill. The king explained the work of the Royal Irrigation Department. The department had already dredged and enlarged a canal in the Chainat-Pasak Irrigation Project. The canal, now 140 kilometers long, provided water for a large agricultural area in the dry season and discharged surplus water in the rainy season. He suggested that people meet with officials from the Royal Irrigation Department to solve their problem.

The royal mission then went on to visit flooded rice fields. Before returning to Bangkok, the mission stopped at a pottery project, where villagers made clay dolls under the queen's initiative. The aim of the project was to create supplementary income for the villagers during the off-season. Skills training had been provided to the villagers. Trainers and skilled workers under royal patronage helped the villagers with making the dolls. The project also helped with the distribution of the products. The royal family returned to Chitralada Palace at about 8.15 p.m. that evening.

Just as the king reached the palace, he had to leave again. The head of the National Governing Reformation Group requested a royal audience. The coup leader requested the king's approval for the appointment of Thanin Kraiwichian as prime minister.

The reason I detail the king's visit upcountry on 8 October 1976 is to emphasize that even during political crisis, with coup d'etat and change of government, the king and his family did not allow political events to become an obstacle in their work. His Majesty was able to perform his duties as a monarch and to integrate them with his responsibility toward the government without sacrificing one or the other.

34

Security concerns were generally not serious for His Majesty and the royal family inside the Grand Palace, which is surrounded by high walls, making it easier to maintain security. Also at the Grand Palace, the royal guards and security officers have a good working relationship with all of the court officials. As for the people who come for royal audiences, they were usually few in number and many were frequent visitors.

After I was appointed as royal court security police officer, I reviewed security measures at the Grand Palace and made a recommendation to the lord chamberlain (at that time, Khun Poonperm Krairirk) that royal court security police officers should take greater part in devising and enforcing security measures in coordination with other court security officers. My recommendation was approved.

Since then, apart from court police officers dressing in a white royal pattern jacket over traditional Thai Jong Krabane pants, wearing a ceremonial sword, walking in process in front of the king, uniformed royal court security police officers also walk in the procession. Other royal court security police officers in private dress are also on duty.

One regular ritual that the king performs three times a year at the Grand Palace is the ceremony of changing the seasonal robe of the Emerald Buddha. This ceremony takes place at the Emerald Buddha Temple, or Wat Phra Kaew, in the Grand Palace. I have accompanied the king to this ceremony a number of times. The details of this ceremony are not well-known, so I will mention some details about this ceremony.

This is uniquely a Thai ceremony. There is no such ceremony in other Buddhist countries. The ceremony was first introduced during the reign of King Rama I. Originally the Emerald Buddha's robes were changed only twice a year—at the beginning of the summer and rainy seasons. Later, King Rama III added the changing of the robes for the winter season as well.

At the present time, the three changing ceremonies take place according to the lunar calendar. Each seasonal ceremony is performed on the first day of the waning moon: in the fourth month for the summer, in the eighth month for the rainy season, and in the twelfth month for the winter.

Changing the seasonal robes of the Emerald Buddha is an important ceremony that the king must perform himself. In the event that he cannot do so, he designates another royal family member to act as his representative to perform the ceremony. For example, one year the king designated Crown Prince Vajiralongkorn to perform the ceremony on 17 July.

According to custom, when the king reaches the Emerald Buddha Temple, he enters the *ubosot* and walks behind the masonry base of the Emerald Buddha. Then he walks up the stairs behind the pavilion where the Emerald Buddha is placed. The king prostrates himself and takes off the crown or the hair of the Emerald Buddha (the hair is of course a wig and I cannot remember in which season the Emerald Buddha wears a crown and in which a wig) and then removes the old robe.

After removing the robe, the king pours fragrant water over each shoulder of the Emerald Buddha. There is an order to the ritual. First, the king pours the fragrant water from Phra Sang Thaksinawat (meaning the conch that has a clockwise pattern). This particular conch had been in use since King Mongkut's time. Next, the king pours fragrant water from Phra Mahasang Phet Noi (a great diamond conch). Afterwards, he dries the fragrant water off the Emerald Buddha with a piece of white cloth and finally puts on the new seasonal robe on the Emerald Buddha.

The king then walks downstairs and sits on a chair on the northern side of the masonry base. From this position, he dips the same white cloth into the fragrant water again and squeezes the cloth to allow the fragrant water to drop into a glass jar, then adds some water to make lustral water that he will later sprinkle on royal family members, royal servants and people waiting for him both inside and outside the *ubosot*.

After preparing the lustral water, the king walks to the front of the masonry base and changes the top of the radiance of the statue of Phra Sambuddha Phanni. He lights candles and incense sticks to worship the Emerald Buddha, Phra Sambuddha Phanni, King Rama I and King Rama III and finally proceeds to sit on his throne.

An officer hands the king Phra Mahasang Phet Noi, the great diamond conch, which contains the fragrant lustral water left after the bathing of the Emerald Buddha. The king first sprinkles the lustral water on his own head and on other royal family members. He subsequently walks around to do the same for the people attending the ceremony inside the *ubosot* and returns to his throne. The head Brahman priest anoints the Emerald Buddha and lights candles that are passed around three times. Before the present reign, the ceremony ended with this Brahman ceremony.

In King Bhumibol's reign, the king walks outside the *ubosot* to sprinkle the lustral water on the people waiting outside as well. This is the only occasion for the public to receive lustral water from the king's hand. As mentioned, the security job inside the Grand Palace, such as this changing robe of the Emerald Buddha, poses no serious concern for court security officers. However, we are not careless or complacent about the job.

The word 'security' is a broad term, which isn't necessarily limited to the danger of ill-intentioned people but includes many possible situations that may pose a danger to the king, even pot holes in the way on which the king would walk, falling coconuts on the side of the roads, or poisonous snakes, of which there are plenty in Thailand. The stairs behind the masonry base of the Emerald Buddha was another place for security officers to test every time before the king would use them.

The old stairs were built of wood. Because the masonry base is located close to the western wall of the *ubosot*, the foot of the stairs could not be extended beyond the wall, resulting in very steep stairs to navigate.

I raised my concern about this with Khun Poonperm Krairirk, the lord chamberlain. He agreed with the idea to design a new staircase that would be less steep, with a landing at the middle point of the climb, and would extend further to either the south or the north side.

Before this renovation could be made, Khun Poonperm fell ill and was no longer in a position to continue with this project. However, the problem was later resolved, with two new staircases, made of stainless steel, finally built. Instead of one long stretch, the new stairs are divided into three sections, and there is a landing between each section to allow the king to stop before continuing onto the next. An elevator has also been added as an alternative to the stairs.

I had witnessed the ceremony a number of times, and noticed that every time the king always paid attention to the people who were waiting outside the *ubosot*. The king always made sure that they got their chance to be blessed by the lustral water. Sometimes there were a great many people and he did not stop sprinkling the lustral water until the last person had received it. He shook his wrist so much from sprinkling the water that it hurt and his fingers were blistered from the friction with the metal handle of the sprinkler. Later, the officers covered the metal handle with cloth.

On Friday, 19 November 1976, the king went to stay at Bhuban Palace in Sakon Nakhon. I like to travel by car because you can see and learn a lot watching from the road. I left the Royal Thai Aid-de-Camp Department in Chitralada Palace at 7.30 a.m. My companion was Captain Decha Bunnag, now an admiral and deputy chief aide-de-camp general. After we reached Sakon Nakhon Province, we stopped for lunch at the market in Baan Phai district, Khon Kaen. At 1 p.m., we were back on the road, going through Maha Sarakham and Kalasin provinces. We arrived at Bhuban Palace in Sakon Nakhon at 5 p.m., two hours before the king arrived at Chiang Khrua Airport.

Bhuban Palace is located on Bhuban Mountain, northwest of Sakon Nakhon and about twenty kilometers from the provincial center. This wasn't a great distance, and it was convenient enough for me to get up early to buy food at the provincial market to offer the monks during their morning alms.

A feature I liked about Sakon Nakhon was its many temples. An important and well-known temple is Wat Phra That Choeng Chum (*choeng* is a Khmer word meaning foot. The temple was given that name because, as the story goes, this was a place where many Buddhas had gathered and left imprints of their feet).

I bought food and desserts from the market and waited for monks to pass. Other court security police officers and royal aides were also doing the same. Two of my regular companions in the morning offerings of alms were Pol. Lt-Gen. Thep Supasamit and Gen. Teanchai Janmookda.

Another temple located near the provincial government offices was Wat Pa Sutthawat. The temple is significant because it was where Ajarn Man Phurithatto was cremated. The cremation site is now the *ubosot*. There is a museum commemorating the life of Ajarn Man on the temple grounds. Among the objects displayed in the museum are the items he once used. There were also his relics, some parts of which have crystallized. The faithful come to worship them.

Outside the provincial center were many temples where we liked to visit to make offerings to the monks and to listen to their sermons. Among them was Wat Doi Thammachedi in the then Khok Sri Suphan subdistrict, about thirty kilometers southeast of Sakon Nakhon.

The abbot of the temple was Ajarn Ban Thanajaro, who later became a Chao Khun, and whose followers always called him Than Ajarn Ban. This temple was where I later came to practice dharma after I was ordained in November 1982 at Wat Boworniwet. Somdej Phra Yannasangvorn, my ordainer, permitted me to spend time practicing dharma here until January 1983.

It is well-known that Their Majesties liked to visit local monks to discuss dharma and meditation. For court security officers, surveying and getting to know local monks was part of our job.

A temple that the king visited while in the northeast was Wat Tham Klong Pane in Tambon Nong Bua Lamphu, Udon Thani's Nong Bua Lamphu district, now Nong Bua Lamphu province. The head monk of the temple was Phra Ajarn Khao Analyo, known widely as Luang Puu Khao. Their Majesties visited this temple on Saturday, 27 November 1976.

Another important monk in the area famous for his meditation was Luang Puu Chob Thanasamo at Wat Sammanusorn in Wang Saphung district, Loei province.

On Tuesday, 30 November the king visited another temple, Wat Pa Phurithattawat in Baan Nong Phue in Tambon Na Nai, Phanna Nikhom district, Sakon Nakhon, where Ajarn Man had spent time meditating until just before he passed on. It was said that when he became seriously ill and realized that he had entered the last phase of life, he asked for medical treatment in the province. He was afraid that if he had died at Wat Pa Phurithattawat, a large number of people would attend his funeral, forcing villagers to find food and kill animals living in and around the small village where the temple was located.

After I first visited this temple and found Ajarn Man's living quarters to be in excellent condition, I informed the director general of the Fine Arts Department (Khun Decho Suwananon). The temple was subsequently registered for conservation as a monument.

35

In 1976, His Majesty the King and the royal family returned from Bhuban Palace in Sakon Nakhon to Bangkok on Thursday, 2 December.

I returned to Bangkok by car, this time with Captain Decha Bunnag, who presently is an admiral and deputy chief aide-de-camp general. Actually the car was a Royal Thai Police Department pick-up truck that had been fitted out as a van, making it convenient for transporting luggage, equipment and weapons for our security duties.

We left Sakon Nakhon about 8 a.m., stopped in Renu Nakhon district of Nakhon Phanom to buy some gifts for the family, and then went on to pay our respects to Phrathat Phanom in Nakhon Phanom's That Phanom district, before driving further to Ubon Ratchathani.

Our stop in Ubon Ratchathani was Wat Nong Paphong to visit Ajarn Cha Suphattho, who was later given the rank of Phra Phothiyan Thera and has since passed on. The temple is located in Warin Chamrap district. I had known and visited Ajarn Cha before. He always made the time to meet with me.

We arrived at the wat at around 2 p.m., and quickly saw a notice in front of the temple, which read: 'Luang Phor would like to take a rest from 12 a.m. to 3 p.m.'

Khun Decha and I looked at each other with disappointment. This meant we had to wait for one hour. At this time Bangkok remained in crisis after the coup and the junta government had announced a midnight curfew. Anyone found outside after midnight would be stopped by the police and searched. Although I was a police officer and Khun Decha a soldier, we had no desire to explain the presence of heavy and light weapons in our van.

We quickly discussed the situation and agreed to make just a quick visit to his *kuti* (his living quarters) to pay respects to him without going inside and then we would be on our way. We walked to his quarters and were surprised to see him sitting on a chair under his *kuti*. We quickly paid our respects and asked if he were waiting for someone. He said he was not.

I asked him for some dharma teaching and asked Khun Decha to make a run to the van for fetch a tape recorder. He gave us a dharma teaching for about forty-five minutes. We left at 4 p.m. and got home at 1 a.m. Fortunately, we were not stopped by the police.

I transferred Ajarn Cha's recording to another cassette and gave it to the king. He told me later that this was one of the best dharma teachings he had ever listened to.

Once during one of my visits to Ajarn Cha—at a time when I was having a serious problem. I related it to him and asked for his suggestion how to solve it. A new *ubosot* of the temple was under construction. He pointed to a big rock near his *kuti* and asked me, 'Can you lift it, that rock?' I looked at it, seeing the rock large enough for a person to put his arms around, and said that it was so big and heavy that I wouldn't be able to lift it, but I could try to roll it. He solved my problem with a short response: 'That's right. You know that it's heavy. Then don't lift it.'

On Wednesday, 22 December, the royal family moved to Bang Pa-In Palace in Ayutthaya, but the family members still traveled back to Bang-kok regularly. The crown prince had some engagements in Bangkok, and his two younger sisters were still attending university. This meant court security officers were divided into smaller units, some in Bangkok and some in Bang Pa-In.

On New Year's Eve of 1976, Friday, 31 December, a casual party was organized, as customary, for the inner circle of the royal family and court officials. The party was held at Bang Pa-In Palace. After dinner, the king played music. The queen and the children danced (in both the Thai and western styles) until 7 a.m. of the New Year. The king played the clarinet and led the queen and the 'Aor. Sor.' Band to the top floor of Withun Thasana Throne Hall. Those who have visited the palace might remember that the shape of the throne hall was similar to that of a tower or lighthouse. The party stayed there until 7.30 a.m. and then went down to offer food to the monks in front of the Waraphatphiman Throne Hall.

On every New Year's Day, the Royal Household Bureau also provided books for people to write their New Year's wishes to the king and the royal family. These were placed in a tent in front of Sala Sahathai Samakhom, located behind the Emerald Buddha Temple. The books for government officials were inside the Royal Household Bureau on the left side when entering Phimanchaisri Gate. Each well-wisher was given a royal calendar.

❖

Three days into the New Year, there was bad news: Ajarn Fan Ajaro, a venerable monk, had passed away. On Wednesday, 5 January at 12.45 a.m., the king and the queen flew to Chiang Khruea Airport in Sakon Nakhon. They arrived at Chiang Khruea Airport around 2.45 a.m. and from there took a helicopter to Phanna Nikhom, where Ajarn Fan's temple, Wat Pa Udom Somporn, was located.

Traditionally, after the king had performed the funeral bathing ceremony, other people were not permitted to do so. But that day, the king allowed others, Ajarn Fan's disciples and the general public, to join the bathing rite of Ajarn Fan after him.

A week later, on Wednesday, 12 January, His Majesty and the royal family moved again to Bhubing Palace in Chiang Mai. After a week's rest, His Majesty resumed his work—visiting the people in the area. I accompanied him until Sunday, 30 January, when I came down with body aches and a fever. Court doctors were always available, but mine, Dr. Pramot Sophak, was for some reason not in the palace that day.

A doctor who was available that day was Dr. Samran Wangsapha, an ophthalmologist, who examined me and prescribed some medication. The next day my condition had not improved, and in fact it had worsened. I wasn't able to go to work and had to stay in my room. I am not sure if it was the mountain chill that made me worse. My doctor visited me in my room and, after an examination, said that I had an infection in my lungs. He prescribed new medication.

In the evening, Khun Aphiradi Yingcharoen, a queen's attendant, now a Thanpuying (Lady) and still working in the queen's court, delivered a bunch of yellow roses from the queen. After saying my thanks to Her Majesty from my room, turning in the direction of her court, I put the roses into the vase and placed the vase on my bed table.

In my 1977 diary, on the page between Tuesday, 1 February and Wednesday, 2 February, there are still three rose petals, which have turned dark brown after twenty-three years. The queen's kindness did not stop with only this gesture. She had lunch and dinner delivered to my room on Wednesday, 2 February.

On Thursday, 3 February, I received flowers and notes from Princess Sirindhorn and Princess Chulabhorn, brought by a royal page. On Princess Sirindhorn's homemade card was her own drawing of a man sleeping on the bed with a quicksilver thermometer in his mouth. Below a caption read: 'So fine'. The message on Princess Chulabhorn's card above her signature read: 'Hope you get well soon. Otherwise, I will have to synthesize a medicine in the lab for you (instead of a lab mouse).' With all these wonderful get well wishes, it was hard to stay ill. I was back on my feet on Tuesday, 8 February, and resumed my escort duty to Ang Khang.

On Tuesday, 1 February, while ill in my room, I was given a note from MC Vibhavadi Rangsit. It was on a small official memo pad. In the space underneath the garuda and above the word 'official', she wrote 'roughly'. There was no date, only the subject: 'Important message from Busarakham (her radio handle), who has to leave CM tomorrow.'

> Khun Vasit,
>
> On the day the king visits Wat Phrabat Huaytom, please present the following group of coordinators working to help Karen people to His Majesty:
>
> 1. Dr. Narin Thongsiri, Chiang Mai University
> 2. Doctor Usa Phanangkoon, Suan Dok Hospital, pediatrician and nutritionist
> 3. Mr. Chalor Buranaphan, technician, Royal Irrigation Department
> 4. Khun Ob Preeyakraison, Royal Forestry Department

Before the king leaves the palace, please inform Doctor Usa to tell the other three to wait for His Majesty at Wat Phrabat Huaytom, Li.
Doctor Usa's home phone: 221-xxx ext. xx.
Office: 221-xxx, 221-xxx, 221,xxx.

Neither she nor I knew that this would be the last letter I would receive from her. Fifteen days later, on Wednesday, 16 February 1977, Thanying Vibha was killed in an attack by the communist insurgents during her mission in Surat Thani province. She was shot while the Royal Thai Police helicopter, on which she was a passenger, was landing to pick up police officers injured in the battle.

The day after she was killed, the entire royal family left Bhubing Palace for Bangkok to attend the bathing rite and the funeral of MC Vibhavadi at Wat Benchamabophit. They returned to Chiang Mai the same day.

If Their Majesties were experiencing sadness and sorrow at Thanying Vibha's untimely death, they did not show it to the public. Thanying Vibha was a very close royal relative who had worked on the royal family's behalf, carrying out duties in both domestic and foreign affairs, throughout her life. Their Majesties still continued with their work as usual.

On Friday, 18 February, the king drove himself from Bhubing Palace to visit the Pa Pae Agricultural Cooperative, in the First Unit of the Royal Water Sources Development Project under royal patronage in Huay Thung Cho, and the Third Unit under the same project in Mon Ang Ket in Mae Taeng.

On Saturday, 26 February, ten days after the death of MC Vibhavadi, the crown prince visited soldiers and police officers on duty in Surat Thani and Nakhon Si Thammarat. He stayed at the operations base in Baan Na Sanya in Nakhon Si Thammarat's Phipun district.

The next day, while visiting Border Patrol Police 8th Subdivision in Nakhon Si Thammarat's Thung Song district, the crown prince was informed that there had been a clash between authorities and the insurgents in Baan Nuea Khlong and that officers had been injured. He immediately dispatched a helicopter with doctors to take the injured to Surat Thani Hospital, and later visited them there.

Baan Nuea Khlong was the village where MC Vibhavadi had been killed.

36

The markets in Chiang Mai were large and the business areas scattered throughout downtown area. Chang Phueak Gate is the northern gate of Chiang Mai's old city. Outside the gate, along the side of Manee Nop-pharat Road were a number of department stores and boutique shops.

I regularly went to a shop called Samanchai and became acquainted with the shop owner. The shop specialized in equipment for soldiers and police and war memorabilia, such as field uniforms, winter jackets, blankets, raincoats and the like. The shop owner knew that I liked to browse through and buy such items, so when new inventory arrived he would keep something for me.

I went to the shop again in early March 1977. The shop owner showed me a compass that he had saved for me. With 'made in the USA' engraved on it, it had an unusual shape, quite different from the standard compass used by soldiers. I suddenly thought of the king, and how he liked to use compasses and maps. I paid the shopkeeper 400 baht for the compass and took it to the palace. I asked someone to take the compass to the king.

A couple of days later, the king told me that the compass I had given him was not a compass intended for general navigation use but for measuring the angles to identify targets for cannon fire.

I'd like to explain a bit about history of my writing. After I was appointed as a royal court security police officer, I had begun to reflect on my 'writer' status. I had written for a living since I was a junior in the faculty of Political Sciences at Chulalongkorn University, and continued to write books up to the time I became a police colonel.

In the early years of my writing, I wrote mostly comedies and social satires, and later got into short stories and long fiction. But when I became chief royal court police officer in 1970, I felt that it was inappropriate for me to continue to produce pieces of writings that might affect His Majesty and that I should devote all of my time to the king and the queen.

I therefore stopped writing almost completely, saving only occasional pieces that I might write about the king's duties upon request. Because I stopped writing, I no longer had to stay up and get up late. My daily routine changed and I began to go to bed before midnight and to get up around 5 a.m. After waking up, my new habit was to turn on all my radio receivers and tune in all networks to check for news updates.

At 5 a.m. of Saturday, 26 March 1977, I got up and turned on the radio. The transmission from the Royal Aide-de-Camp Department called Gen. Teanchai Janmookda, at the time chief of VIP Protection Branch, informing him to 'avoid Suan Ruenruedee'. Suan Ruenruedee was where Internal Security Operation Command was located. I thought that something must be wrong.

I called the Royal Aide-de-Camp Department and was told to immediately go to Chitralada Palace. I spent little time getting ready and arrived at Chitralada Palace just a little past 6 a.m. There I learned of another national crisis. Military forces from the 9th Infantry Division of Kanchanaburi province had seized Suan Ruenruedee, 1st Infantry Division of the King's Guard, and the Front Command of Central Security Operation at Sanam Suea Pa (Suea Pa Field) near Dusit Zoo. I also learned that Maj-Gen. Aroon Thawaathasin, commander of 1st Infantry Division, had been taken into custody.

Later that morning, the Public Relations Department radio announced the first Notification of the Revolution Council, stating that the 'Revolution Council' had seized power. The radio report identified the leader of the revolution council as Gen. Prasert Thammasiri.

At about 11 a.m. came more bad news. Maj-Gen. Aroon, who had been taken into custody, had been shot and killed at the Command of

1st Infantry Division, King's Guard. He had refused to cooperate with the members of the revolutionary group.

In the afternoon, the Revolution Council, led by Gen. Chalaad Hiransiri, surrendered to the government. Gen. Chalaad asked for exile in exchange for the release of the hostages—Gen. Prasert Thammasiri and Gen. Pralong Wirapri—but no country would accept Gen. Chalaad and four others in his group. As a result, the group were finally arrested and charged according to the law.

Maj-Gen. Aroon was a well-known figure among the royal court staff because he had been in court service for a long time. His sudden death caused great sadness among his family and friends.

On Sunday, 27 March, at about 3.40 p.m., His Majesty and his family attended the funeral bathing rite of Maj-Gen. Aroon, which was held at his home, Baan Yung Khao, in Soi Anamai, Suksawasdi Road in Bang Pakok district, Bangkok.

❖

As before, the political crisis did not stop His Majesty from working. On Monday, 28 March, the king gave an audience to the departing Finnish ambassador and his wife to say their farewells because the ambassador had finished his term in Bangkok. Then Mr. James A. Linen III, with Time Company and also executive director of the Asian Institute of Technology, and his wife were given an audience with Their Majesties.

In the afternoon of Tuesday, 31 March, the king, the queen, the crown prince and the two princesses went to a religious ceremony (to set the monastic boundaries of the *ubosot*) at Wat Sattha Prachakorn (Wat Khao Ruak) located in Tambon Na Phralan, Sara Buri's Muang district. The king and the royal family met with a large number of people, as usual, who gave contributions to the royal charity. The family stayed at the temple for a long time and returned to Chitralada Palace at 8 p.m.

On Friday, April 1977, at 4 p.m., His Majesty and his family attended the royally sponsored cremation of Maj-Gen. Aroon on the seventh day of his funeral. On this occasion, the king conferred the rank of general and awarded several royal decorations, including Knight Grand Cross

(First Class) of the Most Exalted Order of the White Elephant (*Maha Paramophorn Chang Phueak*) and Class II 'Maha Yodhin' (Knight Commander) of the Honorable Order of Rama, to the deceased in front of his urn.

The leader of the Revolution Council, Gen. Chalaad Hiransiri, was stripped of his rank of general and charged for his crimes. On 2 April 1977, the prime minister ordered his execution, according to Section 21 of the Constitution of Thailand.

The king was a little late to move to Klai Kangwol Palace that year. It wasn't until Saturday, 7 May 1977 that he arrived in Hua Hin, and after only four days he had to return to Bangkok to perform the Royal Ploughing Ceremony. This is an ancient ceremony of Brahman origin, performed annually in May, to mark the auspicious beginning of each new planning season.[1] The king returned to Klai Kangwol Palace on Thursday, 19 May.

When in Hua Hin, the king enjoyed sailing in the afternoon. When he sailed, the VIP Protection Branch, the Royal Thai Navy and the water police jointly provided security. Pol. Maj-Gen. Sunit Panyawanit, from the royal court police, took duty in this case. As boating and sailing were not my area of strength, I simply watched on the shore.

Sunday, 3 July was an important day for me personally. At 4.10 p.m., the king and the queen received Dr. and Mrs. William J. Ronan in an audience. Dr. Ronan had been my teacher and dean of the faculty of public administration at New York University where I earned a master's degree. After he left this position at the university, he became president of Port of New York Authority and Port of New Jersey Authority, responsible

---

[1] The auspicious date and time for the Ploughing Ceremony is set each year by the Royal Brahman astrologers. The king no longer performs the ploughing rites himself, but appoints the Ploughing Lord to carry out the rites on his behalf.

for the air and seaports in both states, including John F. Kennedy Airport and all underwater tunnels linking the two states.

I had wanted to honor my former teacher when he visited Thailand. I therefore consulted with MR Kukrit Pramoj, who suggested that I asked for the king's permission for an audience for Dr. Ronan and his wife.

Another important day came on Friday, 15 July, when the king handed diplomas to new graduates at Chulalongkorn University. Princess Sirindhorn was among them. She graduated that year with first class honors in the arts.

Court security officers, myself included, had been escorting Princess Sirindhorn to and from Chulalongkorn University during the four-year course of her studies. We thus felt like honorary students, as though we had shared her studies. We were naturally very proud.

After the ceremony, Princess Sirindhorn had her family pictures taken with the king and the queen, Crown Prince Vajiralongkorn, Princess Chulabhorn and HRH Soamsavali (then the crown prince's royal consort) in front of the building of Faculty of Arts. She also took some photos with us, her security officers.

The graduation ceremony lasted three days and Princess Sirindhorn received her diploma on the second day. On the last day of the ceremony, 16 July, she also received the Gold Medal for her extraordinary performance as a history major.

The next day, Sunday, 17 July, was somewhat anxious. The royal family was at Phramongkutklao Hospital, where the queen had an operation to remove a tissue from her left chest.

A team of doctors started operating on the queen at 10.10 a.m. It turned out that what was thought to be a tumor was only a cyst. Although the queen had some discomfort, the operation was considered a success. The family stayed at the hospital until evening and returned to the palace at 6.40 p.m.

37

During my time of service in the royal court, there were a few special duties that I performed for the king. One was writing news about the royal missions, particularly the upcountry ones. Actually this job was the responsibility of the Office of His Majesty's Principal Private Secretary but at that time there was a shortage of staff. There were also usually only a limited number of seats on the royal aircraft and I was almost always on the royal escort duty. The Office of His Majesty's Principal Private Secretary therefore entrusted me on occasion with writing the news for distribution to the media.

The second special duty was to record a voice over (using my voice) for the video recordings of the royal affairs on special occasions such as the birthdays of the king and queen and the royal children.

I forget exactly how I got this job. However, I had had some experience in sound recording. As a student in the United States between 1952 and 1954, MC Yingruedee Worawan, whom I called Thanying Noi, and Khun Phakorn Pachinphayak helped me get a part-time job as a translator and news announcer for Voice of America. After I returned to Thailand, I continued my involvement in the audio and video media, having been invited regularly to go on radio and television programs. Finally, I was asked by the royal court movie technicians to record my voice over the videos of the king and the royal family performing their duties. The sound recording was done at the office of the king's movie technicians in Chitralada Palace, or sometimes at a private sound studio.

Another duty that I occasionally was involved in was to conduct fact-finding into complaints sent to the king. Sometimes I worked on my own and other times with other people such as Khun Kwankaew Watcharothai, who is now the vice lord chamberlain, Special Affairs Division. I enjoyed this duty the most because it allowed me to travel to many places, to meet with many different people, and to study the situations and the topography of the places I visited. What's more, I also got to apply my knowledge in the investigation.

This part of the job made me realize the extent of the suffering and difficulties experienced by the people who sent their complaints to the king. Many cases were resolved. The king often lent his own money to people to deal with their immediate problems. I had to follow up on the progress of those who had been helped.

The main duty of royal court security police officers was to provide security to the king and his family and to protect them from danger. Danger did not necessarily mean from ill intentions to the king, but could be anything that happened in the course of natural events or simply an accident.

Danger could also be something less dangerous, but if occurring often enough, could become an annoyance. These usually involved the two young princesses, who had a great many admirers, some to the point of extreme infatuation.

Each year, the palace received scores of letters to the princesses. It was the duty of royal court security officers to investigate the background of every writer. The investigation might be carried out either by the local police or the Special Branch. The investigations usually concluded that the writers had no ill intention but simply a severe crush on one of the princesses.

Some wrote letters, but others used the telephone. The phone numbers of Chitralada Palace were not secret and were there to be seen in every Thai phone directory. It wasn't too difficult dealing with telephone calls because the princesses did not answer the telephone themselves. Officers screening the incoming calls could easily end the unsolicited ones.

We were particularly concerned about certain individuals who habitually followed the princesses to various places, even on their trips to the provinces. Some of these people had a genuinely high degree of loyalty and dedication to the princesses and tended to follow them everywhere. When possible, they tried to get a close audience in order to present some gifts or flowers. They usually preferred to come in a larger group and after several times we got to know them by sight.

But the fact that we knew them by sight and knew who they were did not mean that we could trust them. There were times when security officers had to block some men from approaching the princesses. These were likely to be those who had written letters or telephoned the palace, and who had popped up in places where the princesses visited. This kind of incidents fortunately did not occur that often. But when these individuals did appear, security officers kept close watch and remained on guard.

In some cases the royal security officers had to give such persistent people an explanation and a clear warning that if they continued to try to get closer to the princesses, the officers would have no choice but to arrest them and that they would suffer from adverse publicity. Usually, serious and stern warning put a stop to the behavior.

His Majesty moved to Thaksin Palace again on Monday, 22 August 1977. The following day, he attended to an important and ancient ceremony that is rarely seen these days. It was the ceremony of offering 'important elephants' to the king. The ceremony was held at the governor's mansion in Narathiwat.

'Important elephants' are white elephants. Actually, the elephants that are totally white, or albino, are rare. Some are only partially white. White elephants were traditionally regarded as a sacred animal and befitting only for kings. If one were found, it would be offered to the king and become a royal elephant.

The important elephant being offered to the king on 23 August was a female elephant named Chitra. Royal Household officials examined her and confirmed that she was indeed a white elephant, so the ceremony to offer her to the king was going to be held.

At 4.30 p.m. on the same day, the king, the queen and the princesses traveled by car to the governor's mansion. The ceremony began with the king lighting candles and incense sticks to pay homage to the Triple Gem and reciting the Buddhist precepts. The interior minister, Khun

Samak Sunthonrvet, then read the elephant's history and presented the elephant on behalf of people of Narathiwat to the king.

The king subsequently walked to the white elephant in her house, climbed up the mounting platform, and sprinkled lustral water on the elephant. He also presented the elephant's costume used in the procession ceremony to Mhuen Siriwang Ratana (*mhuen* or *jamhuen*—one of the lower ranks, usually held by relatively junior officers). The queen then *garlanded* the elephant.

The ceremony ended with the king making offerings to the monks and the monks giving him the Adirek blessing. Following the ceremony, the governor called people who had a part in acquiring the white elephant for an audience with the king and the king gave them medals. Before their departure, the royal family visited with a large number of people attending the ceremony.

Earlier that day, at 9.00 a.m., a related ceremony was held that the king did not attend. It was the ceremony of inscribing the elephant's name on a piece of red sugarcane. In this ceremony, Phrarajkhru Wamathepmuni, the Brahman head of ceremony, also inscribed the spell of Devas on the red sugarcane.

On Wednesday, 24 August, the king presided over another ceremony at the Narathiwat Sports Stadium, installing the white elephant 'Chitra' as the principal royal female elephant.

The king had entered the stadium. The white elephant was led in front of the pavilion where the king was seated, then to take a stand on the platform in the ceremony hall. The pageantry consisted of three processions, the front procession, the royal decoration procession, and a provincial procession. As the elephant ascended the platform, *Aphiroom* officers—*aphiroom* are royal parasols used in royal processions—took five-tiered parasols and tied them to the main column of the northern side of the elephant's hall.

Each set of these parasols, called Phrakan Phirom, contained three parasols, namely, Phra Semathipat, Phra Chatchai and Phra Kowpham. The parasols were made of white cloth, covered with cabbalistic writings in gold, and kept in Pastu bags, red, loosely woven wool bags. Usually in a grand royal barge procession, royal officers would remove the five-tiered parasols from the Pastu bags, open them, and carry them ahead of the royal vehicle. But in this elephant ceremony, the officers simply used the parasols to lead the royal elephant into the celebration hall and tied them to the elephant hall's main column without removing them from the bags.

As the elephant entered the ceremony hall, twenty monks chanted stanzas for the blessing. Then, the king entered the ceremony hall and lit a candle and incense sticks to worship another Buddha statuette called Phra Buddha Patimachai, which had been positioned on the elephant's back. He also lit a candle and incense sticks to worship another Buddha statuette called Phra Devakamma. The Brahman head of ceremony subsequently conducted the devotional offering to Phra Devakamma.

At the auspicious moment, a royal astrologer struck the gong of victory. The king then stepped up a staircase to pour lustral water on the elephant as the monks continued to chant stanzas for the blessing. The king stepped down from the staircase and anointed both sides of the elephant's head and gave the elephant the red sugarcane on which her royal name was inscribed: Phrasrinaraarat Raatchakirini Chitravadi Rojanasuwong Phromphong Atthitsaphisan Phisettharn Thoraniphithak Khunarak Kittikamjorn Amornsarnlertpha.

On this occasion, the king allowed Phrarajkhru Wamathepmuni, the Brahman head of ceremony, to anoint the elephant with lustral water. He also presented Mhuen Siriwangrattana with the elephant's costume and a gold boundary marker from a temple to put on the elephant. Next, he anointed the elephant's nameplate before making an offering to the monks and handing out souvenirs to the Imams.

A highpoint of the ceremony occurred when a pair of Brahman priests read a poem in praise of the elephant and Department of Fine Arts musicians played the wooden rhythm clappers (*khab mai*) and the three-stringed fiddle (*sor sam sai*) to calm the elephant. Princess Sirindhorn had composed the poems. The king gave more medals to more people in recognition of their work. After the king had departed from the ceremony, the procession continued for the elephant, which quickly became known as Khun Phrasri.

There were still more ceremonies to celebrate the white elephant. On the following day at 6.30 a.m., Khun Phrasri was taken for a bath and to make food offerings to thirty monks who had assembled in front of the ceremony hall for their morning alms. Then the elephant was taken to her platform.

At 10.30 a.m., MC Chakrabandhu Bensiri Chakrabandhu, a privy councilor, went on the behalf of the king to offer food to the monks. Afterwards Phrarajkhru Wamathepmuni led a ceremony, in which a candle was lit and passed by those attending the ceremony in celebration of the new royal elephant. Phrarajkhru Wamathepmuni anointed the elephant and fed her young coconut juice. The ceremony ended with this flourish.

Later on, Khun Phrasri was moved to the elephant's house at Chitralada Palace to join ten other white elephants. Chitralada Palace houses the most white elephants in one place in the world. However, today the king has the officers transfer these white elephants to the care of the Royal Forestry Department. They now live in natural surroundings, in a mountainous and forested area, a much more appropriate place for them.

Following the white elephant ceremonies, the king resumed his usual affairs, visiting people and projects under royal patronage in Narathiwat and other southern provinces.

An important project under his initiative that was coming along well was the drainage canal project implemented in a number of districts. One was in Baan Shuwo, Tambon Bare Tai in Narathiwat's Bajoh district. The aims of the project were to drain water from Pru Bajoh, a large marsh, and to increase the number of useable agricultural lands for the villagers. Other drainage locations included Pru Toh Daeng, Tha Pru, and Toh Lang in Tak Bai district. The latter two projects solved the flooding problem in the rice fields.

On his visits to these project locations, the king employed whatever means of transportation necessary to get there; he drove, walked, and went by boat. He usually spent as much time as necessary in each place, often amid unforgiving weather. He also gave generous time to the villagers.

Following the king during the heavy rains in Narathiwat made us creative in finding various ways to keep dry. A kind of raincoat that we police and soldiers had adopted was sort of a rain poncho, worn over the head. Though quite effective in keeping us dry, it made us a little clumsy.

I had a long raincoat with a hood. It had a mid-thigh length and its hood covered my hat, but dealing with the machine gun and the sidearm was still a problem, because they could get wet. As for the machine gun, there was no way to deal with it except to heavily oil the weapon and hope that that would protect it against the rain. We wrapped our radio receivers and side arms with plastic.

38

An unfortunate incident is almost always unexpected.

Normally, the king's visits to local people and projects under royal patronage did not require an advance program to be set by the Royal Household Bureau. In such cases, the welcoming officials were not required to wear official uniforms, only their normal uniform, or standard field uniform if they were soldiers. However, the traveling route would be predetermined and the soldiers and police were stationed at points along the route to provide security for the king. When the king departed the palace or elsewhere, the officers responsible for security were informed by radio.

On Wednesday, 21 September 1977, the king along with the queen and the two princesses left Thaksin Palace at 2.55 p.m. for a trip to visit the Lipa Sa-ngo Irrigation Project and the land allocation project for farmers living in Lipa Sa-ngo Field in Pattani's Nong Chik district.

The king drove as usual but the program was somewhat special in that the ambassadors of the United States, Germany and Egypt and the charge d'affaires of Japan were also on the mission.

At 4.10 p.m., the king arrived at the first line of the main ditch of Baan Yabi, Tambon Yabi, which had been dug by the Royal Irrigation Department. The king, the queen and the princesses walked along the dike above the ditch. When all the digging of the canals was completed, the canals would discharge the water from the area, and in effect increase the agricultural area by an additional 10,000 *rai*. Before the project, the total arable land measured 21,040 *rai*.

The king suggested that the low land between the drainage canal and irrigation canal, which remained wet all year, could be used as a large pond for freshwater fish breeding. This project would be beneficial for local farmers. He also suggested that before the reclaimed land was allocated that the officials hold a meeting with the villagers and explain the basic principles of land and water use to them.

The villagers from Baan Yabi and nearby villages waited for the royal audience around the ditch. The king and the queen stopped to talk with them before moving on to Baan Lipa Sa-ngo where the Pattani deputy governor gave a report on the land allocation project for the farmers of Lipa Sa-ngo Field. Initiated on the king's recommendation, the project aimed to establish a village cooperative, entitling its members to make use of the land for generations. Among the king's suggestions was that the size of the allocated pieces of land should not be uniformly fixed but vary according to the topography and soil quality. A detailed survey of the land was recommended before making the actual allocation.

Here also, a large number of villagers came for royal audience from all over Nong Chik district. Royal doctors examined and prescribed medicine to the ill. Some were taken as patients under royal patronage.

The king stayed with the villagers until 6.35 p.m. and returned to Thaksin Palace.

In downtown Narathiwat, officers had been stationed at different points. They were informed of the king's return and had stopped traffic along all routes until the king had passed. However, as the royal motorcade arrived at the intersection of Phichitbamrung Road in front of the Special Operation Unit of Narathiwat Provincial Police Station, a motorcycle, charging at high speed passing the group of officers, broadsided the king's car. The king was in the driver's seat.

After the collision, the motorbike skidded to the side of the road. The driver and two passengers were thrown off the bike and lay still.

I was in a police escort car, just one car ahead of the king's, and could see what was happening in the rearview mirror. I jumped out as soon as the car stopped and ran to the king's car, thinking that it was a deliberate act. I was fully prepared and on the ready without any hesitation to use my weapon, if my suspicions were confirmed.

Security officers from other cars also ran to the scene. Once we got there, we found all three of the bike riders still unconscious. They were given first aid immediately and later sent to the hospital for further treatment. The driver suffered a severe wound to one foot, which later had to be amputated. They were later retained and charged with reckless driving.

While the officers were busy dealing with the injured, the king sat watching the incident quietly. After the injured had been evacuated from the scene, he drove the car back to the palace.

After having escorted the king back to Thaksin Palace at 8.40 p.m., I immediately drove to the Special Operation Unit of Narathiwat Provincial Police Station to meet Pol. Lt-Gen. Thep Suphasamit, vice director-general of the Royal Thai Police Department, who was investigating the accident.

I was ashamed to learn that the driver of the motorcycle was a police private attached to the Special Operation Unit. Apparently he had gone for drinks and may have been drunk when he took two of his friends on the back of his motorbike and collided with the king's car. I was also ashamed that none of the police officers on security that day, rows of us, were able to stop that motorbike from approaching the royal motorcade and broadsiding the king's car. Needless to say, no one had done their job well.

Before the Royal Thai Police Department imposed a penalty on the motorcycle driver, the king asked that he not be punished too heavily. His Majesty even paid for his medical treatment.

After the accident, the Royal Thai Police Department made an announcement and ordered a meeting to review measures to prevent such incidents from happening in the future. I had no responsibility to follow up on whether the rules had been strictly observed. But I can say that, twenty-three years later, measures and plans adopted in Thai bureaucracy still remain simply words on the page. There are still no training and simulations for the officers to learn how to confront and cope with this type of situation. As a result, when they face a real incident or emergency, they just freeze in their tracks, not knowing what to do next.

The feeling of shame arising from such an incident that had not resulted in any serious harm was somewhat tolerable, but if the incident had caused more serious harm, especially to His Majesty, nothing could have been put it right. No one expected that after that motorcycle accident, another unfortunate incident would occur the next day.

❖

On Thursday, 22 September 1977, at 8 a.m., the Royal Security Division at the Narathiwat provincial police headquarters convened a meeting. Pol. Lt–Gen. Thep chaired the meeting. I attended the meeting as a royal court security police officer. The chair of the meeting emphasized the need to be proactive about security measures. There was also a security briefing that there had been some concerns about possible disturbances during His Majesty's mission to Yala province on that day. Security officers from all units were advised to be especially vigilant during the Yala trip.

At 1.28 p.m., the king drove the queen and the princesses from Thaksin Palace toward Yala province. At 2.45 p.m., the royal family arrived at the white elephants' ceremony hall in Tambon Sateng of Yala. After the king and the royal family members had entered the hall, the education minister reported on the affairs of private Islamic (*pondok*) schools, and identified those schools selected by Ministry of Education for excellent educational management. The secretary of the Office of the Private Education Commission called Islamic teachers representing the schools to receive awards from the king.

Then the interior minister called the members of Islamic Committee of thirteen southern Thai provinces to receive pins inscribed with the king's initials. After that, following the Yala governor's briefing on the affairs of village scouts, the king gave village scout banners to nine groups of village scouts and visited with the villagers.

Suddenly, two successive explosions went off in the tent set up for the villagers. The tent had been positioned fifty meters to the left of where the royal family was seated. After the explosions, the air was filled with the cries of fear and pain. People hurried from the tent to avoid the danger.

It was a nightmare for me. I had asked myself what I would do if such an incident occurred. For all royal court security officers, the most important thing in such a situation was the safety of His Majesty and the royal family. We had agreed that in such a situation, we would protect their safety with our own bodies.

I stepped up to the platform that was especially set for the royal family members to sit. I moved quickly to stand in front of the king, effectively blocking him from any danger that might be approaching. Other royal aides and court police officers closed ranks and did the same thing with other royal family members. I believe that this was the first and only time that we had to provide security so physically close to the king and other royal family members.

According to VIP security procedures, if such an incident occurs, the first duty of the security officers is to remove the VIPs from the scene as soon as possible to minimize further danger. However, at that time, no one dared to tell the VIPs to leave. The king and the queen remained still and calm.

What I didn't expect to see was the officers and leaders of the village scouts quickly gaining control of the situation. They used a loud speaker to calm the terrified crowd, advising them not to move in order to prevent possible contact with explosives. Meanwhile, the injured were immediately taken to the hospital. Another thing I hadn't thought I would witness was that after the crowd had been pacified, the king walked over to the microphone and started to give his speech to the people in his normal tone of voice.

He said that in case of a bad incident, if we acted calmly and in harmony, giving each other encouragement and moral support, we would be able to stay in control of a situation and eliminate its danger.

The events then followed according to the original agenda. Local people presented their donations to the king in support of the village scouts' affairs. The king then gave the donations to the local village scout operation center.

By choosing to stay at the event instead of leaving for their personal security that day, His Majesty the King and his family showed their kindness and commitment to the people.

At 5.40 p.m., the royal mission left the ceremony hall to return to Thaksin Palace. As the motorcade was crossing the railway toward Pattani's Yarang district, the king called me on the radio and inquired about the conditions of the injured people who had been taken to hospital. I checked with the officers who were still at the hospital and relayed the information I received from them to the king that most victims suffered only minor injuries and that the doctors had already treated them and had sent most of them home.

The king ordered that the car procession to head to the hospital. When the king arrived, it appeared that among the forty injured people, there were those who were in serious condition and remained as patients at Yala Hospital.

39

After arriving at Yala Hospital, the king visited the injured and their relatives, and talked to the doctors and nurses. He also allowed specialist doctors on the mission to consult with the local doctors and aid in medical treatment. The patients from the explosions were placed under his patronage. At 7.05 p.m., the royal mission left the hospital and headed for Thaksin Palace.

There was no doubt that the incidents in Yala caused considerable anxiety in the government, particularly the Royal Thai Police Department. Pol. Gen. Monchai Phankhongchuen went down to Yala many times to supervise interrogation of the four suspects. I was also ordered to join him in the investigation.

The authorities found evidence connected to the suspects to the explosive devices, including electrical wires of the same kind found at the scene of explosions. The suspects confessed their role in the bombing. The charges were brought to court and some of them were given prison terms. The convicted did not expose any mastermind. For security officers, the incident showed clearly their disloyalty and ill intention toward the king and their disregard to all Thai people.

One would be wrong to believe that the Yala incidents had changed the way the king and his family performed their affairs. They continued to carry on with their major and minor duties as usual.

In the following afternoon, on Friday, 23 September, the king, the queen and the two princesses left for Banthorn Airport to board a royal plane to Hat Yai, Songkhla where they performed a ceremony of mounting the *chaw fah* (gable finial, the top most decorative part at the top of a roof) of the *ubosot* of Wat Khok Samankhun. After the ceremony, the king and his family visited with the local villagers on the temple ground as they had done in other places. The security officers were particularly vigilant and carefully examined everyone entering the temple and there was no incident. The royal family left the temple at 5.35 p.m. to board the plane to Bangkok.

I followed in a C-123 and arrived at Don Muang Airport at 9.05 p.m. While on the way home from the airport, I was informed by radio that the royal family had arrived Chitralada Palace at 9.15 p.m.

His Majesty and the family returned to Bangkok temporarily because the king had to preside over the celebration of Mahidol Day, and to hand out diplomas to graduates of Mahidol University at Siriraj Hospital the following day. On Sunday, 25 September, the king returned to Thaksin Palace to complete his unfinished work, and returned to Bangkok again on Friday, 30 September 1977, marking the end of his stay at Thaksin Palace for that year.

I and other security and court staff were scheduled to return on the C-123 as usual, but there were some mechanical problems with the left engine. After waiting for the technicians to work on the engine until 7 p.m., the entire crew and the passengers decided to stay overnight at Thaksin Palace and leave the next day. The plane was repaired and flew us back to Bangkok the next morning.

There was another political crisis on Thursday, 20 October 1977.

The royal family was expecting a royal guest: Princess Alix Napoleon, sister of Queen Fabiola of Belgium. She was invited to dinner at Ruan Ton, a traditional Thai building in Chitralada Palace. At about 6 p.m., just before Princess Alix Napoleon arrived, the Revolution Council—claiming to be supported by the army, navy, air force, police and civilians, and led by Adm. Sa-ngat Chaloryu—seized power.

The Revolution Council reasoned that they had to seize power to address the political and economic situation of the country and to 'preserve the royal institution.' The leader of the Revolution Council abolished the constitution. In effect, therefore, the cabinet and the

National Governing Reformation Council, acting as the National Legislature, became invalid.

Adm. Sa-ngat Chaloryu was the leader of Revolution Council that had seized power on 6 October 1976, just a year before. A new government was subsequently formed and Thanin Kraiwichian was appointed prime minister, and Adm. Su-gnat minister of defense.

It was customary that after a coup, the person or persons seizing power would request an audience with the king. That day, at about 8.05 p.m., Adm. Sa-ngat had an audience with the king at Chitralada Palace. Gen. Kriangsak Chamanan, so-called general secretary of the Revolution Council and the commander of the army, navy and air force also accompanied Adm. Sa-ngat.

That night, the queen welcomed Princess Alix Napoleon alone. At 11 p.m., the king and the prince joined the dinner.

The new political crisis, like the previous ones, did not intervene with the king's affairs. At 4 p.m. the following day, the king gave an audience to several groups of people at Chitralada Palace and they made donations to a number of charity foundations under his patronage. In the evening, free from the obligations of the day, the king jogged and the queen exercised at Dusidalai Hall as usual.

On Saturday, 5 November 1977, the king, the queen and the princesses moved to Bhuban Palace in Sakon Nakhon. Officers from the Office of His Majesty's Principal Private Secretary and Royal Household Bureau, as well as royal aides and court police officers followed the royal family as usual.

Thailand's northeast was home to many temples where many monks practiced meditation and where important sacred objects could be found. That year, the king had a schedule to visit both old and new places, allowing me to get to know more places and to pay respect to more monks.

On Saturday, 26 November, Their Majesties and the princesses visited villagers and soldiers in Udon Thani's Nam Som district, which was at that time a red zone, or an area with high activities of communist insurgency. Nam Som district was on the west of Udon Thani and the insurgency problem also extended to Na Klang and Suwannakhuha districts. Transportation in the area was difficult because road construction had not been completed. Security was critical because there were frequent clashes between the authorities and the insurgents, with regular deaths and injuries on both sides. Given this background, the king's visit was meaningful for people and authorities in the area.

The king, the queen and the princesses arrived by helicopter at the field in front of Nam Som Police Station at 12.15 p.m. They met with a large number of people right away. The royal medical unit, which had arrived in advance, attended to the local people in need of attention. The royal family remained at this site until about 2 p.m. and then took a helicopter to the Operation Base, Infantry Battalion, Special Task 132 in Baan Nam Song Noi, Tambon Nam Som.

Once there, the king placed a wreath at the shrine of King Naresuan and gave gift bags and medicine to the representatives of the battalion. And then he went to pay respect to Luang Puu Khrueang Dhammajaro, the abbot of Wat Thep Singhan in Tambon Na Yung. Highly revered, Luang Puu Khrueang, at the advanced age of 100, was truly a human institution. The king donated money to Luang Puu Khrueang as a contribution toward the construction of the *ubosot* and the monk gave the king Buddha amulets.

Afterwards, the king listened to an official briefing and studied the maps showing the area of responsibility assigned to the Infantry Battalion, Special Task 132. It wasn't until 4 p.m. that this part of the visit ended and the mission enjoyed a lunch break. The king and the mission toured around the Operation Base after lunch and left the base at 5 p.m.

❖

Two days later, 28 November, at 1 p.m., the royal family went to Wat Pho Chai in Muang district, Nong Khai to perform a ceremony of mounting the gable finial of the *ubosot*.

Wat Pho Chai was one of the most important temples of Nong Khai province as it enshrined an ancient Buddha image, known as 'Luang Phor Phra Sai'. A story had it that this particular Luang Phor Phra Sai was one of the three Buddha images made for a Laotian princess who had been taken from Laos during the reign of King Rama III. The biggest of the three Buddha images was called Phra Souk. When Phra Souk was transported across the Mekong River, the raft that carried Phra Souk broke apart and Phra Souk fell and disappeared into the river, and had never been found. The second image, called Phra Serm, was smaller. Today, Phra Serm is enshrined at Wat Pathum Wanaram, or Wat Sra Pathum, in Bangkok. The smallest image was Phra Sai, or Luang Phor Phra Sai, and is now at Wat Pho Chai in Nong Khai.

Many years ago, when a plane of Thai Airways crashed in Lam Luk Ka district in Pathum Thani, it was said that a passenger who carried a replica of the Phra Sai image survived the crash without a scratch. People believed that was due to the magical power of the Buddha image.

After the ceremony, local people made donations to the king's charity, which were given as contributions toward the building of a new *ubosot*. Then the king and the royal family went to pay homage to Luang Phor Phra Sai, the principal Buddha image of the temple. The royal family then presented a package of medicine to the temple and their own donations for the *ubosot* to the abbot, afterwards visiting with the villagers on the temple grounds.

The next day, the royal family visited two districts for the first time: Khamcha-E, in Nakhon Phanom (which is now under the jurisdiction of Mukdahan province) and Kham Muang in Kalasin. On a map, you will find these at the foot on the southern side of Bhuban Mountain and opposite of Nakhon Phanom and Sakon Nakhon provinces on the northern side of the mountain. Communist insurgents took hold on the Bhuban mountain range and the security situation in the area was therefore acute.

I left in advance of the royal mission at 8.50 a.m that morning with the royal guards and royal photographers. We dropped off the guards in Kham Muang and arrived in Khamcha-E at 10 a.m. to receive the royal mission. At 11 a.m., the royal helicopter set down on the field in front of Khamcha-E Withayakarn School in Baan Nam Thiang, Tambon Baan Song, Khamcha-E district.

The activities here were the same as in other places. The royal family visited with a large number of waiting villagers, and the royal medical team attended the ill, and some of whom were admitted as patients under the king's patronage. At this place, textbooks and medicine were given to the students at the school as well.

At 1.20 p.m., the king and the royal family continued to Kham Muang. They reached the field in front of Kham Muang Police Station at 1.55 p.m. After disembarking, they immediately set off to walk across the field to meet the waiting crowd of villagers. I was in the group of officers walking in front of His Majesty. The king unexpectedly walked into the police station. It was obvious from the faces of police officers and staff working there that an unexpected audience with the king that afternoon gave them great joy.

After meeting with the villagers and officials, the king and the group went to the district meeting hall to observe the work of the royal medical team and the mobile medical unit of the province, which had arrived prior to the royal arrival. The royal family also stopped to see traditional fabric weaving and local products, before going to the 41st BPP headquarters. Pol. Col. Wipas Wipulakorn, commanding officer, Border Patrol Police Region 2 (now a police general and before retiring the deputy director-general of the Royal Thai Police Department) was waiting to welcome the king and the royal family.

40

The king had known Pol. Col. Wipas Wipulakorn. Khun Wipas and I also had known each other since we were low-rank officers. We had history together. We were almost captured by insurgents while delivering food and medical supplies on behalf of the king to Surat Thani. Later, Khun Wipas was promoted to strategy commander of BPP Region 2, under the Second Army, which was at that time under the command of Lt-Gen. Prem Tinsulanonda, whom I call Phi Prem.

During that time, Phi Prem had two strongmen playing a major role in combating communist insurgencies. One was Khun Wipas and the other Khun Phisan Moolasartsathorn, my former classmate at Chulalongkorn University. Khun Phisan had been a governor in many Isan provinces and was later promoted to director-general of the Provincial Administration Department and permanent secretary of the Ministry of Interior. After retirement, Khun Phisan entered politics and was elected as an MP of Surin province. He later served as a minister before he passed away.

On Tuesday, 29 November, after the king finished his visit to the BPP 41st Subdivision, he provided gift bags, medicine, and King Naresuan medals to the division's representative. He then joined a briefing of activities carried out by the division. He met with Khun Wipas until 3.50 p.m. and had a late lunch. After lunch, the king took a walking tour around the division, returning to Bhuban Palace at 6 p.m.

The following morning, the king presided over a ceremony to cut the boundary-marking stone ball at Wat Sirisukhaphibaan in Udon Thani's Muang district and had lunch at Senee Ronnayut Camp of the BPP 4th Subdivision. After lunch, an American consul from northeastern Thailand (Mr. John D. Finny, Jr.) and village scouts from Khon Kaen province had an audience with the king. Next, the king traveled by helicopter to Romklao School at Baan Huay Duea, Tambon Nong Bua Lamphu, Nong Bua Lamphu district in Udon Thani. (Nong Bua Lamphu district has since become Muang district of Nong Bua Lamphu province.)

The Baan Huay Duca School is another one of the many Romklao schools established according to the king's initiative to give access to education for youths in remote rural areas. The one at Baan Huay Duea was located at the entrance to Wat Tham Klongpane, a monastery where a leading monk named Luang Puu Khao Analayo lived. After the school visit, we accompanied the king to visit Luang Puu Khao at his monastery.

The king, the queen and the princesses spent a long time with Luang Puu Khao. Before returning, the king made offerings to the senior monk. Because it was already night when the royal family began to head back to the palace, they flew on the C-123, instead of a helicopter, from Udon Thani Airport to Sakon Nakhon and then traveled by car, arriving at Bhuban Palace at 9.30 p.m.

On Friday, 2 December 1977, the king and his family returned to Chitralada Palace in Bangkok.

I returned to Bangkok one day in advance. For some reason, which now escapes me, I came back alone. I left at 7.30 a.m. and stopped at the Tor Kaankha market in downtown Sakon Nakhon to buy food to offer to the monks. After having made an offering to the monks at their morning alms, I walked around the market to look for an animal to buy for release and spotted a brown wild rabbit that had been tightly roped. The female merchant said the rabbit cost 80 baht and that it could be kept as a pet. I paid the 80 baht without bargaining and carried the rabbit to my car, intending to release it somewhere along the way.

My first destination was Sri Songkhram district north of Nakhon Phanom. I drove a long way around because I wanted to visit Khun Wichit Iamsawat, Sri Songkhram district chief and a former colleague from the People's Assistance Team Training Center.

I drove to Baan Tharae in Sakon Nakhon's Muang district and then turned north. Before reaching Sri Songkhram, I crossed a brook. It was a scrub area and looked like a suitable place to release the rabbit, so I pulled over, cut the ropes around the rabbit, and put it on the ground. It was immediately clear that the poor creature was not well. It could only move by dragging itself forward on its front legs. Left along the roadside, it surely would have been easily caught and eaten. I quickly picked it up and carried it back to the car and continued the trip.

The trip was not a particularly successful one. I missed Khun Wichit in Sri Songkhram, and when I went further to Baan Phaeng district to visit an aunt, I missed her as well. I drove on to Nakhon Phanom and had lunch there at 12.45 p.m., reaching Ubon Ratchathani six hours later.

I stayed in a hotel that night and left the rabbit in the car. The next morning, Khun Suwanai Thongnop, an old classmate from Chulalongkorn University and director of Development Center in Ubon Ratchathani's Community Development Department, recommended a veterinarian.

It was bad news at the vet's office. The rabbit had been either snared in a trap or hit to break its back legs. Whatever the cause, the injury was severe and the hemorrhaging was so bad that blood came out of its anus. After the veterinarian treated the rabbit, Khun Suwanai asked me not to take the rabbit to Bangkok, because it was not in the best condition to travel a long distance, and offered to look after the rabbit for me. It was a kind offer and a reasonable option, given the circumstances. I left the rabbit with him.

Not long afterwards, I learned that the rabbit had died.

The story of this wild rabbit at first blush doesn't appear related to my duties to the king; however, I couldn't ignore feeling that if I had not been in service to the royal court, had not accompanied the king on that trip, and had not visited the market in Sakon Nakhon, I might not have seen the rabbit and taken it to die in Ubon Ratchathani. I believe in karma but I don't know how complicated my karma had been with the rabbit in our previous lives. Even today, I still think of that rabbit and continue to make merit for it.

I got back to Bangkok just in time for the king's 1977 birthday celebration. The day began with an oath of allegiance ceremony and the parade of the royal guards at the Royal Plaza. The king's birthday

parade was a spectacular ceremony. The royal guards appeared in full
dress uniforms according to their groups and units. Those having an
audience with the king were also in full dress uniforms with all of
their sashes and decoration ribbons and medals. After the royal guards
took an oath of allegiance, the king gave his birthday speech. Then,
the royal guards marched in front of the king, unit by unit. Following
the last unit in the royal guard procession was a band, playing many
songs, including 'Happy Birthday to You'. After all units of the royal
guards had returned to their positions, the king departed from the
ceremony.

The king turned fifty that year, and the celebration was special.
On Sunday, 4 December at 4.40 p.m., on the premises of the Emerald
Buddha Temple, a ceremony was conducted to unveil a special Buddha
image. This Buddha image had been molded on 1 November. In the
ceremony, the king allowed the officers to place three sets of *bai sri*,
offerings in glass, silver and gold containers. A Brahman priest then
passed the candles to the government officials for the circumambula-
tion ceremony.

Before the king went to the Emerald Buddha Temple for the ceremony, he had allowed me to introduce four new royal courts security
officers at about 3.30 p.m.

Introducing a person to the king may be done through a superior or by
self-introduction. The first method is convenient but can be difficult for
the superior, because he or she would have to remember by heart all the
details of each person to be introduced: rank, name, surname, position
and affiliated agency. Self-introductions make it easy for the superior, but
the persons to be introduced to the king must remember all the protocol,
including specific greetings and utterances in the royal language, which
can be quite intimidating for those not familiar with it.

The utterance for introducing oneself to the king is as follows: '*His
Majesty the King, I* (indicate the rank, name, surname, position and
affiliated agency such as Police General Vasit Dejkunjorn, Vice Director-General, the Royal Thai Police Department). . .'

The utterances at the beginning and at the end of the introduction
were only two sentences in the royal Thai language, but some people
have been known to forget their name and surname in the presence of
the king. A wise person has suggested a way to keep calm and focused
in the presence of the king; when the king is right in front of you, do

not look at his face or into his eyes but at the first or second button of his jacket, and speak in a normal voice.

❖

The king's birthday, 5 December, fell on a Monday that year. At 11 a.m., the king went outside for Mahasamakhom at the Amarindra Vinitchai Audience Hall in the Grand Palace.

The word 'Mahasamakhom' does not exist in the dictionary of the Royal Institute of Thailand, BE 2525, that I am using. The word *'maha'* means 'great' or 'grand' and *'samakhom'* means 'meeting'. Mahasamakhom thus means a grand meeting of royal families, cabinet, members of parliament, justices and civil servants, who assemble to give wishes to the king on his birthday.

Mahasamakhom was not often convened. If I remember correctly, there were only two occasions each year, on Coronation Day and on the king's birthday. On these occasions, when the king left for Amarindra Vinitchai Audience Hall, he left Paisan Taksin Hall through the Thewarat Mahesuan Gate and entered Amarindra Vinitchai to sit on the throne beneath the nine-tiered Great White Umbrella of State. The king wore a royal gown over the full dress of the head of the country's three military forces. As he ascended the throne, royal pages carried the king's regalia, hat, and club. A curtain separated the king from the audience, and they could not see him at this time.

At the auspicious moment, officers opened the curtain. Royal police officers lifted a golden bouquet as a signal. An officer played the Mahorathuek Horn. Meanwhile, a horn band played the royal anthem, extolling the king and the queen's virtues. The guards of honor paid their respect to the king, followed by officers of the army and navy presenting a twenty-one-gun salute.

As soon as the curtain opened and the king was in full sight, the royal attendants and the audience gave a bow to greet the king and another bow at the end of the royal anthem. Next, the attendants gave their blessings to the king, beginning with a senior royal family member on behalf of royal members, the prime minister on behalf of civil servants and people, and the speaker of parliament on behalf of members of parliament. Finally, the king gave his reply.

When the king's speech ended, royal police officers lifted a golden bouquet as a signal. Royal pages played wooden rhythm clappers and the officers closed the curtain. The horn band played the royal anthem again. Guards of honor paid their respect to the king and the king descended from the throne and returned to Paisan Taksin Hall, marking the end of the ceremony.

However, because the ceremony in 1977 was an auspicious one, after the blessings were given to the king, the king remained on the throne. Princess Sirindhorn took a seat on Phra Sutni (a piece of silk cloth woven with golden threads) in front of the Great White Umbrella of State. Next, a royal scribe read the royal command, giving Princess Sirindhorn the rank and name inscribed on the gold parchment: Somdej Phrathepharat Ratchasuda Chaofa Maha Chakri Sirindhorn Rathasima Khunakorn Piyachat Siamboromarat Chakumari.

When the royal scribe finished reading the royal command, Princess Sirindhorn stepped on the staircase to the throne and the king poured lustral water on her head. Royal astrologers played the gong; Brahmans blew the conch; a royal page struck the small two-faced drum; and officers blew the conch and played the horn.

The king gave a bale fruit leaf to the princess, which she put over her left ear. He then anointed her forehead and gave her the gold parchment bearing her name. The parchment was in an enameled gold case, decorated with diamonds, and engraved with her initials. The princess was also bestowed the royal decoration of Ancient and Auspicious Order of the Nine Gems (*Nopharatratchawaraphorn*) and given an enameled gold betel nut set decorated with diamonds as part of her promotion.

41

As part of Princess Sirindhorn's promotion to a higher rank, there were also several other gifts from the king that he did not present to her himself but had later been presented to her. These gifts were royal utensils that had traditionally been given to sons and daughters of the king, signifying their rank and status. The set of royal objects bestowed to Princess Sirindhorn on that occasion included an enameled gold beetle nut pedestal tray, a gold pedestal tray for the beetle nut box, enameled gold, a gold cylindrical kettle with a gold tray, an enameled gold bowl, a gold cup and an enameled bathing bowl.

Before the end of 1977, on Monday, 26 December and Tuesday, 27 December, another important ceremony was held for soldiers and police officers—a ceremony to bestow the Ramathibodi decorations (royal decorations in the Honorable Order of Rama). King Rama VI had created this order of decorations to be bestowed on those who have rendered special military services in peace or in war. These decorations were first given to Thai soldiers who saw action in Europe during World War I and have not been known to be given to any officers since—until King Bhumibol's reign.

Numerous soldiers and police officers have since done great services to the country; many showed their bravery in combat and even died on the battlefield, both in and outside Thailand. King Bhumibol decided to present the class of decorations to these soldiers and police officers or their descendants.

I didn't understand why the Ramadhibodi decorations were offered to officers, because they certainly would have been given medals for acts of bravery. I had a chance to ask His Majesty about this. He explained that this order of decorations was given to officers who had not only shown their bravery but also exemplified superior decision-making ability and leadership.

The king gave me an example of Capt. Yutthana Yaemphan, who is now a retired general. At that time, he was the commander of a Thai company that had taken part in combat during the Vietnam War. The Viet Cong had attacked his company. Though outnumbered, Khun Yutthana maintained his calm and held the ground and had not let his company be defeated by the enemies. In recognition of his bravery and leadership, Khun Yutthana was given a Ramathibodi decoration.

The decorations in the Honourable Order of Rama comprised four classes, namely, *Senangapati* (Knight Grand Commander), *Maha Yodhin* (Knight Commander), *Yodhin* (Commander), and *Asvin* (Companion). The other two medals, the two lowest classes in the order, are called the 'The Rama Medal for Gallantry in Action' and 'The Rama Medal'. These decorations are recognized as more special than any other orders of decorations because the recipients of decorations in this Order also have the honor of attending an oath of allegiance ceremony.

On Monday, 26 December, the ceremony to bestow the decorations began about 4.40 p.m. Their Majesties, Crown Prince Vajiralongkorn, Princess Maka Chakri Sirindhorn, Princess Chulabhorn and Princess Soamsavali, then the crown prince's consort, went to Dusit Maha Prasat Throne Hall in the Grand Palace, where the ceremony was to be performed. Once they arrived, they placed garlands in front of the photograph of the decreased officers who would be bestowed a Ramathibodi decoration. The king lit candles and incenses to worship the Triple Gem and a court secretary read acknowledgements of good deeds of the dead soldiers and police officers. Then the court secretary called the descendants of four of the deceased to receive the Companion in the Honourable House of Rama decoration and the descendants of six of the deceased to receive The Rama Medal for Gallantry in Action.

After the presenting of the royal decorations, the king lit candles and incense sticks, and Somdej Phra Maha Veeravongse instructed the Five Buddhist Precepts and gave a sermon in dharma. The king poured water of dedication to transfer merit to the deceased officers, presented the offerings for the sermon to the monks, and laid down the robes in the memorial ceremony. The monks then took the memorial robes, gave an Adirek blessing to the king, and a farewell blessing.

The next day at around the same time, the king went to Amarindra Vinitchai Auidence Hall to give more decorations, but to those who were still alive. The court secretary read the acknowledgements of good deeds of the officers who would receive the royal decorations in the Honourable Order of Rama. The king bestowed on five soldiers the Companion decoration and The Rama Medal for Gallantry in Action on sixteen soldiers and police officers.

The oath of allegiance ceremony that followed the bestowing of the decorations was performed at the *ubosot* of the Emerald Buddha Temple. The king entered the *ubosot* and lit candles and incense sticks to pay homage to the Emerald Buddha Image, the Buddha image in the costume of King Rama I, and the Buddha image in the costume of King Rama III. The king and the queen lit candles and incense sticks to worship the Triple Gem and chanted the Buddhist precepts. After that, Phrarajkhru Wamathepmuni, the royal Brahman priest, read the command for drinking consecrated water ceremony to be performed in the presence of the king. He pierced the royal arrow and the royal sword into the consecrated water. Then nine monks began to chant.

All the recipients of the Honourable Order of Rama decorations drank the consecrated water, as a symbol of an oath of allegiance, and the Brahman took the consecrated water to the king.

What happened next is what the public usually is not aware of. Unlike the previous kings, King Bhumibol also drinks from the consecrated water. This action by the king showed that though he is the giver of all royal decorations, he is also willing to take an oath of allegiance along with the rest of the other oath takers. Then, the rest of the oath takers drank the oath of allegiance water. After that, the king offered basic necessities to the monks. The monks then gave an appreciation and the Adirek blessings to the king.

At 7.30 p.m. on the same day, Their Majesties hosted dinner for the recipients of the Honourable Order of Rama decorations at Dusidalai Hall in Chitralada Palace.

On Tuesday, 3 January 1978, the king moved residence to Bhubing Palace again. As I have said, moving residence for the king did not interrupt his duties and functions. If there were important matters to attend to in Bangkok, he would temporarily return to Bangkok. Usually, the royal guests were invited to the place where the royal family currently resided. In January 1978, for example, Crown Prince Reza Pahlavi II of Iran was a guest at Bhubing Palace from Friday, 6 January to Sunday, 8 January, when he left for Bangkok to continue his travel to Australia.

While in Chiang Mai, Crown Prince Reza Pahlavi II went on a royal visit with Crown Prince Vajiralongkorn and his consort by car to Baan Pong Khrai, Baan Mae Saa Mai, and Baan Pang Chang, Tambon Pong Yaeng of Chiang Mai's Mae Rim district. In Baan Pong Khrai, the royal hosts and guest visited a reforestation project. In Baan Mae Saa Mai, they visited the villagers' cultivation of crops such as coffee and tobacco, cultivated in substitution for opium, and observed the technique of step farming to prevent soil erosion as well as the water and irrigation system in mountainous area. In Baan Pang Chang, they watched the elephants at work, pulling timber. This was a rather short and hasty study trip of projects under the royal initiatives.

Crown Prince Reza Pahlavi II was a young man, still only 18 years of age at that time, and very attractive. During his visit he enjoyed a lot of attention, especially from women, both young and old.

On a day inauspicious for westerners but not for Buddhists—Friday, 13 January—Phi Thep, Phi Teanchai and myself were on duty on a Royal Thai Air Force helicopter, making an advance survey in advance of His Majesty's visit to Nan. Our first landing was near Mor Muang Weir, in front of Mae Charim District Office, Nan province. The helicopter set down at 10.25 a.m. and we surveyed the route on the royal agenda.

Our second destination was Operation Base of Cavalry Troop 301, Baan Nam Phang, Tambon Mor Muang, Mae Charim district. There, while Phi Thep was greeting the soldiers, he was introduced to a young monkey, who was dancing, still tied to a rope, in a tree in front of its owner's dwelling. Its owner was a soldier and stood near the monkey.

Phi Thep was kind to all animals. He thus couldn't pass without greeting the monkey and its owner. I had no idea what Phi Thep said to the soldier but he walked back to the helicopter with the monkey. He said the monkey's name was Ai Saep and he paid 100 baht for it.

I was right in thinking that Phi Thep planned to release the monkey. Both of us disliked seeing animals in chains or in cages. Phi Thep believed that birds with the most beautiful voice were those singing outside a cage. On Wednesday, 25 January, after having kept Ai Saep for ten days, I went along with Phi Thep, his children, and Ai Saep to an open zoo of the Royal Forestry Department, located near Wat Umong just outside of downtown Chiang Mai.

Releasing Ai Saep back to the wild was no complicated task. When we saw the trees with monkeys, Phi Thep let Ai Saep climb up on the tree. But what happened unexpectedly that was so touching we couldn't hold back our tears was that Ai Saep did not want to leave Phi Thep and his children. It jumped back to embrace them and would not let go. It took some time and some pulling of limbs before Ai Saep joined the other wild monkeys.

We went back to see Ai Saep after his release. The first time he recognized us and came straight down from the tree to greet us and let us embrace him. But after a few visits, the monkey society seemed to have accepted Ai Saep and he no longer come down from the trees to greet us.

The story of Ai Saep is like the story of the wild rabbit in Sakon Nakhon. If it had not been for our work for the king, Phi Thep would not have had the chance to meet Ai Saep and I might not have such a touching tale to tell.

❖

On Saturday, 21 January 1978, a royally sponsored funeral was held for Ajarn Fan Ajaro at Wat Pa Udom Somporn in Sakon Nakhon's Phanna Nikhom district.

I went in advance along with other security officers in a C-123. We left Chiang Mai Airport at 11 a.m., an hour later than scheduled due to some mechanical problems, and arrived at 1.10 p.m. at an airport in the Second Army Area Command (or Siwara Camp) in downtown Sakon Nakhon. As soon as our car reached the Second Army Forward, the royal plane landed at the airport.

At 2.20 p.m., the security officers arrived at Wat Pa Udom Somporn. We hurried to get out of the car to prepare for the king's arrival. We had learned by radio that the royal car had already left Sakon Nakhon and was approaching. The king arrived at 2.25 p.m. I didn't know if he noticed that some of his security officers were still panting.

The king, the queen and Princess Maha Chakri Sirindhorn entered the pavilion and then walked up to the crematorium in front of the pavilion. Their Majesties presented ten sets of monk's robes in dedication to the deceased. The monks then meditated and received the funeral robe. The king placed a banana-leaf cup containing flowers and popped rice in front of Ajarn Fan's coffin. He then picked up candles and wooden funeral flowers and lit the fire fuse. After cremation, the king left the crematorium for the pavilion, allowing a large number of government officials and the general public to enter the crematorium. Their Majesties and Princess Sirindhorn left the funeral in late afternoon and arrived back at Bhubing Palace at 7.15 p.m.

42

I have said before that serving the king had given me the chance to meet many famous and highly respected monks. Kruba Chaiwongsa Pattana, known widely as Kruba Wong, was another monk I visited in 1978. His monastery was at Wat Phrabat Huay Tom, Tambon Na Sai of Lamphun's Li district. I had visited him while accompanying MC Vibhavadi.

In 1978, the king visited the temple on Sunday, 15 January, and then again on Thursday, 26 January, with the queen and the two princesses.

The villagers of Baan Huay Tom were ethnic Karen. But unlike other Karen, they were vegetarians. The villagers followed the example of Kruba Wong in abstaining from eating meat, believing that it aided and abetted the killing. However, they lacked knowledge on how to supplement their vegetarian diet with protein.

During the previous visit, accompanying MC Vibhavadi, I could see that most of them, adults and children alike, looked sickly and pale from protein deficiency. On the king's first visit to the village, he advised the villagers to raise soybeans for consumption. On this visit, they appeared healthier.

On this visit, the king walked to the Huay La Reservoir, which the Royal Irrigation Department had built following the king's advice. The reservoir provided water supply all year round to five hundred households covering about 2,500 *rai*. Apart from the reservoir, there was also the Agricultural Development Project, carried out by the Faculty of Agriculture and the Faculty of Medicine, Chiang Mai University, in collaboration with the Royal Forestry Department, the Royal Irrigation Department, the Department of Public Welfare, and Lamphun province.

Another important monk the king visited was the late Luang Phor Kasem Khemako, who lived and practiced dharma in solitude at Trailak Graveyard, in Lampang's Muang district. His solitude, however, was often disturbed by those who arrived with a request for him to consecrate their Buddha amulets or water.

The first time I visited him, I saw a lot of offerings at his *kuti*. Some of the food had even gone bad. He always offered food and snacks (the offerings) to his guests. He offered me a cracker. Normally, I didn't eat snacks but one of his disciples asked me to eat it. I learned that every day, many people asked him to consecrate their Buddha amulets and to make holy water. Some people couldn't wait in a long queue. The impatient ones put their Buddha amulets on a tray as they walked past his *kuti*, and came out telling people that Luang Phor Kasem had consecrated their Buddha amulets. As for the holy water, some people would give him bottles of water, which he would keep in his *kuti*. A day or two later, one of his disciples gave the bottles of water back to the owners and said that it had been consecrated.

Luang Phor Kasem had a strange habit. He couldn't bear the sight of people walking on written letters. When he went outside his *kuti*, he would stop and pick up all the pieces of paper with letters—typed or written—on them.

The king visited Luang Phor Kasem to perform a ceremony to cut the consecrated boundary-marking stone balls at Wat Khatuk Chiangman, Lampang's Muang on Monday, 6 February 1978. Luang Phor Kesem had been invited to attend the ceremony. The king conversed with Luang Phor Kasem for a long time after the ceremony, then presented village scout banners to the local village scouts at Nong Krathing Sports Stadium.

I have written about Ajarn Ngoan Sorayo, another well-known monk. The king gave him another visit on Sunday, 29 January 1978, during his visit to Kamphaengphet, where he was to give banners to the local chapters of the village scouts. As usual, I arrived ahead of the king and met with Khun Kaj Raksamanee, the governor. Khun Kaj, who was also an alumnus of Chulalongkorn University's Faculty of Political Science, was the person who first introduced me to Ajarn Ngoan.

Ajarn Ngoan gave me Buddha relics. I knew little about relics but when a widely respected monk gave me such objects, I respectfully accepted them. I later placed the relics in a small case on the altar with the Buddha images at my house. One day for some reason, the principal Buddha image on the top table fell down on the incense pot and the relic case, causing the case to spill open and the relics to scatter among the incense ashes. I searched for the relics among the ashes in vain. This is a phenomenon I haven't been able to find an explanation for.

The communist infiltration was not confined only to the north and the northeast, but had spread to the southwestern region of the country, including Kanchanaburi and Tak. Especially in Mae Sot district in Tak province, the insurgents' activities were so aggressive that many ethnic hill tribe villagers fled to the lowland areas and the government had to provide them a new settlement and assistance center.

On Saturday, 4 February 1978, the king, the queen and the princesses visited Mae Sot to visit members of the assistance center in Baan Chedi Kho. They also observed metal forging work, the local industry of the villagers. During the visit, Mr. Changphong Sae-ma, a Hmong villager, invited the royal family to visit his home. He presented to the king a Hmong costume and other ethnic articles, and gave each of the royal guests traditional Hmong blessing by tying holy threads around their wrists.

Later that afternoon, the royal family continued to Sapha Wit-thyakhom School in Mae Sot and gave banners to nineteen groups of village scouts. The king's speech to the village scouts was a spontaneous one, emphasizing the scout's commitment to conduct themselves for the benefits of the society and all Thai people.

Following his speech, the local people made voluntary contributions to the fund for the village scouts' affairs. The king and his family visited with the people until 4 p.m., when they had a chance to get lunch, then at 6 p.m., they had to continue on to another function, to perform yet another cutting of consecrated boundary-marking stone balls at Wat Weruwan, Tambon Mae Pa in the same district. Finally, the royal visit to Tak ended at 7 p.m. and the family returned to Bhubing Palace at nearly 9 p.m.

Given his schedule of daily duties, returning to his residence late at night was a normal event for the king. Officers had to be prepared with lighting equipment on the ready functions after dark, and be prepared for overnight stay during any royal visit.

On 10 February, at 10.50 a.m., Their Majesties and Princess Maka Chakri Sirindhorn left Chiang Mai Airport for Lom Sak district in Phetchabun province. The royal transport was changed to a helicopter in Phitsanulok. A little after 1 p.m., the family arrived at Somdej Base at Khao Khor, Tambon Camp Son in Lom Sak.

Somdej Base was a strategically important base. The 909th Infantry Division and Joint Civilian-Police-Military Headquarters (CPM 1617) were located at this base. Communist insurgency was the most active here.

Their Majesties and the princess spent a long time at the base, listening to the briefing of the situation. Then they took a car to Baan Thai Noi 1 and Baan Thai Noi 2 of the Thung Samor Project—a project of land allocation for agricultural purposes. They visited the villages and reservoirs. The king recommended that the reservoir should be modified to a multilevel style to prevent soil erosion. He also asked for a list of the villagers who might be interested in getting chicken breeders to breed with local chickens. The cross-breeding would result in bigger and stronger chickens.

There was another temple visit on the agenda that day, but the royal mission didn't arrive at Wat Petch Wararam in Muang, Kamphaeng-phet until nearly 6 p.m. The team of security officers couldn't reach the destination in advance and had to follow the royal motorcade. We reached the wat in the late evening. The king sprinkled holy water and pasted gold leaves on consecrated boundary-marking stone balls of the temple, then performed a ceremony of cutting two stone balls: one in front of the *ubosot* and the other inside it. Next, he lit candles and incense sticks to pay homage to the principal Buddha image and conversed with Somdej Phra Yannasangvorn and Phra Kittisan Sophon, the abbot, to whom he made offerings.

By the time the king left the *ubosot*, it was already very late and pitch dark outside. Lights were lit all through the temple grounds. The king planted pink cassia and then returned to the pavilion. Next, he made an offering to the monks. The monks expressed their appreciation and gave the Adirek blessing to the king. Then people gave donations for the construction of the *ubosot*. Afterwards, the king, the queen and the princess visited with a large group of local people who were waiting for an audience with them.

While the royal family was having a visit with the people, security officers held a rather serious and anxious meeting. A helicopter pilot had informed us that the way that the king intended to use for his return to the palace ran through the high mountains and deep forests of Phetchabun and Phitsanulok, an area prone to insurgent activities. There were reasons to believe that some groups of insurgents had high-capacity weapons capable of shooting down helicopters.

After the pilot's briefing, the trip planners, who were the chief aide-de-camp general, the Third Army commander, Phi Teanchai (chief of VIP Security Detachment attached to the Royal Aide-de-Camp Department), and I had a consultation to find a safe route for the return trip. Finally, we agreed on returning by car, but to avoid Highway 12 (Lom Sak-Pitsanulok). We would recommend the royal motorcade to use Highway 21 (Phetchabun-Wang Chomphu), 113 (Wang Chomphu-Khao Sai), and 11 (Khao Sai-Wangthong) and to enter Phitsanulok by Highway 12 (Wangthong-Phitsanulok).

Yet the king disagreed with our recommendation to take an alternate land travel. He suggested that the return trip could still be made by helicopter, using the suggested land route—Phetchabun-Wang Chomphu-Khao Sai-Wangthong-Phitsanulok. The highway police radio cars would stop periodically, especially at intersections, and turn on the light to signal the helicopter pilot that safe passage was possible.

At 7.40 p.m. the royal helicopter left Phetchabun following the light signals by the highway police cars below. Forty minutes later, the king's helicopter arrived at Phitsanulok Airport. Security officers arrived shortly thereafter. When the royal plane left Phitsanulok province, we followed on a Royal Thai Air Force C-123 back to Chiang Mai.

❖

On Thursday, 23 February 1978, the king and queen returned to Bangkok to anoint a new airplane the Royal Thai Army had offered as a royal transport. The king also presented swords and certificates to graduates of the Army Cadet Academy of Phrachulachomklao, the Naval Academy, and the Royal Thai Air Force (RTAF) Academy.

The same day, the king also bestowed ranks and commissions to new police generals. The ceremony was held in Chitralada Palace at 6.35 p.m. I was among the officers who were given the rank of police lieutenant general.

Rank promotion often came with a higher position. I had previously been appointed by a royal command to the position of chief royal court police officer, a newly created position equivalent to the rank of a commissioner, who holds the rank of police lieutenant general. Before that promotion I was assistant commissioner of Border Patrol Police and held the rank of police major general. Once I had been appointed to a permanent position in the new Office of Royal Court Police Officers, my affiliation with the BPP also came to an end.

With the new rank and position I returned to Chiang Mai on the same day as Their Majesties, back to the duties I had handled before.

43

The weather in February could be unpredictable as it falls between the cool and hot seasons—rain is not infrequent and can be an obstacle for royal travel.

On Saturday, 25 February, the king and the queen visited Nan province again. This time the destination was Baan Suad, Baan Luang subdistrict and Baan Pa Klang, Tambon Sila Daeng, Pua district. They left Chiang Mai Airport at 11.15 a.m. On arrival in Nan Airport, the king and queen transferred to a helicopter for their onward journey to Baan Suad and Baan Pa Klang.

Baan Pa Klang was a big hill tribe center. Before they came to live in the center the hill tribe people had previously lived on various mountains in the north. As communist insurgencies became more aggressive, the government evacuated the people from the mountains to the center. Once many people had been transferred to the center, a need arose to expand the existing facilities.

The king had visited the same hill tribe communities when they lived in the mountains, so he was familiar with them and their way of life. He had advised them about work possibilities. When these people were taken to the center, the king was concerned about their well-being.

His Majesty had asked the Royal Irrigation Department to dig a pond near the center for water storage. The department built a weir in Huay Phi Ba and diverted water to the first pond. When the first pond was filled, more water was diverted to nine other ponds, providing enough water sources to support an area of about 2,000 *rai*.

The king left Baan Pa Klang at 6.12 p.m. on a helicopter and arrived at Nan Airport at 6.30 p.m. He still had to visit with government officials and with the local people waiting for him at the airport. He finally boarded the royal plane for Chiang Mai at 7 p.m. Royal guards, court police officers and royal servants followed ten minutes later in a C-123.

During the return flight the weather, with heavy rainstorms, was a challenge. Neither the royal plane nor our C-123 was able to land at Chiang Mai Airport. The pilots therefore headed to Phitsanulok Airport and arrived there at about 8.25 p.m. Their Majesties waited in the plane at Phitsanulok Airport for the weather to clear until 9 p.m., when we were able to finally return to Chiang Mai. The royal mission got back to Bhubing Palace at 11.25 p.m. that night.

The next morning, Sunday, 26 February, we planned to conduct a survey in preparation for a royal visit, Tambon Mae Tuen of Chiang Mai's Om-koi district. In northern Thailand, there are many unusual names for the tambons, districts and provinces like Om-koi. Phi Thep, who had worked in the north for a long time, explained to me that *om* was a borrowed word from Lua language, meaning water, but I forgot the meaning of *koi*. Ethnic Lua people had historically lived in the area, which was once prosperous. Today, there are still remains of ancient cities believed to have been built by the Lua, and these ruins are scattered throughout the region, especially in the west.

At 10 p.m., we reached the airbase of 411th air squadron, Chiang Mai Airport. The airport was our meeting point. At 10.30, MC Bhisatej Rajani, the most important officer in charge of the survey, arrived. But then our pilot informed us that we couldn't fly to Om-koi according to our plan because we were running low on fuel.

We took the opportunity to do other things on that day. We took a car to the Faculty of Agriculture at Chiang Mai University, which was located at the foot of Doi Suthep in Chiang Mai's Muang district, to inspect a packaged food factory, scheduled for the king's visit on 28 February. We arrived at the factory after 11 a.m. and we found that many pieces of equipment in the factory that would be offered to the king were either old or used items.

We finished our inspection duties by midday and still had enough time for a rest and to prepare ourselves for another task at Chiang Mai

Sports Stadium. I got to the stadium at 3.30 p.m. At about 4.15 p.m., the king and Princess Maka Chakri Sirindhorn arrived to give banners to ninety-four groups of village scouts from around Chiang Mai. Afterwards, as usual, the king gave a speech and received donations for the fund to support village scouts' affairs. And as before, the donations went to the local village scout operation center. Afterwards the king met with the people, leaving the stadium at 6 p.m.

On Tuesday, 28 February, at 4.15 p.m., the king drove Queen Sirikit from Bhubing Palace to Chiang Mai University to visit the packaged food factory. This factory was a project under royal patronage, operated under the supervision of the Department of Food Science and Technology in the university.

It may be appropriate to mention here again that many development projects under the king's patronage are usually part of a complete circle of initiatives to help the people. For example, he encouraged the hill tribe villagers to abandon opium cultivation and plant alternative cash crops. That is, he initiated projects to process local products to ensure that the villagers would make income from their new cash crops. The factories, like the one being visited that day, typically were a fruit canning operation. The king advised the people on how to find markets for the canned fruits and how best to distribute the products.

At the factory, the royal couple observed operations, and the king gave a talk about the value of integrated service operation. He suggested that the factory project produce simple and cheap food processing machines using human labor. Such machines could then be installed in village and settlement cooperatives so that the villagers would have a local means to process fruits that otherwise rotted quickly and were difficult to transport. Processing the fruits locally could solve the spoilage problem and reduce both transportation costs and a great deal of the product loss.

Among hill tribe villages in the north, Baan Mae Pun Luang in the mountains at Tambon Wiang of Chiang Rai's Wiang Pa Pao district was one of the most impoverished. The village was accessible by helicopter or by car via Highway 118 (Chiang Mai-Chaing Rai) through Doi Saket. However, the road beyond Chiang Mai's Doi Saket ran through steep mountains with sharp switchbacks, very dangerous for those unfamiliar with the terrain. Baan Mae Pun Luang was located on one of the hilltops of the mountain range. The steep slope of the exit from Highway 118 to the east caused a Chiang Rai Provincial Police car on royal security survey duty to overturn, killing one police officer and injuring others.

On Friday, 3 March, the king and queen went by helicopter to Baan Mae Pun Luang. The helicopter landed at a temporary landing site on a nearby mountaintop. The villagers were Lahu Yi, an ethnic group generally referred to as 'Muser Daeng' by Thais. The king and queen went into the village temple, where Pu Chong, the village wise man, performed a blessing ceremony according to Lahu Yi custom.

The king and queen visited with the waiting villagers and then watched as the royal medical unit attended to the villagers. The king also gave basic necessities such as blankets and medicine to Royal Forestry Department workers stationed there. The royal couple then watched as villagers sun dried the tea leafs before packaging. Processing tea leaves was principal occupation of the villagers. Those who have been in Thailand's north may know that fermented tea leaves—or *miang*, as known locally—are a favorite pastime for northern Thai people.

The royal couple stayed at Baan Mae Pun Luang until 1 p.m. and then got back on the helicopter to Baan Sa Ngo, Tambon Pasak in Chiang Saen district, Chiang Rai.

The hill tribe people at Baan Sa Ngo were ethnic Akha ('E-gor' in Thai) and had a reputation for eating dog meat. Their taste for dog caused many Thai dog lovers to dislike them. Dog eating reminded me of another village, Baan Tharae, Sakon Nakhon, where most villagers were ethnic Vietnamese. Like the Akha, they also ate dog meat. Today at Tha Rae Market, you can buy raw dog meat, which is sold together with pork and beef, a sight that dog lovers find very disturbing.

Baan Sa Ngo was located on a small mountain, also named Sa Ngo. Ajarn Pol. Lt. Saeng Monwithoon told me that this word *'sa-ngo'* was actually distorted from the words *'chang ngu'* ('elephant and snake' in Thai). There was a legendary origin to the name. The legend had it that the area where now the village was situated was once a place where King Phrom Kuman, son of King Phangkharat, ruler of Nakhon Yonok Nakburi, came to capture three white elephants. King Phrom Kuman had dreamed an angel told him of his chance to catch three white elephants. The angel said that if he could catch the first white elephant, he would rule all four continents. According to a Thai legend Trai Phumi ('Three Worlds'), the four continents include Chomphu Thaweep, Amornkhoyana Thaweep, Uttarakuru Thaweep and Buphawitheha Thaweep. If he could catch the second one, he would rule only Chomphu Thaweep. If he could catch the third one, he would conquer Thai Lanna states and the Black Khmer empire.

While King Phrom Kuman was waiting to catch the white elephants, he saw two big snakes swimming. According to the legend, they were the same size as a palmyra tree trunk, but because they were not the elephants, he let them pass by. However, when the third snake swam past, he had an inkling and, along with his servants, jumped into the river to catch the snake. It turned out that what they had seen as snakes were in fact white elephants, only one of which he was able to catch. So the mountain was called Doi Chang Ngu, according to the legend. Akha people couldn't pronounce the Thai words correctly, the pronunciation was distorted and the name of the mountain came to be known as Sa Ngo.

To continue with the legend, after King Phrom Kuman conquered all of Lanna, he invaded the Khmer. His plan caused Indra God to send Phra Vetsanukam Dhevabutra to build a stone wall to block King Phrom Kuman from wiping out the Khmer from the face of the earth. The stone wall would become Kamphaengphet province (which translates to 'diamond wall'). Later, King Phrom Kuman built Chaiprakan city, where he later died. Chaiprakan is now a district in Chiang Mai.

Here at Baan Sa Ngo, the king gave basic necessities, including medicine, stationery and textbooks to teachers, students and public welfare and land development workers stationed there. In addition, nineteen sacks of rice were given as the capital to establish a rice bank in the village. Akha villagers made their living working as day laborers for low wages, so the government agencies encouraged them to grow field crops for livelihood.

Next, the king and queen met with the people at Prasit Thawisin School, where the royal medical unit was providing medical services to the villagers. Then, they went on to inspect a pond used for cultivation, fish farming and pens for cattle and buffalo provided under the royal patronage.

The royal couple had lunch at 3 p.m. and after lunch went to Huay Pha Laad Weir, which had been built to preserve the water source and distribute the water supply to the adjacent agricultural areas. They visited the Chiang Rai Land Development Center to see land development plots, where coffee, green beans, string beans, Chinese morning glory, and lychee were cultivated. There were also pineapple and vegetable plots and storage facilities for manure and compost. He suggested that the center construct a series of small weirs in all ditches, around the mountain, to preserve moisture from the headwater. The recommended project would also allow for irrigation in the lower lying areas, which had the advantage of dissuading people from encroaching on the forest upstream.

At 5.03 p.m., the king and queen left Baan Sa Ngo by helicopter for Mae Lua Weir, which was not far away. The flight took only seven minutes. After meeting with the waiting crowd, the royal couple inspected the weir that had been built as a temporary measure to prevent flooding in farming area. The Royal Irrigation Department was in the process of conducting a survey and drawing up a plan to further assist the people. The royal couple left Mae Lua Weir at 6 p.m. They flew on the helicopter to Chiang Rai Airport to board a plane waiting to fly them back to Chiang Mai.

On Sunday, 5 March 1978, I accompanied the royal couple to McKean Hospital on the occasion of its seventieth anniversary. McKean Hospital, located in Tambon Pa Daed, Chiang Mai's Muang district, was a rehabilitation center for people with leprosy operated by the Church of Christ in Thailand.

I must admit that accompanying them to McKean Hospital made me a little anxious. I thought that leprosy was both a severely infectious disease and incurable. In my hometown in Isan, people unlucky enough to have contracted leprosy were banished from their family and community, and had to live in isolation until death.

44

I was enlightened about leprosy after listening to a report presented by Professor Richard Brian at McKean Hospital. Professor Brian, the hospital director, said in this briefing to the king and queen that leprosy was not the frightening disease that many people, myself included, had thought. I also learned that it was curable. At that time, the hospital provided both in-patient and out-patient services.

After the briefing, the royal couple received souvenirs from the director, which had been made by the patients. Next, the king accepted donations that people in attendance had made for the hospital, and walked around the hospital buildings to visit patients. The royal couple also bought lacquer ware and carvings made by the patients and made their private contributions to the hospital. Ever since that visit I have been completely cured of my fear of leprosy and leprosy patients.

The northern climate in March was hot and arid. The region was susceptible to forest fires in the hot season. In some nights from Bhubing Palace, which is situated on Doi Suthep overlooking Chiang Mai City, we could see flames of forest fire in many places.

On Friday, 10 March, at 5.30 p.m., Queen Sirikit traveled by car from Bhubing Palace to Doi Pui, where she walked down to the mountain ridge below. It was one of her most favorite places. That day, there was a forest fire and smoke enveloped the area.

It is well-known that the queen loved nature, especially forests. She hated to see or know about bad things being done to the environment. The queen was upset, seeing the smoke of the forest fire. She told us that the fires were usually a result of human recklessness, and the smile so often seen on her face disappeared. This made all of us escorting her unhappy.

I have always wondered why the government seemed unenthusiastic about the problem given how common forest fires were in the hot season. Usually no one other than the villagers who lived there extinguished the fires. Sometimes the palace fire fighters had to go out and help the villagers.

Foreign countries, especially western countries, recognized the seriousness of forest fires and provided significant resources to deal with the problem. For example, in the United States, planes carry water and chemicals to extinguish such blazes, and rangers and firefighters are specially trained to extinguish forest fires. But in Thailand, forest police are there only to arrest illegal loggers. I wonder if such ignorance and neglect have played a part in the sharp reduction in forest area in the country and the resultant climate changes. There are not enough forests to withstand the floods, and the areas that never had flooding problems are now often flooded, causing much hardship and grief to people.

Their Majesties moved back to Bangkok on Sunday, 12 March 1978. I saw them off at Chiang Mai Airport at 6 p.m. and stayed overnight in Chiang Mai before leaving by car the next day. I did not return to Bangkok right away but went farther north for a short trip and to pay homage to some Buddha images in Chiang Rai's Mae Sai and Chiang Saen district and Phayao district (which has since become a province). I stayed overnight in Phayao. The next day, 14 March, after having paid homage to Phrachao Ton Luang at Wat Sri Khomkham in the morning, I headed back to Bangkok and arrived home that night.

The royal couple stayed in Bangkok for only a little over a month. On Sunday, 16 April, the king and queen moved residence to Klai Kangwol Palace.

The king continued his usual visits and functions while staying at Klai Kangwol Palace. When he had to visit other provinces, he would take a plane at Bo Fai Airport in Hua Hin. If he had to come back for any duty or function in Bangkok, it would be a day trip by car. When he finished his work in Bangkok, he would return to Hua Hin.

In Hua Hin he usually went sailing in the afternoon. The queen enjoyed swimming in the sea in the evening. Apart from male security officers, most of the queen's attendants were women. I had never accompanied the queen to swim but I knew that she liked water and was very good at swimming. She would be in the sea for an hour at a time, so her attendants had to be good swimmers.

❖

On Tuesday, 16 May, the king was scheduled to visit Chumphon province for the gable finial mounting ceremony of the *ubosot* of Wat Pak Nam and gave banners to village scouts. Phi Thep and I had gone there in advance, leaving Hua Hin at 4.40 p.m. We stayed over night at Sri Chumphon Hotel.

The weather was terrible that day. The heavy rainstorms continued into the night. Many areas in downtown Chumphon and highways leading to Chumphon were reported to be flooded. At about 11 p.m. an officer from the Royal Household Bureau knocked on the door of my room and told me that the king had cancelled his trip to Chumphon.

The king and queen seldom cancelled their trips. The flood would be the obstacle not only to the royal travel but also for the many people who would want to come to meet the royal couple. The trip was therefore cancelled.

Chumphon Governor Khun Aroon Rujikanha was understandably anxious by such a sudden change of plans. The following morning, Tuesday, 16 May, I went to see him. After a little bit of chat, he asked officers from the Public Relations Department of Chumphon to tape a radio interview with me to broadcast the reason for the cancellation. Then, at 9 p.m., I met with the committee that was preparing a welcoming ceremony for the royal visit. Finally, Phi Thep and I traveled to Wat Pak Nam to meet the village head and members of the temple committee to tell them about the cancellation.

I have already written about the ceremony of offering the white elephants in Narathiwat. There was another such ceremony in Phetchaburi province that year. This time, there were three important elephants—Chang

Phlai Phrasri, Chang Phlai Daorung and Chang Phang Khwanta (*phlai* is male, and *phang* is female).

The ceremony was held on Thursday, 25 May in front of Phra Nakhon Khiri Palace. All three white elephants were given a royal rank of Khun Phra. The poems in praise of the elephants, read by a Brahman priest and performed by artists from the Department of Fine Arts, were again composed by Princess Maka Chakri Sirindhorn.

The Hup Kaphong Agricultural Cooperative in Cha-am district, Phetchaburi had earned its reputation years earlier. Hup Kaphong had once been plagued by drought and its land was now infertile. It was believed that nothing could grow in Hup Kaphong. Sometime before 1971, the people of Hup Kaphong had made a complaint to the king, telling him about their hardships stemming from the infertility of their land. The king then had an initiative to make the place fertile again.

In 1971 the king had an initiative to establish Hup Kaphong Agricultural Cooperative to allocate the land believed to unusable to 296 farming households. With the help of various government agencies directly responsible for land development and foreign experts, particularly Israeli experts, who were famous for turning the desert into fertile land, the king advised and supported the villagers to develop their soil for growing crops.

Finally, Hup Kaphong became fertile again and the villagers grew vegetable and field crops such as pineapple, sugarcane, Roselle and even asparagus, which then had to be imported. The cooperative progressed and the livelihood of its members improved. The Faculties of Economics and Business Administration at Kasetsart University estimated that the net monthly income of the cooperative's members was higher than 20,000 baht per household. Some of them could even afford to send their children to study overseas.

The king had been visiting Hup Kaphong every year. On Saturday, 27 May 1978 at 3.20 p.m., the king, the queen, Princess Maka Chakri Sirindhorn and Princess Chulabhorn arrived in Hup Kaphong. Director-General of the Cooperative Promotion Department Khun Adul Niyomwiphat, Chairman of Hup Kaphong Agricultural Cooperative

Khun Chiang Thanomphaladisai, and Chairman of Hup Kaphong Crime Prevention Volunteers Lance Corp. Sanit Prangson had an audience with the king to present a report.

The king said that he was satisfied with the progress of the cooperative, thanks to the collaboration between its members and relevant government authorities. He compared a cooperative and its members to a body and organs, which had to depend on each other and remarked that strong organs could make a body healthy. Afterwards, the king went to see Hup Kaphong Reservoir while the queen and the princess went to see members of the cooperative in the village.

At that time, the dike of the reservoir was extended to ten meters in height and 275 meters in length. When this was completed, the reservoir would have a capacity of 260,000 cubic meters, an increase of 215,000 cubic meters. The king saw the construction and the spillway. He advised officials of the Royal Irrigation Department, the Cooperative Promotion Department and the cooperative committee to conduct a survey of channels for small-scale dam construction to block a brook to allow water to be absorbed into the soil, which would increase the groundwater level.

On the occasion, the king expressed his satisfaction with the increasing number of trees and firewood to the director-general of Royal Forestry Department, Khun Thanom Premrasmi. The king said that this was a very good way to preserve headwater.

The king subsequently rejoined the queen and the princesses at land plot 67 and then went to see a basket weaving demonstration by the Hup Kaphong Women's Group at the cooperative. The royal family departed at 7.30 p.m.

Many cooperatives like Hup Kaphong Agricultural Cooperative have been established according to the king's initiative in the north, northeast and south. Near this one were Don Khun Huay Cooperative in the same district and the Nong Phlap Cooperative in Hua-Hin, Prachuap Khiri Khan. Those in other provinces include the Pong Krathing Cooperative in Ratchaburi's Suan Phueng district, Baan Chao Nen Cooperative in Kanchanaburi's Si Sawat district, Huay Manao Cooperative in Chiang Mai's San Pa Tong district, Thung Luilai Cooperative in Chaiyaphum's Khon San district and Thung Lipa Sa Ngo Cooperative in Pattani's Nong Chik district.

The cooperatives were centers for demonstration and testing of growing different types of crops suitable for the local soil condition and market demand. Apart from selling their own agricultural products, the cooperative members sold products under occupational development and household industry such as basketry products and earthenware.

45

Another impoverished village not far from Klai Kangwol Palace was Baan Khao Tao, Tambon Nong Kae, located on the seaside in Hua Hin. The village was only four to five kilometers south of the palace. Beyond the village, there was a beach called Hat Sai Yai, giving an image of a big banyan tree on the beach (*sai* means Banyan tree and *yai* means big). Later, the name of the beach became Hat Saai Yai, meaning a beach with a lot of sand (*saai* means sand).

The soil in Baan Wat Khao Tao was salty as is usually found at seaside villages. Therefore the ground was not suitable for growing crops. Apart from coconuts and pineapples, there were a small number of mango trees, hardly enough to sustain a livelihood for the villagers.

I remember when the king and queen were walking along Hat Sai Yai, the villagers in shabby clothes came out to welcome them and offered them what seemed to be stunted, undernourished mangoes. I am sure the appearance of the place, the villagers, and their apparent substandard living conditions were not lost to the royal couple.

Not so long after this visit, there were some changes in Baan Wat Khao Tao. The king had a reservoir constructed. As for the land near Hat Sai Yai, instead of being simply a beach for pleasure, it became the king's private farm, where cows were raised and many crops were cultivated that were suitable for the climate and soil conditions. The farm was a demonstration project for the villagers. Also a weaving workshop was built according to the queen's initiative with the purpose of training female villagers to learn local cotton weaving.

Because the village was near Klai Kangwol Palace, the villagers had many opportunities to meet the king, the queen and the princesses.

This was one of the areas where the king liked to go jogging. Usually he ran about three kilometers from Baan Wat Khao Tao to his private farm at Hat Sai Yai. When he jogged past the farm, he would take the opportunity to see the progress of the project.

There was a school in Klai Kangwol Palace—Wang Klai Kangwol School. The only other palace with a school is Chitralada Palace—Chitralada School.[1] Initially Wang Klai Kangwol School had only primary school level education but it later expanded to the secondary school level.

While at Klai Kangwol Palace, the king usually gave awards to students with good academic performance. After that, he would make a speech. This was a special occasion for the students, their teachers and their parents.

The year 1978 seemed to also be the year of white elephants for Phetchaburi province. In June, a male elephant with a strange color was discovered in Tha Yang. He was called Phlai Wanphen. After its characteristics were confirmed to be those of a white elephant, it was offered to the king according to tradition.

On Tuesday, 13 June, at 4.20 p.m., the king, the queen and Princess Maha Chakri Sirindhorn went to receive Phlai Wanphen in Kaeng Krachan, Tha Yang district. The ceremony to offer this white elephant was not as elaborate as the previous three white elephants. It began with the king giving holy water to the elephant. Next, the queen placed a garland over its head and Princess Sirindhorn fed it bananas and grass, and that was the end of the ceremony. I am not certain about the cause of the shortened ceremony and do not know whether Phlai Wanphen lacked any of the white elephant characteristics.

The royal family stayed at Hua Hin lasted until Thursday, 15 June.

---

[1] Chitralada School was established to provide education for King Bhumibol's children and the children of the royal couple's entourage. It has been gradually opened to the public.

After returning to Bangkok, the king and Princess Maha Chakri Sirindhorn attended the graduation ceremony at Srinakharinwirot University, where they handed certificates to graduates. The ceremony lasted six days. The reason for this extraordinarily long ceremony was that Srinakharinwirot University was an open university with a huge number of graduates from many campuses throughout the country. Also, the ceremony was held for graduates of two academic years, 1975 and 1976. The ceremony was held at Suan Amphorn near Chitralada Palace. On each of the six days, the king and the princess handed out certificates continually for as long as four hours at a time.

I don't know if anyone noticed that during the ceremony the king never changed his posture or fidgeted despite being in a sitting position for a long time. He took a certificate from an officer and gave it to one graduate after another with consistent rhythm and grace, without any signs of tiredness, boredom or drowsiness. After the ceremony and his return to the palace, he exercised as usual.

The king had said on a different occasion that during graduation ceremonies, he always observed all of the graduates' manners. Therefore, when a graduate paused or delayed stretching out his or her hand to receive the certificate, he would hold the certificate until the individual stretched out to take it. At first, I didn't know how he could do it but I later came to understand that he could maintain such concentration through meditation.

Normally, after the king finished handing the certificates, he gave a speech, reminding the new graduates of the responsibility awaiting them in the real world and that they should prepare themselves for it. His speeches usually reflected his personal circumspection and comprehensive knowledge.

As for his speech to the graduates of Chulalongkorn University on Thursday, 13 July, he said that graduates were usually regarded as possessing *satipanya*. *Sati* means awareness and *panya* means wisdom; *sati panya* usually means intelligence only. The king elaborated on the meaning of *sati* as excerpted here:

> . . . As for the word *'sati panya'*, when carefully considered, it comprises two parts, *'sati'* and *'panya'*. Each word has a meaning that varies according to the context in which it is used, for example, *'sati*

pattathan', 'sati sampachanya', 'sati winai, 'sati sompradi, 'sin sati', 'mot sati' and *'maidai sati'.*

The first three usages of the words are found in a religious context. *'Sati pattathan'* means 'recalling one's own condition'. *'Sati'* in *'sati sampachanya'* means 'awareness' since *'sampachanya'* means 'awareness at all moments'. *'Sati'* in *'sati winai'* means conscience. As for the last four words, *'sati'* is used in general terms. *'Sati'* in *'sati sompradi'* is a redundant word. *'Sati'* derives from Pali and *'sompradi'* is from Sanskrit, both meaning consciousness resulting from an awakening status. But in *'sin sati'*, *'sati'* means conscience, resulting from sanity. When it comes to *'sia sati'*, *'sati'* then means awareness that is not damaged by insanity. And when we say *'maidai sati'*, which is a modern vernacular, it encompasses a larger and distinctive meaning. I think all of you know it as an expression to suggest that you are not acting mindfully.

In conclusion, *'sati'* is a good thing in all contexts. No matter how it is used, if one lacks *'sati'*, there will be problems. I would like to advise those with good intention, who will work for the benefits of both themselves and the public, that when you are regarded as one who possesses *'sati'*, you should have *'sati'* in all its characteristics. This will result in desired success in its entirety.

The king gave another speech on the next day, Friday, 14 July, to graduates of Chulalongkorn University. Here is the part of the speech concerning the word *'panya'*:

'Panya' literally means general knowledge. If considered in context, it has several different meanings. One meaning is all knowledge learned from other sources or from one's reflection and training, which enhances one's skill. On the other hand, one's skill results from one's intelligence. An important point is that knowledge, when combined with intelligence, becomes talent—knowing things accurately, clearly, and thoroughly results in the ability to see through thought, conduct, theory, intention of others and situations encountered. When one has this ability to understand and see through, one will see ways and means to overcome obstacles, problems, degradation and failures, and to walk on the right path toward achievement and progress. . . .

On Saturday, 15 July, the third and last day of the graduation ceremony at Chulalongkorn University, the king gave another speech on resolutions, stating that besides *sati panya* one should also have a resolution or a sincere determination to fulfill one's responsibility and duties. The right way to establish one's determination is to apply *sati panya* to consider whether what one does is useful and right before committing one's determination to a course of action. If one doesn't see usefulness and righteousness, one should not take that course of action, because it will bring about immeasurable trouble and loss.

Some parts of three speeches presented here illustrate His Majesty's profound knowledge of the Thai language and Buddhism, and show his thoughtful preparation for each of the speeches. He carefully researched the subject matter, independently seeking out the appropriate information. He didn't just read what other people had prepared for him. Those who have had a chance to listen to any of his speeches should keep in mind the considerable effort that he puts in every speech and listen to it with mindfulness. A speech he gives can be a true blessing.

All security officers, whether soldiers, police officers, or civilians, share a curse: we cannot trust anyone and must be skeptical and vigilant at all times, especially when someone approaches those we are to protect, in this case the king, and during times of crisis.

I have talked about the bombing in the king's presence in Yala Province on 22 September 1977. That was the only time that we suspected ill will toward the king, but we have never been able to find any evidence to confirm our suspicion. Another group that security officers have to be careful about are those with mental illness.

On Saturday, 22 July 1978, around 9.30 a.m., I left home for Chitralada Palace for work. When I arrived at the Royal Aide-de-Camp Department, which doubled as the Office of Royal Court Police Officers, I was informed that a woman had been asking for a meeting with the queen and that she was waiting at Phra Kuwen Yufao Gate. The northern gate of Chitralada Palace was used as the entrance and exit point for royal staff and servants, and for other people who had business at the palace.

The woman also claimed that she had been commanded by Phra Phrom (a Brahman God) at Erawan Shrine to meet the queen. I hurried to see the woman. When I met her and she insisted on the command of the Brahman God to meet the queen, I had no choice but to ask a royal court security police officer on duty to take charge of her, to investigate her and to contact a police lieutenant on duty at Dusit Metropolitan Police Station. Meanwhile, I needed to inform the private secretary to the queen about the incident.

In a case like this, instead of an audience with a royal family member, the person would be sent to Srithanya Hospital for a medical examination and mental status check. If anyone in this situation were found to have mental health problems, they would be given treatment. But in many cases, the hospital allowed the patients to return home. Then, they would seek other opportunities to meet members of the royal family as they leave the palace grounds. The officers had the responsibility of remembering their faces and taking suitable preventive measures.

The Dusit Metropolitan Police Station has had regular experience with this kind of situation. In some cases, such individuals would successfully climb over the fence and get inside the palace. Once they were caught, the metropolitan police officers keeping surveillance outside the palace and the king's guards inside would be investigated and reprimanded.

All chief inspectors at the Dusit police station would be understandably frightened on receiving news of another mentally unstable person having entered Chitralada Palace. They could not be certain whether the incident would have an adverse affect on their position. However, what needs to be mentioned is that when such an event occurred and even after I no longer worked for the royal court, none of those who trespassed the palace were ever found to have harbored any ill intentions toward the king or queen. All had some mental problems in need of medical treatment.

On Saturday 18 August 1978, the king, the queen, Princess Maha Chakri Sirindhorn and Princess Chulabhorn moved residence to Thaksin Palace in Narathiwat.

46

The king and the royal family took a rest at Thaksin Palace for two days. In the evening of Monday, 21 August, they left the palace to visit villagers in Baan Thorn, Tambon Khok Khian, Muang district, Narathiwat. The royal doctors were also on the visit to provide medical assistance to the villagers.

On Friday, 25 August, at 3.20 p.m., the king drove his family to Tak Bai district in the same province. The destination was Nam Tha Pru Drainage Project, which was under the king's patronage, and Wat Phra Phut. Ambassadors of the United States, the Netherlands and Malaysia and a BBC reporter were also on the visit.

Foreign reporters from many countries have accompanied royal visits in the past. Each time, security and logistic officers had to inform the reporters about Thai culture and traditions. Before each visit, we had to clarify the rules with the reporters to avoid unnecessary confusion and misunderstanding. I was assigned on occasion to make the necessary explanations.

A common problem with reporters was that at the time of the explanations they would nod and say 'yes, yes' but when it came to the real situation they seemed to have forgotten about the advice or ignored it completely. The main problem was their attempts to approach the king too closely. Some just interviewed the king without asking for and receiving permission to do so.

Once, in a northeastern province, a reporter asked the king a question, which might be viewed as inappropriate by Thais: 'Do you think your visit and support to these people will decrease the number of the communists?' The king gave a prompt response: 'I don't know if it will reduce the number of the communists but I hope that I am making them less hungry.'

Some foreign reporters were young. Once, during a visit to Moo Baan Saen Kham Lue in Mae Hong Son province, as the king walked, a young female reporter about eighteen or nineteen years old followed him vigorously. But as the hike progressed on the slope leading to Moo Baan Saen Kham Lue, her speed gradually decreased. When the group reached the hilltop where Baan Saen Kham Lue was located, she could hardly move any longer. After she caught her breath and was able to speak again, she asked me: 'How old is your king? How can he keep up such a pace?'

The name of the BBC reporter on the Tak Bai visit was Brigitte Winter. A cameraman and a sound recording technician accompanied her. I have already forgot their names. I remember, however, that the two men who came along with her caused us a great deal of trouble. The cameraman always approached the king, the queen and the princesses too closely for filming. Worse, the sound recording technician stretched a long microphone very close to the king's face to record his voice. Understanding the news business, I sympathized with them, but still I couldn't allow them to carry on in such an inappropriate fashion. It didn't seem to occur to any of them that their conduct was dangerous as well as inappropriate; they were literally sticking the microphone in the king's face.

The first time this happened, I appealed to Ms. Winter but that approach didn't work, so I took a more direct one. Again, when I saw that the cameraman and sound recording technician had gotten too close to the king and stuck the microphone in his face again, I walked in front of the camera. They protested, making gestures and loudly whispering to me to move out of the way. But I didn't move and said in my accented English without caring whether or not my voice would be recorded: 'I don't give a damn! You are too close to His Majesty.' This tactic worked. The sound recording technician pulled back the microphone and the cameraman hurried to turn off his camera.

Brigitte and the BBC team had also been allowed to make a documentary film in the Grand Palace during several important ceremonies. The Royal Household Bureau facilitated their work and allowed them access to high scaffolding at nearly the same level as the royal throne. I don't know what other people think, but as a conservative man, I felt uneasy about it.

A foreign ambassador once said to me: 'There is probably only one king like yours in the entire world.'

During his stay at Thaksin Palace, the king attended graduation ceremonies and handed out certificates to graduates of several universities in the south, such as Prince of Songkla University and Srinakharinwirot University (Songkhla Campus) in Songkhla and Prince of Songkhla University (Pattani Campus).

The king returned to Bangkok on Friday, 9 October 1978.

Once back in Bangkok, the king handed out yet more certificates, this time to lawyers who had passed the bar examination set by the Law Training Office of the Lawyers Council of Thailand for 1977 and 1978. I didn't follow the king to the ceremony in Suan Amphorn that time, but when I later read his speech presented on that day, and I found that his message contained his views on Thailand's legal system and the role to be played by lawyers to ensure justice:

> Living with the law may make one feel too attached to the letter of the law and believe that the law alone will bring about total justice. The fact is, law is only a tool for determining right and wrong, and a principle applied in administering justice, not the sole element of justice. Therefore, we cannot depend solely on the law and the testimonies in court because the law and facts presented in the court can be distorted by misleading evidence, prejudice or ill intention, diminishing and destroying righteousness and true justice.
>
> Administering justice should therefore also depend on those applying the law as much as on the law itself. In performing duty that can either positively and negatively affect the lives of the people, it is critical that a lawyer must first be just through determination to maintain neutrality, objectivity and strictly preserving the spirit

of the law and, second, demonstrate a sense of honesty, ethics and conscience as though these were the lawyer's life. One must perform one's duty with circumspection, equanimity and clear wisdom. Then one will have an accurate, just and fair consideration and can become a genuine refuge for people who live under the law of the land.

❖

On Monday, 6 November, there was a special royal ceremony—the ceremony for the ordination of the crown prince.

At 1.30 p.m., the king, the queen, the prince and Princess Sirindhorn entered the Grand Palace. Arriving in Paisan Taksin Hall, the king and the crown prince lit candles and incense sticks to worship Phra Siam Devathirat before entering Phrathat Monthian Hall. They lit candles and incense sticks to worship relics of their ancestors. Afterwards, the family rode the royal limousine to Wat Phra Kaew or the Emerald Buddha Temple.

They walked up the stairs to a pavilion behind the *ubosot*. The prince went behind a screen in the pavilion. The king and queen entered the *ubosot* and lit candles and incense sticks to pay homage to the Emerald Buddha, Phra Sambuddha Phanni, King Rama I and King Rama III. Their Majesties then left the *ubosot* through the back exit and went behind the curtain to cut the prince's hair.

Once the prince's head had been shaved, he emerged from behind the screen in an ordination costume and came to pay respect to his father, offering the king flowers, candles and incense sticks. In return, the king anointed the prince with holy water from a conch. Next, the king escorted the prince along the balcony filled with candles to enter the *ubosot* from the front. The king guided the prince to the offerings. The prince offered flowers and golden candles inscribed with holy writings to pay homage to the Emerald Buddha. The prince then lit candles and incense sticks to pay homage to the Triple Gem and prostrated to the king. Finally, the prince received a set of monk's robes.

Next, the prince joined a group of monks, presided over by Phra Ariyawongsakotayan, the supreme patriarch. The prince made offerings and asked for ordination to become a novice. The supreme patriarch paid homage to the Triple Gem, gave the prince an instruction, and then helped dress the prince in a white robe. The prince went behind the screen and, with the king's assistance, changed into a monk's robe.

247

Wearing a monk's robe, the prince made offerings to the supreme patriarch. He was instructed about the Triple Gem and the Ten Precepts (Sila) for the ordination to become a novice. After this final act completing the prince's ordination, he received an alms bowl from the king.

The prince then proceeded to request a place of residence and ordination as a monk from the supreme patriarch. The monks in attendance performed the ordination ceremony. The supreme patriarch acted as the senior monk, asking about the qualifications of the prince to become a monk. Somdej Phra Thirayanmuni gave the instructions during this questioning. Next, the prince offered monk's robes and bags to the supreme patriarch and to the monks in attendance, and returned to his seat among the monks.

What followed was His Majesty the King offering of necessities to the newly ordained prince. Then, the Princess Mother, the queen, HRH Princess Galyani Vadhana, Princess Maha Chakri Sirindhorn and ML Bua Kittiyakara, mother of the queen, offered a set of robes, books, candles, flowers and incense sticks to the new monk.

After the offerings by the royal family members, Ajarn Sanya Dharmasakti, Privy Council president, made a similar offering on behalf the Privy Council, followed by Gen. Kriangsak Chamanan, the prime minister, on behalf of the cabinet, civil servants and the public, Air Chief Marshal Harin Hongsakul, president of the National Legislature, on behalf of members of parliament, and Mr. Prapot Thirawat, Chief Supreme Court Justice, on behalf of the judicial committee. A special guest on that occasion, Deng Xiaoping, deputy prime minister of China, was given the honor as a guest of the government to make an offering to the prince. The monks then gave thanks to the people for their offerings and the Adirek blessing to the king. The king, the queen and Princess Sirindhorn left the *ubosot* of the Emerald Buddha Temple and took a car to Phra Bhuddarattanasathan at the Grand Palace.

At the Grand Palace, the newly ordained prince performed a ceremony according to royal tradition at the *ubosot* of Phra Buddha Rattanasathan. After the ceremony, Their Majesties and Princess Sirindhorn returned to their car and continued on to Wat Boworniwet. The prince rode in a car with the supreme patriarch. When they arrived, the king lit candles and incense to worship Phra Buddha Chinasi and paid homage to Phra Sirirarangkhan of King Mongkut. When the prince arrived, he entered the *ubosot* and monks chanted stanzas for the blessing. The new monk lit candles and incense to Phra Buddha Chinasi and left the *ubosot* to Panya Court, where he would reside during the period of his monkhood. The royal family then left Wat Boworniwet for the palace.

Two days later, Wednesday, 8 November, a group of royal aides and court police officers visited the new monk at his monastery. The visit was a simple affair in light of his status as a monk. The chief aide-de-camp general offered candles and incense sticks to the monk and then we paid respect to him. The prince was solemn and composed and said only a few words. I don't know how others felt, but having known the prince since his childhood, I could not help but feel delighted seeing him in a monk's robe.

47

After a month at Chitralada Palace, His Majesty moved his residence again. On Friday, 10 November 1978, the king and queen moved to Bhuban Palace in Sakon Nakhon.

Soon after I started serving as a royal court security police officer to the king, I realized that royal court security work, whether in the capacity of court security police officer, royal aide, or royal attendant and staff, required a lot of travel. For most people, it meant frequent separation from family. In my case, I was lucky because Her Majesty the Queen had allowed my wife to accompany her and help with her private affairs, even during royal visits upcountry. This allowed me to see my wife more often than otherwise would be possible, although we would have to live in separate quarters; she with the other female staff and I with other security officers in the Royal Aide-de-Camp Department accommodation.

As for my two children, my son studied at Chiang Mai University and his younger sister was old enough to take care of herself at home. We therefore had no serious worries about our children.

I had been a field officer in Sakon Nakhon for a number of years and was familiar with the province, its topography and people. For this reason, I was well aware of the severity of the situation in the province and the extent to which we could not take lightly the safety of the king.

The authorities and we officers always kept the king informed about the situation, especially when there was cause for concern. However, it was clear that the king gave priority, not to the seriousness of the situation or his own safety, but to the well-being of his people and his duty to them. The king always put the people who needed help first. He and his queen would go to any place where people were facing hardships. Their Majesties believed that they could help to alleviate the people's suffering. They would make every effort to see the people even in the face of serious security concerns.

Fortunately, there had never been any serious incidents during countless royal visits in the northeastern region, except for a few minor accidents that might have happened anywhere.

On Wednesday, 22 November, I visited Wat Chetiyaram, known locally as Wat Phu Thok (the name comes from the mountain where the temple is located). The abbot of the temple was Phra Ajarn Juan Kulachettho. I had heard of his reputation as a rigorous ascetic monk.

Phu Thok was in Nong Khai's Bueng Kan district not far from the Mekong River. It was a mountain with strange shape, looking like an immense rock plunged into the ground. Instead of gradual slopes toward the ground like other mountains, high cliffs on all sides surrounded it. Going up and down the mountain must have been very difficult before Phra Ajarn Juan constructed a circular bridge around the cliffs to the mountaintop where the temple stands.

The bridge was made of wood—two parallel wooden boards with bamboo bars to hold on to. I imagined that it was built with a solid structural design of engineering, but it did not seem too stable. Apart from the circular bridge, the abbot also had a very steep staircase from the bottom of the mountain leading directly to the temple. One needed a great deal of energy to climb those stairs. There was even a notice, informing potential climbers that those who were not up the challenge should use the circular bridge instead.

I felt I was not up to the challenge, so I chose the circular bridge. Yet I quickly discovered that I had made the wrong decision. Although the bridge was not steep, it skirted the high and steep cliffs. Furthermore, some parts of the bridge were as unstable as they appeared. Before the climb up the bridge, someone had played a psychological game, telling the story of a nun who had fallen from the bridge but did not die.

I had been a parachutist. But at Phu Thok, you had to walk without a parachute or any other safety accessory. I admitted that I made my way on the bridge with a heightened sense of insecurity. I mustered effort and concentration and focused only on the pacing—step up, put foot down, step up, put foot down—one step at a time, without thinking about the bridge or the ground below. After some time, all became silent. I turned around and looked back; there were my companions coming behind me, crawling on all fours, trying not to look down the steep mountain.

After we arrived at the top, Ajarn Juan was not in. He had already gone outside the monastery. The serenity of the place was exceptional. I decided, after the adventure of the bridge, that I might as well spend the time enjoying the serene quietness. I sat in meditation there for about half an hour, which was the most peaceful I had experienced. It was worth risking my life up there. On our way down the mountain, we chose to use the stairs.

On Sunday, 26 November 1978, at about 3 p.m., the king drove the queen and the two princesses to Huay Hin Laad Reservoir in Baan Na Nai, Tambon Na Nai. I didn't much care for the route we took that day because it passed Baan Nong Sanai, Tambon Na Mong, Baan Phak Kham Phu and Baan Un Dong, Tambon Na Nai, Phanna Nikhom districts, where communist insurgency was aggressive. This was also the case at Baan Na Nai and Baan Nong Phue—the village where the monastery of Phra Ajarn Man Phurithatto, a renowned monk in Vipassanadhura, was located.

The royal family arrived in Huay Hin Laad at about 4.20 p.m. The king and Princess Maha Chakri Sirindhorn first visited with the waiting crowd of villagers and then went to see the reservoir. The queen and Princess Chulabhorn went to visit a temple in Baan Nong Phue.

At the Huay Hin Laad Reservoir, Royal Irrigation Department officials who were planning to build a dike for the reservoir reported to the king on the progress of the construction. The dike would be built to store water to ensure an adequate water supply for two villages, Baan Na Nai and Baan Nong Phue, covering an agriculture area of about 1,000 *rai*.

Two officials from the Royal Irrigation Department who had an audience with the king that day were Khun Lek Chinda-Sanguan and Khun Rungruang Chulachat, both of whom later became director-general of the department, one at a time, of course. Khun Rungruang was the chief mechanic for the Nam Un Dam Project and had known me well since the time I worked in Sakon Nakhon.

At Wat Phurithatthirawat in Baan Nong Phue, the queen and the youngest princess met with the villagers and monks. They stayed at the wat until later that evening and joined the king and Princess Sirindhorn at the entrance of Baan Nong Phue. The family got back to Bhuban Palace after 7 p.m.

Another sacred place the king visited was Wat Phrathat Bang Phuan in Nong Khai's Muang district. Prathat Bang Phuan was an ancient sacred *chedi* (stupa or pagoda) believed to contain a relic of the Lord Buddha, which his disciple had taken from Rajakur. Khun Term Wiphakpojanakit wrote in his *History of Isan* that the name Bang Phuan was derived from the word 'Bang Khon'. Isan people called the pagoda Khi Phon, meaning intestine.

This stupa was restored many times. The original one was Indian made from laterite, believed to be from the same era as Phra Pathom Chedi in Nakhon Pathom. In his book, Khun Term also noted that in 1970 that the new top of Bang Phuan Stupa inclined by forty degrees, and predicted that it was likely to fall down. It did fall, and was restored. The ceremony of lifting its top tiered umbrella was held on Tuesday, 28 November 1978—by the king.

The king went to perform the ceremony at the restored stupa with the queen and the princesses. He also gave banners to eighty-five groups of local village scouts.

❖

During the royal stay at Bhuban Palace, whenever possible, I took the opportunity to visit villagers I had worked with in Sakon Nakhon and Nakhon Phanom. These were members of People's Assistance Teams that I had trained during 1967 and 1968. Many had since become members of various agencies established by different governments, such as the Territory Protection Volunteers Division.

I had a bond with these villagers. One of my concerns was that, as they got older or the political situation changed, they would no longer be able to use the weapons or would be relieved of their duties. The problem was that, unlike official civil servants, there were no pensions for these volunteers. How would they make a living?

Other than my job, I had no other occupational skills. I tried to use common sense and advised them to prepare themselves for the future by finding work based on their existing skills. I had seen the king's work helping poor villagers develop their livelihood. I therefore began telling my former students about the king's idea of cooperatives. Instead of working individually, they could work together to increase the scale of the local economy by collectively increasing production, producing products according to market demands, and thereby increasing their bargaining power.

A village that took my advice was Baan Khok, Tambon Rai, Sakon Nakhon's Phanna Nikhom district. The village's business seemed to be progressing. My former students in the village grew mint. Mint leaves can be distilled for oil and extracted for menthol used in cigarette, toothpaste, perfume and the like. The seedling plants were provided by Khun Kamon Khusakul's farm in Nakhon Phanom.

At the beginning, the villagers only grew mint for fresh supply to deliver to Khun Kamon's factory in Nakhon Phanom. However, when Khun Kamon saw that the villagers were committed, he set up a distillation factory in the village. At that time, mint oil cost as much as 400 baht per kilo, so Khun Kamon helped the villagers earn a very handsome income for a time.

On Thursday, 30 November 1978, I visited the distillation factory at Baan Khok and was happy to see firsthand that their business was going well. Unfortunately, they later ran into problems. A few middlemen in the country controlled the market and kept the price so low that the villagers had to stop production although mint oil was still in great demand in the world market.

Today, if you visit Baan Khok and see pots of mint at some houses, know that the mint originally came from Khun Kamon's farm.

❖

A few days later, the king returned to Bangkok temporarily for his birthday celebration, which started on Sunday, 3 December. The celebration began with the oath-taking ceremony and a parade of the king's guards at the Royal Plaza around the equestrian statue of King Rama V. That year, Crown Prince Vajiralongkorn joined the celebration as deputy commander of the King's Guard Regiment.

On Tuesday, 5 December at 10.45 p.m., the king attended the grand meeting at the Amarindra Vinitchai Audience Hall as was the custom. At 4.35 p.m. the king, the queen, the prince and the princesses were at the Grand Palace. They paid homage to the Emerald Buddha and proceeded to Paisan Taksin Hall and Amarindra Vinitchai Audience Hall, respectively. The king presented a set of commissions and royal decorations to high dignitary monks and decorations and sashes to government officials.

As the king was walking to Paisan Taksin Hall, something happened that usually happened only during royal visits on the countryside. I never thought I would see the scene in Bangkok. Many people had lined up on both sides of the path along which the king walked. Many of them offered donations of five or ten baht each to the king's charity. The king stopped to accept all the donations, causing a significant delay in the schedule.

48

Thais of all ages, genders and occupations would like to have an audience with the king and the queen and be in their presence for as long as possible. One way to have that opportunity is to present something to them. Normally, security officers try to gather the articles that people wish to present at one point along the route the king and queen will follow. This enables the officers to inspect the articles and makes it more convenient for the king and queen to accept all the articles at once, rather than one at a time.

However, there were always some people who wanted to do things their own way and to give money to the king and queen outside the designated point. These people would open their wallets, take out the money, and stretch out their hand with various banknotes to the king and the queen at the moment they passed. When others saw this, they did the same in a chain reaction. The king and other royal family members would stop and be delayed for their next destination.

There is no doubt that the most anxious people when this happened were the security officers, especially when it was getting dark. It was a difficult situation to deal with. The king and the queen never showed any annoyance but always smiled and walked slowly to receive money from those offering it. Many people also took the chance to touch Their Majesties' hands. Such small impromptu donations often caused the royal visits to be delayed and the king and queen to return from their visits late into the night.

On virtually every visit, the officers tried to deal with the problem by making an announcement prior to the royal arrival. The people were always asked to place their presents to the king and queen at the designated place. If people wanted to make a donation (usually as contributions to funds for local affairs or to royal charities), the officers usually provided a big bowl to receive donation money and asked the villagers to choose a representative who would then offer the bowl to the king (or other family members). Still, there would be at least one person who violated the rule and gave a donation personally, which soon caused other people to follow suit. This shows the lack of discipline among Thai people, even though their action is done with loyalty to the king.

There was another important event in December 1978. Air Chief Marshal Harin Hongsakul, president of the National Legislature, requested the king to sign a new constitution to replace the one that had been in place since the coup d'etat in 1977.

The king remained in Bangkok until Saturday, 30 December, when he moved to Bhubing Palace. I had left Bangkok by car a day earlier, stayed overnight in Phitsanulok, and arrived in Chiang Mai at 4.40 p.m. the next day—just in time to receive the king and the royal family that evening.

On Sunday, 31 December, the royal family hosted a New Year's Eve party at Bhubing Palace. His Majesty played the music and gave prizes to those who answered his questions. Music continued until 4.30 a.m. on New Year's Day.

The king's visits to the local communities resumed quickly after the New Year celebration. To plan royal visits in the north, security officers and officers with relevant responsibilities usually held meetings with MC Bhisatej Rajani , who directed many royal development projects for hill tribe people and had extensive knowledge and experience of the topography and the local population.

The meetings with MC Bhisatej usually involved a lot of debate, sometimes heated, and negotiation between what and who the king and queen should see and the safety concerns. MC Bhisatej was not a person who went by convention and strict rules, whereas the security and court officials were by nature of their work wished to follow the rules. This difference sometimes led to disagreements. However, the disagreements or conflicts, though sometimes strong, were always resolved in the end. If there were any disagreement that could not be resolved, the parties

would inform His Majesty of the facts and arguments and counterargu-
ments involved. Once the king had made the verdict, there would be
no more discussion. All deemed the king's verdict final.

For example, there was a development project in Huay Thung Lao,
Tambon Samoeng Tai, Samoeng district, Chiang Mai. The officers
and MC Bhisatej conducted a survey of the place before the king's visit
as usual. A disagreement arose between MC Bhisatej and the security
officers when he proposed that the project's name should be changed to
Huay Thung Rao, because it sounded more appealing and meaningful.
Rao means we or us, and as part of the name Thung Rao, it means
our fields. The other officers and I disagreed. We felt that the existing
name of the village reflected its history or characteristics. *Lao* is a kind
of flower in off-white color, growing widely in the area, and therefore
the local people called their village Thung Lao, the fields of Lao flowers.
We felt that to change the name of the village would be taking away
the history of the place.

Someone must have brought up the dispute with the king. When
the king visited the village, MC Bhisatej still referred to the village
with the king with his preferred choice, Thung, but the king made no
comment on the matter. Later, the village was referred to as Thung Lao
in a royal news item, which was prepared by the Office of the King's
Private Secretary. The matter was resolved.

Another name issue arose in connection with a royal project in
Tambon Ban Pong, Chiang Mai's Hang Dong district. The name of the
project was Thung Loeng. The king visited the project on Thursday,
18 January. MC Bhisatej wanted to change the name to Thung Roeng
(*roeng* means happy). He thought that the new name would give it a
more positive meaning. Again, security officers and myself disagreed.
The word '*loeng*' in northern and northeastern Thai dialects means vast
plains.

In this case, however, I did not followed up to see whether the name
of the second project had been changed to Thung Roeng. Given that
things like names can be arbitrarily changed, one never knows.

The king made his first royal visit in 1979 on Tuesday, 9 January, to
the Cereal Breeding Station under the Royal Development Project for

Northern Thailand in Chiang Mai's Samoeng district. But after that visit, he had to temporarily return to Bangkok.

On Wednesday, 10 January, His Majesty performed the ceremony of fixing pins and offering the Royal Thai Military Flags. I have never known that the king had to do this himself. That day, at 2.30 p.m., the king went to Chitralada Palace to perform the ceremony in the *ubosot* of the Emerald Buddha Temple. The officers stretched the flags in a row and then the king fixed pins on each flag himself. After that, he went to his seat, which was temporarily built for royal functions concerning soldiers, boy scouts and other special occasions. This royal seat, placed in front of Sahathai Samakhom Pavilion, was in a rectangular shape with a roof of cloth and silk strings from it. The king presented the flags to seventeen units of the Royal Thai Army and seven units of the Royal Thai Air Force.

I should also mention that the Royal Thai Military Flags are special not only because the king fixed pins to the flags, but also because the king's hair was on the top of each of them. For this reason the flags are usually not lowered to show respect to anyone but the king. The flags are brought down only in his presence, such as when the king inspects a row of honor guards.

Apart from the army, the only non-military agency that is offered this special flag is the Police Cadet Academy.

On Thursday morning, 11 January, a royal ceremony was held to celebrate the first month and the cradle for HRH Princess Bajra Kitiyabha at Amphorn Palace. At 4.30 p.m., the king, the queen, Princess Sirindhorn, HRH Soamsavali and Princess Bajra Kitiyabha boarded the royal plane at the Royal Air Force Headquarters to return to Bhubing Palace.

On Friday, 9 February 1979, at 10.30 a.m., Their Majesties, Princess Maha Chakri Sirindhorn and Princess Chulabhorn flew to Chiang Rai to visit two hill tribe development and welfare centers, one in Baan Sa Ngo, Tambon Pa Sak, Chiang Saen district, and the other in Baan Pang Sa, Tambon Pa Tueng, Mae Chan district. They would also visit the Mae Salong Basin Development Project.

Again, there was a mechanical problem with the C-123 that would fly the security officers to Chiang Rai, causing a delay. The plane finally arrived to pick us up and we arrived in Chiang Rai at 11.37 a.m. and hurried off to board the police helicopter to Baan Sa Ngo. The royal plane, an AFRO, was landing just as we left the Chiang Rai Airport.

The last visit that day was to Baan Pang Sa. Apart from seeing vegetable plots at the Hill Tribe Development and Welfare Center, the king needed to mediate a village land dispute.

After the mediation, the king rejoined the queen and the princess. Villagers of several ethnic groups—Lisu, Haw, Lahu, Yao (Mien) and Akha—were waiting to have an audience with them.

I can't remember which group did the calling of the spirit ceremony for the royal family. The ceremony was not on the agenda and took such a long time that we started to get worried. It was nearly at 6 p.m. We didn't want the royal family to fly back on the helicopter in the dark. That day, we much appreciated MC Bhisatej's ability to break with the rules and conventions. He intervened, cut short the ceremony and asked the king and the royal family to leave.

The king left Baan Pang Sa at 6.30 p.m. On the way back to Chiang Rai Airport, there was a rainstorm with hail. We were deeply worried about the safety of the king and the royal family. The helicopters landed safely at Chiang Rai Airport despite the rain and hailstones. The royal family stayed inside the helicopter until the storm passed.

At 7.30 p.m., the royal plane was able to fly out of Chiang Rai Airport. The security officers and staff then proceeded to board our plane, the same C-123 that had taken us from Chiang Mai that morning. Yet again there was a problem. The right engine choked. The mechanics tried to fix it but quickly informed us that their attempt was unsuccessful. We then hired a bus and left Chiang Rai at 9 p.m. The bus trip took three hours to Chiang Mai.

Fortunately, the engine had not choked while we were in flight that morning.

49

When I first began serving as a royal court security police officer, I felt that the job was quite heavy because there were so few court police officers. But as more police officers joined the team, I felt that the job became less burdensome.

One thing that had made my job easier was that the Royal Thai Police Department gave me a free hand in choosing police officers to work in royal court security. The court police security team with me as the head therefore had a good working relationship and few problems. I imagined that if I had not been given an authority to select my colleagues, I am not sure that my responsibilities would have run as smoothly as they did.

Before April 1979, the Chinese Embassy in Bangkok extended the Chinese government's invitation to me to visit China. I considered the invitation with interest for two reasons. First, in the past, my work placed me in an adversarial position with Chinese government due to my extensive involvement in the investigation and retaliation against communist insurgents in Thailand. It was well-known that the Chinese government had supported the insurgents. Inviting me was like inviting an ex-enemy. I sincerely wished to accept the invitation but I wanted to know how I would be welcomed.

Another reason to seriously consider the invitation was that at that time Thai-Sino relations were being established. MR Kukrit Pramoj had initiated the reappraisal of the bilateral relations during his term as prime minister. MR Kukrit had led a Thai delegation to visit China earlier and there were now more delegations at different levels visiting China frequently. China also sent delegations to visit Thailand.

Despite these new ties, communist insurgency in Thailand had not abated. Police, soldiers and civilians continued to be killed and injured in fighting the insurgents. The king and queen still had to sponsor and attend the funerals of hundreds of people every year.

I didn't have a chance to consult with anyone. I had thought, however, that when government policies changed and we had resumed friendship with China, considering the friendly exchanges by other government agencies, that Thai police should also have such exchanges. It might help minimize the insurgency in our country. But then I realized that my refusing or accepting the invitation might have extensive or profound repercussion. I was not an ordinary police officer but the chief of the Royal Court Police, directly serving the king.

After that realization, I informed the Chinese Embassy that I would very much like to visit China. However, I was a police officer under the Director-General of Royal Thai Police Department and it would be more appropriate for them to invite the Director-General (who was Pol. Gen. Monchai Phankhongchuen) to head the delegation from the Royal Thai Police Department. And I would be pleased to be part of such a delegation. The Chinese government agreed with my suggestion.

Their Majesties and Princess Maha Chakri Sirindhorn moved to Klai Kangwol Palace on Saturday, 12 May 1979. They left Chitralada Palace by car at 6.10 p.m. I had arrived at Hua Hin at 12.40 a.m. and Their Majesties and the princess at Sala Roeng in Klai Kangwol Palace at 8.30 p.m. I had an audience with the king to say goodbye before my trip to China. At 10 p.m. I said goodbye to the queen.

One week later, on Saturday, 19 May, at 10.45 p.m., I joined a delegation of senior police officers on a flight from Bangkok to Hong Kong. The delegation stayed overnight in Hong Kong and took a train from Kowloon to China the following afternoon. Our visit to China began with a visit to Guangzhou in Guangdong province.

I do not go into the details of the China trip, because they are not so relevant to my duties to the king. The visit featured a study tour of the work activities of the Chinese police, which operated within the Internal Security Ministry. In addition to the study tour, the Chinese government also took our delegation to visit important Buddhist historical sites and ancient monuments. I suspect that they knew of Director-General Monchai's interest in archeology and my interest in Buddhism.

The most important temple visit (for me) was a visit to Xin Xiao Chu Temple on Friday, 25 May. That day was a Buddhist holy day, the fifteenth day of the waning moon of the sixth lunar month. The temple, built in 669 AD, was situated near Xian, an ancient Chinese city.

The stupa at the temple contained the mummy of a Chinese monk called Hian Chang, whom Thai people know well as Thang Sam Chang. After we gave a model of Phra Buddha Chinnarat to the abbot, we paid respects to the Buddha image in the main temple hall and made a donation to the temple. Director-General Monchai then took us for a walk clockwise three times around the stupa for auspiciousness. If I hadn't been a royal court police officer, I would never have had the opportunity to pay respects at Buddhist temples in a communist country.

On Thursday, 31 May, we took a train from Guangzhou back to Hong Kong and observed the work of Hong Kong police as well. The Thai police delegation returned to Thailand on Saturday, 2 June.

Friday, 16 June of that year was an important day for the police. The Royal Thai Police Department was given an opportunity to host a Chinese dinner for the king at Klai Kangwol Palace.

Director-General Monchai and his party came to Sala Roeng in the palace. At 8 p.m., the king, the queen and the two princesses arrived. Five senior officers, including the director-general and myself joined the king's table.

The dinner consisted of cold hors-d'oeuvres, shark fin soup, barbecued suckling pig, crab claws roasted with salt, chicken steamed with chestnuts, Chinese mushrooms steamed with dried fish maw, steamed dollarfish, stir-fried Chinese broccoli with sun-dried salted fish, followed by hot ground cashew nuts and fried buns and fruits.

During dinner there were forty songs, including the royal anthem, and three comedy shows performed by the Royal Thai Police Department and Department of Fine Arts. The king, queen and princesses watched the performances until 0.20 a.m. and turned in.

After the China trip in May, I didn't expect to travel overseas again. However, in August, I requested personal leave to see my father, who was seriously ill in the United States. My father had lived with my younger sister in Honolulu, Hawaii, for ten years. A strong and an athletic person, he played billiard, golf, tennis and football in his younger days. However, his asthma was getting worse as he got older and the discomfort and pain was becoming less tolerable for him. In August my sister called and said that his condition was very worrying and that he had expressed his wish to die in Thailand.

My parents had given me the gift of life and I felt that it was my responsibility to give them whatever they wanted. When my father was seriously ill and wanted to see me, I had to go and see him in Hawaii, probably on his deathbed.

On Tuesday, 7 August, I accompanied the king in his jogging exercise around Dusidalai Hall after 7 p.m. I told the king about my father's situation and asked for personal leave. Princess Sirindhorn joined later, and I jogged with them until 8.20 p.m.

Two days later, at 1.44 p.m., I flew to Honolulu. I prepared a small Buddha image in case there would be a funeral. Yet, as soon as my father saw me, his condition quickly, almost miraculously, improved. The doctors were amazed at his recovery. He didn't need a respirator anymore. After his quick recovery, I felt that I could leave. I returned home on Thursday, 16 August. My father still insisted that he wanted to die in Thailand.

The majority of people in Narathiwat were Muslim. There were more mosques than temples in the province. However, this did not stop me and my close colleagues, Phi Thep and Phi Teanchai, from finding our ways to make food offerings to Buddhist monks in the mornings during the royal stay at Thaksin Palace. Because there were not many monks, we had to go to a temple to make the offering. Wat Lamphu was one temple we regularly visited and got to know the monks and lay people there.

Our activities did not go unnoticed by Princess Sirindhorn. Finally, she told us that she would like to go with us to the temple. On Friday, 14 September 1979, at 6.50 a.m., I had the honor of driving a van taking the princess and my colleagues to Wat Lamphu. The visit was really a personal visit. There was no escort motorcade as in official visits. There were only a few royal attendants of the princess in the company.

At the temple, Princess Sirindhorn made food and other offerings for the monks and went to see a sermon hall inside a monastery that was under construction. She visited monks at the Vipassana School at the temple. Phra Ajarn Daeng Yasotharo was among the monks at the mediation school.

She stayed at the temple until 8.45 a.m. There were not many people at the temple that morning. Most who were there were laymen and lay-women who came to the temple on Buddhist holy days. A few villagers who had heard about the visit hurried to see the princess. The faces of those who met the princess that day showed great delight and joy at meeting her. It was hard to forget the happiness shown on their faces. I believe that the villagers, as well as the princess, probably did not forget that chance meeting either.

That same year, I was again reminded of my own mortality. I was accompanying the king on his regular evening round of jogging in Klai Kangwol Palace on Tuesday, 16 October. It was the first time that I could not keep up with the king and had to stop at intervals. My legs tired and my energy seemed to have dissipated. The next day I experienced the same problem. My legs had given out. After that, I stopped accompanying the king but continued to jog on my own. The pain was lessened but not entirely.

On Monday morning, 22 October, I went to see Dr. Thamrongrat Kaewkan, presently a lieutenant general, at Phramongkutklao Hospital. He x-rayed my spine and prescribed physical therapy.

On Tuesday, 11 December, I was strong enough to resume jogging with the king. The king came down at 7 p.m. and had a talk with me until 7.50 p.m. Princess Sirindhorn joined us. The king jogged with his daughter for seven rounds and I was able to keep up with them.

50

The king and queen spent most of their time outside of Bangkok in 1979. Usually around the time of the queen's birthday in August, the queen stayed at Thaksin Palace. But in 1979, she resided in Bangkok and made merit on her birthday (12 August) there.

As for the king, he did not stay for his birthday celebration in Bangkok. There were always many ceremonies for the king to attend in Bangkok on that occasion. On Tuesday, 4 December 1979, the king and the royal family left for Bang Pa-In Palace in Ayutthaya. When I joined them the next morning, 5 December, at around 11.30 a.m., the entire royal family—including the king, the queen, the prince, the princesses and the prince's wife and baby—were having a family celebration. The monks were having their late morning meal offered by the family.

While the monks were having their meal, the king and queen were paying respect to the ancestors at Waraphatphiman Hall. A Brahman priest read eulogies to former Thai kings. After the monks finished their meal, the king lit a candle to read religious texts. Next, the supreme patriarch gave a sermon. After the sermon, the monks sat in meditation in dedication to the king for about forty minutes. The king, the royal family, and other attendants joined the meditation.

Usually when monks gave sermons during the royal visit, I took the opportunity to mediate. I felt that sitting in meditation in the presence of the king, either at the palace or temples, calmed my mind better than in other places. Also, I usually had a vision in the form of beautiful luminous lights. It was another good meditation experience at Bang Pa-In Palace that day. I supposed that my concentration was especially good because all the others were calm in action, speech and mind and the ambiance was pure. Time passed incredibly quickly. After the meditation, the king offered the monks necessities. The monks gave thanks and blessings to the king.

A special program was organized to celebrate the king's birthday in the afternoon—a boat race between the Ayutthaya and Ang Thong teams. The king and his family went to watch. There were also a boat procession and traditional performances. The king gave prizes and souvenirs to the competitors. Afterwards, the king and the family went to see handicraft demonstrations by the villagers who had benefited from a vocational training program initiated by the queen.

Later that evening, the king gave his birthday audience to groups of people at the Bang Pa-In courtyard. The cabinet, members of parliament, government officials, judges, diplomatic corps and civil servants came to give him birthday wishes and to join a party. I didn't join the party because I had to prepare myself for a talk. I was to give a talk in English entitled 'The King Upcountry' the next day at Grand Hyatt Erawan Hotel in Bangkok before the members of the Bangkok Rotary Club.

Giving talks about the king was becoming a frequent extracurricular activity for me and continued even after my court police duties had ended. In fact, I was not very comfortable talking about the king after I had left court police work. I told those who invited me that my materials were no longer up to date and they should invite others who are still working for him as they would have more current information. Yet, there still seems to be demand for stories about the king in the old days.

On Monday morning, 10 December, I joined a team of security officers on a logistical preparation survey for the king's visit to Khon Kaen University. We had a meeting with relevant parties around lunchtime. After lunch, I took time off to visit Wat Sri Nuan, an important local temple.

My ties with Wat Sri Nuan go back to my childhood when my parents were teachers in Khon Kaen. At that time, the public health services were still poor. There was probably only one doctor with a medical degree in the entire province. Many people therefore relied on traditional medicine and doctors.

One famous traditional doctor was Luang Phor Phang Phakkho. Luang Phor Phang always had all kinds of herbs in his bag. Before he treated people, he would always ask for a bowl of water. Then he would grind up the herb on a small, thin stone and dip the stone in the bowl. This was the monk who was my 'personal doctor'. I drank the herbal water from his bowl or had my head sprayed with it. Considering that I survived my childhood, whenever I was in Khon Kaen I always made an effort to visit the temple and make merit for the late Luang Phor Phang.

Bhuban Palace in Sakon Nakhon is in the upper part of the northeastern region. The distance from the palace to provinces in lower northeast, such as Surin, Buriram and Si Sa Ket, was as far as from Bangkok. Therefore, the people in the lower Isan had fewer chances to see the king and queen than those in the upper Isan. However, they got to see one royal family member more often. The Princess Mother spent a lot of time in the lower Isan.

December 1979 was different. The royal family went for a brief stay at the Saneng Irrigation Project in Surin's Muang district. The purpose was to visit the Princess Mother who was staying at her residence in Surin.

The royal family arrived at Surin Airport at about 2 p.m. on Monday, 17 December, on the C-123. Upon their arrival, the king observed guard of honor and spent about half an hour visiting with the people waiting for him, and then left for Huay Saneng Reservoir Project.

After two hours at the reservoir, at 4.45 p.m., the king and Princess Maha Chakri Sirindhorn went to visit villagers at Wat Phanom Silaram in Baan Phanom, Tambon Na Bua in Surin's Muang district.

The king always made a point of having information about the place he would visit. At Wat Phanom Silaram, apart from talking with monks and villagers of Baan Phanom and Baan Krathom, he had a discussion with the Royal Irrigation Department officials, suggesting that they consider developing Nong Phanom, a natural swamp, into a permanent reservoir because during the summer, the water dried up in the swamp. Developing it into a reservoir would allow Baan Phanom and nearby villages to have a source of water supply for consumption and agricultural activities throughout the year.

In addition, His Majesty the King asked the officials to consider a feasibility study to build a small-scale reservoir in an area around Phanom Sawai Mountain. The aim was to reclaim a deteriorated forest area around the mountain covering as many as 3,000 *rai*, and possibly to create an agricultural park.

In the late morning of the following day, the king and Princess Sirindhorn went together again to visit villagers in Baan Kut Yai, Tambon Nong Teng and Baan Ka Nang, Tambon Ban Prue in Buriram's Krasang. In Baan Kut Yai, the villagers were waiting at the bank of Nong Kut Yai. The king had wanted to see the swamp and another one nearby called Nong Kut Khuang. The two swamps had the same problems as the one in the village in Surin; they were dry during the summer months. The king again advised the Royal Irrigation Department to develop the swamps into a permanent reservoir.

After that, the king and the princess went on to Baan Kanang. They visited with the villagers as usual, and the king talked with monks at Wat Indra Burapha before moving on to see Nong Kanang. The Royal Irrigation Department was advised to construct another reservoir in Chi Noi Basin to store water for an agricultural area of 6,000 *rai*, covering a number of villages in Krasang district. Part of the water could also be diverted to Nong Prue, Nong Kut Yai and Nong Kut Khuang to ensure adequate water supply in the summer months.

On the same day, at 12.50 p.m., the queen, the prince, Princess Chulabhorn and Princess Soamsavali visited Baan Khok Rahoei, Tambon Prasat in Buriram's Baan Kruat district. They also went to Wat Burapharam in Surin's Muang district to visit Phra Ratchawuthajarn (Dulya Atulo) and other monks. The king, Princess Sirindhorn and the king's granddaughter joined the other half of the family at Wat Burapharam at 6.30 p.m. After visiting the monks and meeting a large number of people, they left the temple at 7.30 p.m. to board a plane in Surin for their return journey to Bangkok. They arrived at Chitralada Palace at 9.30 p.m.

That royal visit to Surin showed me that although the king and the queen might not necessarily spend a lot of time in a particular area, but they still attended to the people's needs. The king especially studied the problems that people faced comprehensively and thoroughly and advised government officials of possible solutions to solve local problems.

51

I celebrated the 1980 New Year in Chiang Mai because the king had moved to Bhubing Palace on Sunday, 30 December 1979. While I was stationed in the north before I took up the job in the royal court, I had one special duty, teaching history and political ideologies at the training center in Chiang Mai, called the Chaiya Training Center, and the center provided training to provincial police officers on suppressing communist insurgency and terrorism.

Given the number of years I worked in the north, Chiang Mai is like my second home. This became especially true when my son entered Chiang Mai University. I had more opportunities to see him while accompanying the king to Bhubing Palace.

One distinctive charm of Chiang Mai for us, royal court officers and staff, was its ubiquitous historical sites and ancient monuments. I enjoyed visiting Chiang Mai's many temples to pay homage to a great many Buddha images, although I had done that time and again.

On the New Year's Day, around 2 p.m., I thought to start the New Year with an auspicious and meritorious act by walking up to the Buddha Image Hall near a reservoir at Bhubing Palace. The hall was built after the palace. It enshrines an ancient Buddha image that was discovered in a deteriorated condition and then given to the king. The king had the image restored and placed in the hall. The reservoir was on the mountain above the palace.

Normally, no one would enter this hall except the custodians, so it was usually very quiet. I sometimes went up there to meditate at night. After having paid homage to the ancient Buddha image, I had also planned to meditate there that day. A royal servant had opened the hall to clean it, however, so I gave up my meditation plan. I later learned that the royal family was preparing the hall for a visit following dinner that was to be held near the reservoir.

❖

The following day was a Buddhist holy day corresponding to the full moon of the second lunar month, a period when I observed the Eight Precepts and refrained from eating meat. I left Bhubing Palace early in the morning, at 5.45 a.m. with my fellow officers. We had an appointment with Phi Thep at Warorot Market, where we would buy food to offer the monks at Wat Umong, a historical monument of Chiang Mai. The temple earned its name, Wat Umong, because the monks long ago had drilled a tunnel (*umong*) into a mountain to make a place for practicing meditation.

It was a temple tour that day. After the early morning of food offering to the monks and breakfast, we went to pay homage to a number of Buddha images and holy sites, starting with the Phra Chao Kao Tue image and a Buddha relic at Wat Suan Dok in downtown Chiang Mai. Next we drove to Lam Phun province to pay homage to the Buddha images at Wat Phra Nang Chamdhevi, Wat Mahawan and Wat Phra Yuen, as well as to relics at Wat Phrathat Hariphunchai.

We came back for a vegetarian lunch in a restaurant in Chiang Mai and stopped at Wat Pra Sing, where we were told that the king was going to visit Doi Mae Pang in the afternoon. We cut short our temple tour and hurried back to Bhubing Palace.

At 4.50 p.m., the king and every member of the family including the prince's daughter went to Wat Doi Mae Pang in Phrao district. Arriving at the temple around 7 p.m., they paid respect to Luang Puu Waen Sujinno, the most famous monk of Chiang Mai. They remained until 8.40 p.m. and were back at the palace two hours later.

That was a special Buddhist holy day for me. I paid homage to the most Buddha images and monks, and to Buddha relics at two temples.

❖

On Monday, 7 January at Rin Come Hotel, the National Research Council of Thailand and United Nations Development Project (UNDP) organized a seminar on the application of aerial photography and satellite technology for land use planning in northern Thai basins. This is a subject in which the king had great interest. At 1.20 p.m., the king and Princess Maha Chakri Sirindhorn went to see the exhibitions that were part of the seminar and spent three hours there.

On Tuesday, 15 January, at 11.35 a.m., the king, the queen and Princess Chulabhorn flew to Mae Hong Son to inspect a small-scale irrigation project and a vocational development project under royal patronage, and to see the villagers.

After their arrival, at about 1.05 p.m., the king went to Baan Mae Sakuet to inspect the Huay Mae Sakuet Weir Project. The queen traveled on to a vocational training center at Baan Huay Dua, Tambon Pha Bong. The Royal Irrigation Department was in the process of surveying and considering the site economically to build a small weir that would release water supply to 2,000 *rai* on the left bank of the Pai River in Tambon Pha Bong. The area that the department was surveying was a dense forest. The king observed the development of this project with interest. He rejoined the queen and the princess at the vocational training center in Baan Huay Dua more than an hour later.

At the vocational training center, the members made cement jars, concrete blocks and sanitation equipment. The project provided training and after members finished the course, they received certificates and a share of the production equipment. After graduation, members from each village formed their own group to make products for personal use and for sale to generate extra income. The members with high skills were selected as trainers. At 3 p.m. Their Majesties and the princess left Huay Dua village for the Pai Basin Development Center in Baan Tha Pong Daeng, Tambon Pang Moo in Muang district, and had a late lunch there.

Around 5 p.m., the king went to see three more reservoir projects, one in Huay Sai Lae, Tambon Pang Moo and two others in Huay Dua, Tambon Pha Bong and Huay Chong Chai, Tambon Pang Moo. The queen and Princess Chulabhorn joined the king at the last reservoir in Huay Chong Chai. They left Huay Chong Chai at about 6 p.m.

The royal accommodation in Mae Hong Son that night was a simple one, a small-single story wooded house. It was very cold, by Thai standards, that night with heavy fog and low visibility.

Next morning, I rose early to buy food to offer the monks. My companion was Khun Suphot Khruthaphan, now air chief marshal and deputy chief aide-de-camp general. The trip to make merit that morning was exciting. The fog was heavy and we could hardly see the road. Our car crept along the road to the market. After we made the morning alms offering to the monks and had breakfast, we went to pay homage to the Buddha relics at Wat Yot Doi Kong Moo, an important ancient monument of the province. Built in 1860, the temple was situated on the highest mountain in Mae Hong Son.

At 2.05 p.m., Their Majesties and Princess Chulabhorn visited the Pai Basin Development Center, another project under the king's initiative. There were many project activities, including animal husbandry. The villagers raised buffaloes, cattle, mules, chicken and ducks. Their Majesties and the princess also toured a field under cultivation, fruit groves and vegetable gardens.

There were supposed to be no more visits that afternoon. However, at 2.22 p.m., Their Majesties and the princess boarded a Royal Thai Army helicopter and a group of soldiers followed in another helicopter. Other soldiers, police officers and civilians were told to wait for the king at Mae Hong Son Airport. Court security officers, including me, were puzzled. No one knew the king's destination.

After some time had passed, our puzzlement turned to anxiety and fear for the king, the queen and the princess's safety. A royal trip without a plan is a trip without undertaking a survey to secure the route and area.

We waited and the answer came at 3.45 p.m., over an hour after they had left. We were informed via radio that the king would visit Pang Tong Development Center, Tambon Mok Cham Pae, in Mae Hong Son's Muang district. The center was located twenty kilometers north of Mae Hong Son. The center had been established as part of the Livestock and Agricultural Development Project under the king's initiative.

There Their Majesties went to see Pang Tong Weir. The Royal Irrigation Department had built a dam had been to store water to supply an agricultural area of 1,200 *rai*. They saw the operation of hydraulic ram pumps that relied on the pressure from the weir to pump water to the plots in the high areas. Their Majesties also toured a ranch where cattle were raised for meat, observed a demonstration farming project and a coffee plantation.

While the king was at Pang Tong, security officers and I were uneasy. We weren't sure if the small military force would provide sufficient security, especially in case of an emergency. We appealed to the deputy-commander of the Royal Thai Air Force, who was also among the group of officers waiting at the airport, to call for additional air escort from the RTAF Headquarters in Bangkok. He was clearly reluctant. As we were still making a case with him, a radio message came that the king had already left Pang Tong by helicopter. Eleven minutes later, his helicopter landed at Mae Hong Son Airport. He met the people waiting for him at the airport until 5.18 p.m. and then boarded the plane with the queen and the princess, heading back to Chiang Mai. The security officers and I followed in a C-123.

On the way back to Chiang Mai that night, I remained worried about the unexpected visit. In fact, as I later found out, the king's visit to Pang Tong was planned but only by a small group of officers. The officers directly responsible for the king's security had not been informed. Had the visit been in an area where the situation was stable, there would be nothing to worry about. But it took place in Mae Hong Son, a heavily forested, mountainous border area with a sensitive security situation. It was worrying to think of what might have happened.

I hoped that those with loyalty and concern for the safety of the king would not let such a thing happen again.

52

In late January 1980, the royal family returned to Chitralada Palace temporarily. The Princess Mother was going to the United States for medical treatment for her allergies at Walter Reed Hospital in Washington, DC. She was seen off by at the RTAF Headquarters at Don Muang Airport by her family on Friday, 25 January at 7.30 a.m. The crown prince was traveling with his grandmother.

I did not see the Princess Mother off at the airport but at Chitralada Palace along with other royal servants and staff because I had to prepare for the king's trip to Suphan Buri. It had been known for a long time that the Princess Mother had allergies. She was allergic to dust, cigarette smoke and engine exhaust and always took allergy medicine with her when she traveled. Sometimes she had severe allergic attacks but never let her condition stop her from performing her duties as the king's mother. She traveled to visit people with her son and on her own in all places, climates and topography. On such visits, she was often exposed to harsh sun, dust and rain, but doctors were always available when she needed medical treatment. When we learned that she was to receive medical treatment from American doctors, we were glad and hoped that her condition would improve.

The Princess Mother returned to Thailand on the last day of March. Her allergies still had not gone away but she didn't seem to worry. She still continued to work industriously and visit all places as before. She did not focus on her own comfort and devoted her time and energy to the Thai people. The Princess Mother's conduct was along the lines of the Ten Guiding Principles, the Buddhist concept of the righteous monarch that has been adhered to by the king.

The Ten Guiding Principles for the Sovereign (Tossapit Rajatham) comprise *dana, sila, paricaga, ajava, maddava, tapa, akkodha, avihimsa, khanti* and *avirodha*, as follows:[1]

1. *Dana*: Liberality, generosity, or charity. The giving away of alms to the needy. It is the duty of the king (government) to look after the welfare of his needy subjects. The ideal ruler should give away wealth and property wisely without giving in to craving and attachment. In other words, he should not use his position to become rich.

2. *Sila*: Morality. He must observe at least the Five Precepts, and conduct himself both in private and in public life as to be a shining example to his subjects. This virtue is very important, because if the ruler adheres to it strictly, then bribery and corruption, violence and indiscipline would be automatically wiped out in the country.

3. *Pariccaga*: Making sacrifices for the good of the people. These include personal name and fame and even life if need be. By granting such gifts etc., the ruler spurs his subjects on to more efficient and more loyal service.

4. *Ajjava*: Honesty and integrity. He must be absolutely straightforward and must never take recourse to any crooked or doubtful means to achieve his ends. He must be free from fear or favor in the discharge of his duties. At this point, a stanza from Sigalovada Sutta (Digha-Nikaya), a relevant declaration by the Buddha comes to mind: 'Canda, dose, bhaya, moha—Yo dhammam nativattati. Apurati tassa yaso—Sukkha pakkheva candima.' If a person maintains justice without being subjected to favoritism, hatred, fear, or ignorance, his popularity grows like the waxing moon.

5. *Maddava*: Kindness or gentleness. A ruler's uprightness may sometimes require firmness. But this should be tempered with kindness and gentleness. In other words, a ruler should not be overly harsh or cruel.

6. *Tapa*: Restraint of senses and austerity in habits. Shunning indulgence in sensual pleasures, an ideal monarch keeps his five senses

---

[1] Danister I. Fernando, Virtual Library, Sri Lanka, http://www.lankalibrary.com/Bud/dasa-raja-dhamma.htm.

under control. Some rulers may, using their position, flout moral conduct. This is not becoming of a good monarch.

7. *Akkodha*: Non-hatred. The ruler should bear no grudge against anyone. Without harboring grievances, he must act with forbearance and love. At this instance, I am reminded of how a certain royal pupil, an heir to the throne, who had been punished by the teacher for an offence, took revenge by punishing the teacher after he become King! (Jataka Text). Political victimization is also not conducive to proper administration.

8. *Avihimsa*: Nonviolence. Not only should he refrain from harming anybody but he should also try to promote peace and prevent war, when necessary. He must practice nonviolence to the highest possible extent so long as it does not interfere with the firmness expected of an ideal ruler.

9. *Khanti*: Patience and tolerance. Without losing his temper, the ruler should be able to bear up hardships and insults. On any occasion he should be able to conduct himself without giving into emotions. He should be able to receive both bouquets and brickbats in the same spirit and with equanimity.

10. *Avirodha*: No opposition and non-enmity. The ruler should not oppose the will of the people. He must cultivate the spirit of amity among his subjects. In other words, he should rule in harmony with his people.

❖

After having seen off the Princess Mother, the king and the princesses returned to Bhubing Palace on 26 January. The next day, they went to Chiang Mai University to hand out certificates to graduates for the years 1978 and 1979. The graduation ceremony in Chiang Mai University in that year was especially important for me because my son was one of the graduates receiving a B.Sc. diploma.

The king returned to Chitralada Palace on Wednesday, 5 March.

On Tuesday, 25 March, there was a ceremony at which the king would give royal decoration sashes to officers at Dusidalai Hall. I was among the officers to receive a sash. This was my first in my career as government official. Some people were a little surprised to see that I was receiving it for the first time. I was already a police lieutenant general. They wondered why I received my first sash later than other officers with an equivalent rank, position and salary.

I supposed I had been working too long in the provinces, far away from superiors and those who would request one on my behalf. I hadn't felt troubled by my not having a sash and never thought of asking for one, even after I started working in the royal court, where officials were required to wear full dress uniforms with their highest royal decorations in all official ceremonies.

At one such ceremony I appeared in full dress uniform but without a sash. The chief aide-de-camp general to HM the King, the late Gen. Champen Charusathian, asked me why I didn't wear a full dress uniform according to protocol. I explained that I was already in full dress uniform and I hadn't worn a sash because I hadn't been given one. I felt that a sash was an obstacle to providing security. Security officers had to be able to perform their work without unnecessary obstructive objects in their attire. However, honoring the king was still important.

I proposed to the police department for royal court security police officers to wear a khaki working uniform, decorated with medals and a leather string without a sash, instead of a full dress uniform, in event that protocol required full dress. I also proposed that the royal court security officers dispense with wearing a sword and belt. The Royal Thai Police Department kindly approved both proposals. Since then, royal court security officers have been required to wear only the working uniform with open collars, decorated with medals but without sash and sword.

I would like to mention the green field uniform of the police. According to a previous regulation of the Royal Thai Police Department, this uniform was worn only by the border patrol police and a special task force of the provincial police. Other police, including royal court security police, had to wear their khaki working uniform even in the field, which is not very convenient because the khaki working uniform is not very appropriate for fieldwork.

Finally, I requested that the Royal Thai Police Department allow court security police officers to wear a green field uniform with a jockey cap, and those police officers who had passed the parachutists' course to wear the black beret of the parachutist police instead of the jockey cap.

This uniform matter may seem trivial, but having an appropriate uniform can facilitate the performance of duties. The green field uniform is suitable for security police officers following the king in forest areas, particularly the Westmoreland uniform (named for the American general in the Vietnam War who designed it). In addition to the calf-length boots and many pockets on the shirt and trousers for personal items, it had several useful field accessories, such as a canvas belt with slots for a hanging holster, ammunition pouch, field knife, compass and a canteen strung with a harness.

The 27th of April of every year is an important day—the anniversary of the BPP Aerial Reinforcement Unit, or Naresuan Camp. I had been both a trainee and trainer at this camp. On this date, those who had participated in a training course at Naresuan Camp would join to commemorate those who had lost their lives on duty. Many from all parts of Thailand and from overseas joined the commemoration and a dinner party on that day.

I was not able to join the gathering that year because I had to accompany the king and queen to the funerals of those killed in a plane crash. A Thai Airways flight from Udon Thani to Bangkok had crashed in Patum Thani's Lam Luk Ka district. A number of passengers were killed and others were injured, some seriously. Among the casualties were two famous monks and meditation masters, Phra Ajarn Juan Kulachettho of Wat Chetiyaram (Phu Thok) from Nong Khai and Phra Ajarn Wan Uttamo of Wat Aphai Damrongtham from Sakon Nakhon.

Apart from the two senior monks, there were three other monks I didn't know. One was young but widely respected, Phra Ajarn Sing Thong from Sakon Nakhon. The five monks had been invited to a ceremony on the occasion of the king's and the queen's wedding anniversary on 28 April 1980. Another important person who died in the crash was Khunying Khaisri Na Silawat, the wife of Privy Councilor Khun Chao Na Silawat. Both the wife and husband were in close service to the king and queen.

There were many survivors from the crash. Some were lucky enough to have escaped serious or any injury. Among the survivors were Khun Somporn Klinphongsa, governor of Sakon Nakhon and my former junior at Chulalongkorn University. He was seriously injured and was sent to Bhumibol Hospital, a Royal Thai Air Force hospital in Don Muang Airport.

Due to the accident and the death of the monks and Khunying Khaisri, the king and the queen remained in Bangkok to attend their funerals and sponsor their cremation. This delayed moving to Klai Kangwol Palace until 18 May 1980.

During my stay at Klai Kangwol Palace, my son was sent for training to become a pilot for Thai Airways at Bo Fai Airport, near Klai Kangwol Palace. When off duty, I liked to go and see him taking flying lessons in the early morning. I must admit that my son's becoming a pilot excited me. There had been only one pilot in my family, my late youngest uncle (Lt-Cdr. Chuladit Dejkunjorn), and only one parachutist (me).

The flight-training schedule for my son and his seven friends had them starting at 7 a.m. each day, and the flight was an hour long. They trained in single-engine planes. During the first part of the course, they flew with a trainer and then they had to fly alone. On Wednesday, 28 May, my son passed his test to become a pilot. After that, I still got up to see my son practicing flying almost every day until the king returned to Chitralada Palace on Monday, 23 June 1980.

53

In September 1980, I was admitted to the twenty-third class of the Army Staff School.

The Army Staff School is a postgraduate institution offering a master's degree for senior government officials, including soldiers, police and civilians. In the past, it was assumed that a degree from the institution would lead to a promotion. However, the facts don't affirm this assumption. Most of the students who were already in a high-ranking position would certainly have been promoted with or without the degree from the school. Some were promoted while attending the program.

I had applied to study at the Army Staff School because I had a high position as chief royal court police officer but I felt I would have missed out on something important if I hadn't gone to the Army Staff School. Another reason to attend was that each class was drawn from the ranks of senior officials representing many ministries and government agencies. Having contacts with these groups, I thought, would facilitate my work in the future.

An advantage of the Army Staff School classes was that they were held for only a half day, in the morning, so you could return to work in the afternoon, not posing too much of an obstacle to work.

Gen. Damrong Sikhamonthon, former chief aide-de-camp general to HM the King, who was then a colonel, was also admitted in the same class. I reported to the college and attended an orientation meeting in early August. The day of the class was Thursday, 18 September 1980.

Having attended the classes, I soon realized that I was ignorant about a great many things and that the course would help remedy this. In addition to military subjects, where the lectures were given by military officers, other lectures were given by experts and specialists in management and administration in many other fields, politics, economics and the social sciences. There were also study tours to the provinces around the country to observe the activities of military and civilians, which students would otherwise not have an opportunity to see. Toward the end of the course, there were also group study tours overseas. My group went to Australia, New Zealand, Indonesia and Singapore. The program lasted for a year. I completed the course in September 1981.

In October 1981, after having served the king for eleven years and eleven months, I requested a permanent leave from the Office of Royal Court Police to return to work at the Royal Thai Police Department.

My decision to return to the Royal Thai Police was based on two important factors. First, I felt that I was getting too old for the duties (I had turned fifty-two that year). My body was no longer in top form and my eyesight was no longer strong. I still exercised by jogging but keeping up with the king and others had become an effort. In the field, switching between my prescription glasses to reading glasses to look at the king's map when he wanted to point out something to me was also not convenient.

The other reason was that over a decade of working as a royal court security officer, my work had become such a routine that I found myself beginning to make unintentional mistakes. Although these did not cause any damage, I did not want to make another error. After all, when the job was to protect and provide security for the king, even a minor mistake could have huge consequences.

I felt that it was time to step aside and allow a younger officer with fresh perspective and more energy to take over my position. The eight years I had left before retirement and my knowledge and experience could be put to use to greater benefits in another capacity that would not involve the same risk and security consequences.

I submitted a letter of intent to my superior stating my intention to continue my career in the Royal Thai Police Department and a letter of resignation to the king. My resignation was granted.

What I did not expect, however, was that the Royal Thai Police Department did not appreciate my knowledge, experience and seniority. I returned to the Royal Thai Police Department during a time of appointments and reshuffle. Instead of appointing me to a normal position, the department created a new position for me—'commissioner of the Royal Thai Police Department.'

Later in 1982, in another reshuffle, the Royal Thai Police Department nominated me to the position of deputy director-general. The Police Commission approved my nomination. But after it was sent to the cabinet, it was sent back to the department and my name was withdrawn from the list. Another officer was appointed to the position instead.

Even now I still have no idea why my name was withdrawn. I could guess who might not have liked to see me progress in the ranks, but I accepted my fate completely. In fact, the director-general had been kind to me and assigned me many duties. However, surprisingly, all those assigned to me had already been assigned to others in the department. Therefore no one sent me any work. I had a real taste of being the commissioner of the Royal Thai Police Department.

I didn't know what other people feel when they have nothing to do, but for me, I was depressed, felt useless, and regretted that I didn't have an opportunity to apply my knowledge and experience. At first, I thought I would resign and take up another job. My friends living overseas who knew of my having left the palace to end up doing nothing at the Royal Thai Police Department suggested a research position at an institution overseas. While I was filling in the application form, however, I realized that I would be using a great deal of knowledge and experience for the benefit of a foreign country. It also occurred to me that the reason I had nothing to do was that someone didn't want me to have something to do. If I quit, I would give satisfaction to that person.

I decided not to resign.

During this period, I wrote a novel *Sarawat Thuean (Rogue Inspector),* which became a best-selling novel and was made into a television drama series and film. I then wrote *Mae Lao Luead (Bloody River),* which features the same character as the first novel. It also became a bestseller.

In 1982, it occurred to me that I had never been ordained as a monk. I wanted to exercise my right to take an ordination leave. In the monkhood, I would have a chance to study and practice dharma. However, there was one obstacle. The king had said to me several years before that he would not let me become a monk unless it was for his funeral.

I consulted with Somdej Phra Yannasangvorn to learn whether I could be ordained to dedicate merit to living people. He said yes and that by doing so, I could gain a great deal of merit. When I got the answer, I sent a letter to the king and asked for his permission for my ordination. The king gave it.

I was ordained at Wat Bowornjwet and Somdej Phra Yannasangvorn was my ordainer. After having been at Wat Bowornjwet for seven days, Somdej Phra Yannasangvorn allowed me to study with Tan Ajarn Ban Thanajaro at Wat Doi Dhammachedi in Sakon Nakhon.

The seventy-eight days I spent wearing a monk's robe was the most precious time of my life. I would have never had this experience if I had been appointed deputy director-general in 1982.

Wat Doi Thammachedi specialized in meditation practice. The monks and novices spent most of their time practicing meditation in accordance with strict ascetic discipline and austerity. I had experienced different kinds of difficulties and austerity in my life before the monkhood. After I had experienced an ascetic life of a monk practicing meditation, however, I realized that my previous experience was no comparison to that of an ascetic monk.

I told my police colleagues that the program I studied at Wat Doi Thammachedi was the spiritual Ranger program.

I left the monkhood in January 1983 and returned to work at the Royal Thai Police Department, thinking to continue writing novels. However, somebody was interested in my knowledge and experience after all. The deputy director-general in charge of crime suppression at that time, Pol. Lt-Gen. Suthat Sukhumwat, now a retired police general, asked me to join his team. I accepted.

Finally in 1985, the Royal Thai Police Department and the cabinet saw it fit that I should be relieved from duty as commissioner of the

Royal Thai Police Department and appointed me to the real post of inspector-general.

Even after the long interval since I served the king, I still feel that I am never far away from him. I still see him performing his duties, minor or significant, through the media. I feel that if I so wish, I could always find an opportunity to see him, like any other Thai, on one occasion or another.

The news of the king performing his duties confirms that he still holds to the words he uttered when he became the king in 1950: 'I shall reign with righteousness for the benefits and happiness of the people of Siam', with his queen at his side. Through industriousness, perseverance and dedication, both Their Majesties have continued to find ways to alleviate the suffering of the Thai people. They continue to visit villages that I visited along with them thirty years ago, without signs of discouragement or weariness. The close bond between Their Majesties and the Thai people is a special one—one that can't be found the world over, except in Thailand.

Even in their later years—like everyone else the king and the queen have grown older—old age has not stopped them from continuing to work for the Thai people.

Having spent twelve years working for Their Majesties and having witnessed firsthand their consummate efforts to sustain their work for their subjects, I can confirm that there is nothing that Their Majesties want more than the happiness of the Thai people. For this reason, I feel that it is impossible for me or any other Thai to feel separated or far from our king and queen. It is our blessing to have such an exemplary king and queen.

My personal record of His Majesty's footsteps ended on the king's birthday in 2000. I would like to take this opportunity to ask Thai readers to repay their compassion and dedication by performing their duties with the same full effort, holding the achievement of the task itself as a reward, as our king and queen have long performed their duties.

I would like to direct the power of all merits I have accumulated thus far to Their Majesties and to bestow upon them longevity, good health, happiness and strength, so that they continue to be the ultimate refuge of the Thai people for as long as they live.

GLOSSARY

adirek	special Buddhist blessing reserved for Thai kings and queens
ajarn	teacher, master
amphur	district
anapanasati (Pali)	awareness of inhaling and exhaling (Buddhist meditation concept)
aphiroom	royal parasols used in royal ceremonies
attama or *attamaphap* (Pali)	first person pronoun used by Buddhist monks
ba kud-te (southern Thai dialect)	pork bone soup
baan	village, house
bai sri	beautifully decorated container (usually with banana leaves and fresh flowers for holding food and desserts made in offering) in a traditional Thai rite of *Bai Sri Su Khwan*, an auspicious rite to welcome or strengthen the *khwan* (spirit, soul)
benja	five
Benjamaporn Chang Phueak	The Member (Fifth Class) of the Most Exalted Order of the White Elephant
Benjamaporn Mongkut Thai	The Member (Fifth Class) of the Most Noble Order of the Crown of Thailand

bot	building in a temple complex where Buddhist ceremonies are performed
Chang Phueak	White Elephant (royal decoration)
chaw fah	gable finial, the top most decorative part at the top of a roof (of a temple or a royal house)
choeng (Khmer)	foot
chom (northern Thai dialect)	a hilltop
doi (northern Thai dialect)	mountain
fueang fah	bougainvillea
ha (pronounced in short vowel)	word of acknowledgement, spoken informally by male speakers in Thai, equivalent to "yes" in English
hia	Bengal monitor
Isan	Thailand's northeastern region, northeastern Thai dialect
imam	Muslim religious leader
Jaturathaporn Chang Phuek	The Member (Fourth Class) of the Most Exalted Order of the White Elephant
Jaturathaporn Mongkut Thai	The Member (Fourth Class) of the Most Noble Order of the Crown of Thailand
kammatthana (Pali)	meditation exercise
kamnan	head of *tambon* or sub-district
kathina (Pali)	Buddhist ceremony in which robes are offered to monks after they have dwelled in the monastery for three months during Buddhist Lent in the rainy season
khab mai	wooden rhythm clappers
khiad laew	a type of mountain frog
khlong	word in southern Thai dialect for river which means canal in standard Thai
khrap	word of acknowledgement for male

	speakers in Thai, equivalent to "yes" in English
khru	guru, teacher, master
khun (northern Thai dialect)	water source of a river
kin wor	Hmong New Year celebration
kuti	monk's abode or living quarters
lao	name of wild flower; of Laotian origin
loeng (northern and northeastern Thai dialects)	vast plains
luang phor	Buddhist monk (of one's father's age)
luang puu	elderly Buddhist monk (of one's grandfather's age)
Maha Paramophorn Chang Pueak	The Knight Grand Cross (First Class) of the Most Exalted Order of the White Elephant
Maha Yodhin	The Class II (Knight Commander) of the Honorable Order of Rama
mee sua	stir-fried yellow Chinese noodles
mhuen or *jamhuen*	rank of junior officer in traditional Thai royal court
miang (northern Thai dialect)	fermented tealeaves
mondhop	chapel
Mongkut Thai	Crown of Thailand (royal decoration)
Nopharatratchawaraphorn	Ancient and Auspicious Order of the Nine Gems (royal decoration)
panatipati (Pali)	act of taking away life of living beings
panya	wisdom
patchim owadhi (Pali)	Buddha's last sermon
Pathom Chula Chom Klao	The Knight Grand Cross (First Class) of the Most Illustrious Order of Chula Chom Klao
Pathom Chula Chom Klao Wiset	The Knight Grand Cordon (Special Class) of the Most Illustrious Order of Chula Chom Klao

Pathommaporn Mongkut Thai	The Knight Grand Cross (First Class) of the Most Noble Order of the Crown of Thailand
phang	female elephant
phlai	male elephant
phom	I (for male speaker)
pid tong	to affix a gold leaf on a Buddha image or amulet
pid tong lang phra	to affix a gold leaf on the back of a Buddha image; an idiom, meaning to conduct good deeds without making it known to others
phi	older brother/sister, big brother/sister, person who is older or has higher status
pondok	private Islamic school
phrathat	stupa or pagoda that contains relics of the Buddha or his disciples; *that* in northeastern Thai dialect
pru or *pora*	marsh or swamp
puja	act of reverence or worship, to pray, to make offering in act of worship
rai	Thai unit of area equal to 0.16 hectare or 1600 square meters
Ramathibodi	The Honourable Order of Rama (royal decoration), comprising four classes of decorations: *Senangapati* (Knight Grand Commander), *Maha Yodhin* (Knight Commander), *Yodhin* (Commander), and *Asvin* (Companion)
rao	we, us
roeng	happy
saai	sand
sae (Chinese)	last name
sagai	native tribe in southern Thailand
sai	banyan tree

sala	temple hall for giving religious instruction
sankhara (Pali)	mental formation, the fourth of the five skandhas, or aggregations, which constitute human appearance
sanyabat	royal commission
Sapha Sanam Ma	Thailand's National Convention convened at the Nanglerng Horse Racing Stadium (Sapha Sanam Ma) in December 1973 following the 14 October 1973 political crisis
sati panya	intelligence
sati	awareness
sila	Buddhist precepts
sor sam sai	traditional Thai three stringed fiddle
suan	park, garden
su-ngai (Malayu)	river
takuat	water monitor
tambon	district
Tatiya Chula Chom Klao Wiset	The Grand Companion (Third Class, higher grade) of the Most Illustrious Order of Chula Chom Klao
Thanying	Lady, Dame
Thutiya Chula Chom Klao Wiset	The Knight Commander (Second Class, higher grade) of the Most Illustrious Order of Chula Chom Klao
Thutiya Chula Chom Klao	The Knight Commander (Second Class, lower grade) of the Most Illustrious Order of Chula Chom Klao
tom yam	Thai spicy soup
Tossapit Rajatham	Ten Guiding Principles (in Buddhism) for the (Thai) Sovereign, including: (1) *dana* (charity), *sila*

(Five Buddhist precepts), *paricaga* (making sacrifices for the good of the people), *ajava* (honesty and integrity), *maddava* (kindness and gentleness), *tapa* (restraint and austerity), *akkodha* (nonhatred), *avihimsa* (nonviolence), *khanti* (patience and tolerance) and *avirodna* (no opposition and non-enmity)

ubosot	Buddhist sanctuary, temple hall
umong	tunnel
vihara	temple hall or monastery
vipassana	meditation
Wan Maha Wippayoke	Day of the Great Sorrow
wat	temple
yai	big

INDEX

1st Infantry Division of the King's Guard, 186–87

14 October 1973, 94–96. *See also* Day of Great Sorrow

6 October 1976, 204

9th Infantry Division, 82

9th Infantry Division of Kanchanaburi, 186

Aat-ong Chumsai Na Ayutthaya, 100–101

Adul Niyomwiphat, 235

AFRO, 260

Airavata elephants, 76

Alix Napoleon, Princess, 203–204

Amarindra Vinitchai Audience Hall, 212, 216, 254

Amnuay Kohphet, 154

Amphorn Palace, 6, 259

Ananda Mahidol, King, 166

Anantasamakhom Throne Hall, 93

Ancient City, 72

Andaman Sea, 83, 108

Ang Khang Agricultural Research Station, 126

animal husbandry, 59, 71, 231, 274

Animal Husbandry Research Station of the Hill tribe Development Project, 126

Anne, Princess, 72

Aor. Sor. Band, 6, 180

Aphiradi Yingcharoen, 181

AR–15, 13

Army Cadet Academy of Phrachulachomklao, 133, 225

Army's Special Warfare Headquarters, 82

Aroon Rujikanha, 234

Aroon Thawaathasin, 186–87

Asia Foundation, 164

Atthawatya Khongsuwan, 109–110

Bajoh Farmers Evacuation Project, 141

Bajra Kitiyabha, Princess, 259, 266, 269

Bamrung Sookhabusaya, 161

Bang Pa-In Palace, 114–15, 147–48, 180, 266–67

Bangkok Airport, 89, 103

Banthorn Airport, 111, 140, 202
BBC, 244
Bear Cliff, 58, 127–28
Belgium, 89–91, 203
Benjawan Chakrabandhu, MR, 6
Bhanubandh Yugala, Prince, 158
Bhisatej Rajani, MC, 38, 56, 60,
    122–24, 227, 257–78, 260
Bhuban Mountain, 143–44, 176,
    206
Bhuban Palace, 62, 108, 143, 145,
    176, 179, 204, 208–209, 250,
    253, 268
Bhubing Palace, 17–19, 24,
    46, 53–54, 58, 61, 72–73,
    100–102, 115–16, 119–125,
    128–29, 132–34, 147, 150–56,
    181–83, 217, 228, 232, 257,
    271–72, 278
Black Monkey Ascetic, 46, 115
Bloody River, 284
Bodoin, King, 89–90
Bombing, 67, 141, 200–202, 242
Border Patrol Police (BPP), 1–3,
    19–20, 23, 35, 129, 134, 140,
    183, 206–208, 225
boundary-marking stone balls,
    161, 194, 208, 221–23
BPP Aerial Reinforcement Unit
    (BPP PARU), 1, 9, 12, 29, 81,
    141, 280
BPP Tactical Training Division,
    134–38
Brahman priest, 175, 193–94,
    211, 216, 235, 266
Brian, Richard, 232
British Consulate, 173
Bruges, 90

Brussels, 89
Bua Kittiyakara, ML, 248
Buddhism, 37, 45, 61, 65, 163,
    242, 263
Buddha, 4, 47, 62, 101, 159,
    277
Buddha amulets, 33, 74,
    160–1, 221, 233, 264,
    271–2
Buddha images, 57–58, 66,
    144, 149, 156–57, 194,
    205–206, 211, 216, 263
Buddhist Lent, 36
Buddhist Precepts, 106, 159,
    192, 215–16, 248, 277
Ten Guiding Principles of
    the Sovereign (*Tossapit
    Rajatham*), 277
Triple Gem, 117, 159, 192,
    215–16, 247–48
Burgundy, 90
C-123, 103, 140, 152, 161, 203,
    209, 218, 224, 227, 259–60,
    268, 275
C-47, 158, 161
Carl XVI Gustaf, King, 87–88
Central Investigation Bureau
    (CIB), 24
Cereal Breeding Station, 258
Chainat Dam, 148
Chainat-Ayutthaya Canal, 148
Chainat-Pasak Irrigation Project,
    172
Chaiyong Maekcharoen, 85
Chakrabandhu Bensiri Chakra-
    bandhu, MC, 195
Chakri Dynasty, 17, 33, 76, 113
Chalaad Hiransiri, 187–88

Chalor Buranaphan, 182
Champen Charusathian, 279
Chang Phueak Gate, 185
Chao Na Silawat, 280
Chatra Mongkol Day. *See* Coronation Day
chaw fah. See gable finial
Chertchamrat Chitkarunrat, 136
Chiang Mai University, 124, 182, 220, 227–78, 250, 270, 278,
Chiang Mai University Students Association, 125
Chiang Rai Land Development Center, 231
Chiang Rai Special Branch, 23, 36
Chiang Thanomphaladisai, 236
chief royal court police officer, 186, 225, 282
China, 13, 91, 248, 261–63
Chitralada Garden, 6
Chitralada Palace, 42, 52, 55, 66, 70, 81, 93–95, 102–104
Chitralada Train Station, 104
Cholchan Salaksna, 60
Chop Cholakate, 147
Chote Klongwicha, 85
Chula Chom Klao, King. *See* Chulalongkorn
Chulabhorn Walailak, Princess, 53, 83, 99, 104, 123–24, 128, 132, 139–40, 143, 146, 154, 158, 171, 182, 188, 215, 235, 235, 243, 252, 259, 269, 273–74
Chuladit Dejkunjorn, 281
Chulalongkorn Hospital, 98

Chulalongkorn University, 12, 35, 68, 79, 97, 106, 186, 189, 208, 222, 240–42, 280
Chulalongkorn, King (Rama V), 66, 76–79
Claridges Hotel, 91
communism, 2, 20–21, 29, 135
communist insurgency, 2, 9, 13, 24, 28, 38–39, 48, 67, 98, 108, 136, 204, 223, 226, 252, 262
counterinsurgency, 24, 28, 67, 138, 208, 271
Communist Suppression Operation Command (CSOC), 11, 22–23, 27, 35, 142
consecrated water, 216
constitution, 92–93, 102, 106–107, 116, 188, 203, 257
Constitution of the Kingdom of Thailand B.E. 2515 (1972 AD), 92
Cooperative Promotion Department, 117, 235,
cooperative, 117, 119, 147, 198, 228, 235–37, 254
Coronation Day, 77, 212
coup d'etat, 18, 186–88, 203
Crime Suppression Division, 70
crops (substitute, alternative), 18, 123, 126–27, 147–48, 217, 228–30
Damrong Sikhamonthon, 282
Danai Sanitwongse Na Ayudhaya, 55
Dara Rasmee Camp, 31, 129–130
Day of Great Sorrow, 44, 94–98, 153
Debharidh Devakul, MR, 14

Decha Bunnag, 176, 179
Decho Suwananon, 178
Decho, Phaya, 5
Democracy Monument, 93
demonstration projects, 236–38, 275
demonstrations, 93, 95, 103, 116, 153, 171
Deng Xiaoping, 248
Department of Public Welfare, 221
dharma, 64, 110, 177, 180, 215, 221, 285
Doi Ang Khang, 125–28
Doi Chang Ngu, 230
Doi Inthanon, 120–23, 151
Doi Mae Pang, 116–18, 272
Doi Pui, 58, 150, 232
Doi Suthep, 17, 120, 156–57, 227, 232
Duke of Edinburgh, 72
Dumaine, Betty, 164
Dusidalai Hall, 52, 93, 204, 216, 264, 278
Dusit District Office, 95
Dusit Metropolitan Police Station, 243
Dusit Palace, 77
Dusit Thani Hotel, 69–70
Dusit Zoo, 95, 186
Ecole Nouvelle de la Suisse Romande, 165
Elizabeth II, Queen, 72–73, 91
Emerald Buddha, 173–75, 247, 255
Emerald Buddha Temple, 98, 158, 173, 181, 211, 216, 247–48, 259

England, 72–73, 89, 91, 165
Erawan Shrine, 242
exercise (physical), 17, 52, 58, 150–1, 204, 240, 264, 283
Fabiola, Queen, 89–90, 203
Fah Muang Thai, 86
FBI National Acemdy, 22, 164
Fine Arts Department, 40, 143, 178, 194, 235, 263
Forestry Department, 19, 122, 126
Front Command of Central Security Operation, 186
gable finial, 182, 195, 202, 205, 218, 220, 229, 234, 236
Galwalnadis Diskul, MC, 35, 51
Galyani Vadhana, Princess, 165–67, 248
Grand Palace, 114, 173, 175, 212, 215, 245, 247–78, 255
Great White Umbrella of State, 212–3
Gregers, Count, 153
Guangdong, 262
Guangzhou, 262–3
Gun Trader Association, 154
Gustaf VI Adolf, King, 84, 87–88
Harin Hongsakul, 248, 257
Hat Sai Yai Beach, 52
Haw, 260
Hian Chang, 263
Hill Tribe Development and Welfare Center, 259, 260
Hill Tribe Development Project, 126, 153
hill tribes, 17–18, 32, 55–58, 71–72, 82, 100, 116, 122–28, 150–51, 222, 226–29, 257–60

Akha, 229, 230, 260
Hmong, 19, 58–59, 121, 129, 222
Karen, 44–46, 58, 122–23, 182, 220
Lahu (Muser), 58, 71, 125, 127–28, 229, 260
Lisu, 260
Mien (Yao), 58, 260
History of Isan, 253
Horse Racing Stadium Convention. *See* National Convention
Huay Hin Laad Reservoir, 252
Huay La Reservoir, 220
Huay Mae Sakuet Weir Project, 273
Huay Mai Nai Highland Agricultural Research Station, 129, 153
Huay Manao Cooperative, 236
Hup Kaphong Agricultural Cooperative, 235–36
Indrathep, Khun, 170
Ingrid, Queen, 153–54
Internal Security Operation Command (ISOC), 95
Irrigation, 113, 119, 147, 149, 197, 217, 231, 273
Irrigation Department, 111–12, 126, 147–49, 172, 197, 220, 226, 231, 236, 252, 269, 273–74
Isan, 9–11, 22, 32, 38, 55, 83, 110, 146, 155, 208, 231, 253, 268
Inthawichayanon, Chao, 120
Iyarapot Barge, 115
Jamras Mandhuganond, 25–26

Jandara, 83–84
Jinda Sanitwongs, ML, 84
Joint Civilian-Police-Military Intelligence Center, 23, 35, 223
Isawan Thippaya Throne Hall, 114
Kaj Raksamanee, 63, 222
Kamon Khusakul, 254
Kasetsart University, 79, 171, 235
Khaisaeng Sooksai, 92
Khaisri Na Silawat, 280
Khlong Kolok. *See* Kolok River
Khmer, 176, 230
Khon Kaen University, 267
Khunchaiyanat Narendhara, Prince, 38
Klai Kangwol Palace, 2, 4, 7, 12, 17, 33, 35, 52, 136, 139, 169, 188, 233, 238–39, 262–65, 281
Kolok River, 112
Kor Sor 9, 16
Kotabaru, 112, 136
Kriangsak Chamanan, 204, 248
Kukrit Pramoj, MR, 2, 69–70, 106, 132, 153, 189, 261
Kwankaew Watcharothai, 191
Laeken Palace, 89
Lanna, 230
Laos, 1, 9, 24, 32, 68, 205
Lausanne, 165–67
Lek Chinda-Sanguan, 252
Lek, Princess. *See* Chulaborn
Lipa Sa-ngo Field, 197–8
Lipa Sa-ngo Irrigation Project, 197
London, 91

Lord Chamberlain, 173, 175, 191
Lua, 227
lustral water, 174–76, 193–94,
    213
Mae Lao Luead, 284
Mae Salong Basin Development
    Project, 259
Mae Talai Farm, 119
Maha Chakri Sirindhorn, Prin-
    cess. *See* Sirindhorn
Maha Nikai, 162
Maharat Irrigation Project, 149
Mahasamakhom, 212
Mahorathuek Horn, 212
Makha Bucha Day, 154
Malaysian Police Field Force, 136
Malee Chantharaksa, 163
Manratana Srikranon, 6
Margrethe II, Queen, 91
Marigadayavan Camp, 134, 139
Marigadayavan Royal Residence,
    1–4, 138
Meditation, 37, 46–47, 64,
    105–106, 129, 143, 156–57,
    177, 204, 240, 252, 266–67,
    272, 280, 285
McKean Hospital, 72–73, 231–32
Mekong River, 9, 62, 205, 251
Monchai Phankhongchuen, 202,
    262
Mongkut, King (Rama IV), 1,
    74, 104, 159–60, 174, 248
monks
    Ariyawongsakotayan
        (Supreme Patriarch), 247
    Ban Thanajaro, 177, 285
    Buddhadhasa Bhikkhu, 37,
        105

Cha Suphattho, 179
Chob Thanasamo, 177
Choy Thittapoonyo, 162
Daeng Yasotharo, 265
Fan Ajaro, 145–46, 181,
    218–19
Juan Kulachettho, 251, 280
Kasem Khemako, 221
Khamphandha Kosapanyo,
    66–68
Khanti Thammakhun, Phra-
    khru, 163
Khao Analyo, 177
Khrueang Dhammajaro, 205
Kinnaree, 62–63
Kittisan Sophon 223
Kruba Chaiwongsa Pattana,
    45, 220
Kruba Dhammachai, 46
Kruba Srivichai, 124
Man Phurithatto, 143–44,
    177–78, 252
Nam Kaewchan, 161
Ngoan Sorayo, 63–66, 221–22
Noraratana Rajamanit, Phraya
    (Chao Khun Nor), 74
Phang Phakkho, 268
Phothiyan Thera (Cha
    Suphattho), 79
Pun Punyasiri (Supreme
    Patriarch), 99
Sao Kantasilo, 144
Sim Buddhajaro, 62
Thep Rattanakawi, Chao
    Phrakhun, 162
Thep Sarasuthi, Chao Phrak-
    hun, 163
Udom Pitaka, 160

Veeravongse, Somdej Phra Maha, 215
Waen Sujinno, 116–17, 272
Wan Uttamo, 143, 280
Yannasangvorn, Somdej Phra, 155, 177, 223, 285
Muang Boran. *See* Ancient City
Muslim, 109, 168, 264
Myanmar, 57, 125
Naga Noi Island, 84
Nakhon Si Thammarat Hospital, 140
Nakhon Yonok Nakburi, 230
Nam Som Police Station, 205
Nam Tha Pru Drainage Project, 244
Nam Un Dam Irrigation Project, 143
Nanglerng Horse Racing Stadium, 97
Naresuan Camp, 7, 9, 12, 14, 20, 22, 35, 81–82, 280
Naresuan, King, 205, 208
Narin Thongsiri, 182
National Convention, 96–97
National Governing Reformation Group, 171–72, 204
National Legislative Assembly, 97
Naval Academy, 133, 225
New York City Police Academy, 22, 165
New York University, 69, 188
Nitya Sukhum, 50
Noi, Princess. *See* Sirindhorn
Nong Phlap Cooperative, 236
Nonni Ahlefeldt Laurvit Bille, Countess, 153
Nual Chantree, 61, 105

oath of allegiance, 210–11, 215–16
Ob Preeyakraison, 182
Office of Royal Court Police Officers, 225, 242
On Maithaothong, 139
opium, 18, 59, 123, 127, 217, 228
Operation Base of Cavalry Troop 301, 217
Pa Pae Agricultural Cooperative, 183
Pai Basin Development Center, 273
Pai River, 273
Paisan Taksin Hall, 212–13, 247, 255
Paitoon Muangsomboon, 33, 44
Pang Tong Weir, 274
People's Assistance Teams, 67–68, 142, 144, 253
People's Assistance Team Training Center, 11, 12, 22, 209
Pha Mee. *See* Bear Cliff
Pha Mon. *See* Pillow Cliff
Phakorn Pachinphayak, 190
Phangkharat, King, 155, 230
Phanlert Buranasilapin, 100–101, 123, 156
Phimanchaisri Gate, 181
Phisan Moolasartsathorn, 208
Phoemphun Krairirk, 69
Phra Buddha Chinasi, 248–49
Phra Buddha Chinnarat, 263
Phra Buddha Patimachai, 194
Phra Buddha Rattanasathan, 248
Phra Chao Kao Tue, 272
Phra Chatchai, 193
Phra Devakamma, 194

Phra Kowpham, 193
Phra Mahasang Phet Noi, 174–75
Phra Nakhon Khiri Palace, 235
Phra Pathom Chedi, 253
Phra Phrom, 242
Phra Ruang, 5
Phra Sai, 205–6
Phra Sambuddha Phanni, 175, 247
Phra Sang Thaksinawat, 174
Phra Semathipat, 193
Phra Serm, 206
Phra Siam Devathirat, 247
Phra Sirirarangkhan of King Mongkut, 248
Phra Souk, 205–206
Phra Vetsanukam Devabutra, 230
Phra Warunyujane Entrance, 95
Phrachao Ton Luang, 233
Phrakan Phirom, 193
Phramongkutklao Hospital, 189, 265
Phrao Settlement Cooperative, 117, 119
Phrathat Monthian Hall, 247
Phrom Kuman, King, 230
Pillow Cliff, 150
Pimol Jaraksa, 31
Pisal Silapakarm, Luang, 44
Pisit Nantapaet, 32
Pittayalappruetiyakorn, Prince, 99
Pittayalongkorn, Prince, 38
Piyarangsit Rangsit, MC, 38
Plabplachai Metropolitan Police Station, 107
Pojna Phekanantna, 24, 26

Police Aerial Reinforcement Unit (PARU), 20. *See also* BPP Aerial Reinforcement Unit
Police Cadet Academy, 133, 259
Police Detective Training School, 24–25
Police General Hospital, 98
political crisis, 92, 102, 172, 187, 203–204
Pong Krathing Cooperative, 236
Poonperm Krairirk, 173, 176
Pornpimolpan (Worawan), MC, 38
Pralong Wirapri, 187
Pramot Sophak, 121, 181
Pranetr Ridhipachai, 1, 3, 9, 26, 83
Prapat Charusathien, 170
Prapot Thirawat, 248
Praratchapromayarn, 115
Prasarn Raengkla, 31
Prasartthong, King, 114
Prasert Rujirawongse, 29
Prasert Thammasiri, 186–87
Prasert Thanadpojanamatya, 25
Prasit Kanchanawat, 132
Prasit Srisuchart, 132
Prasit Thawisin School, 230
Prathat (Pagoda) Chom Kitti, 155
Prayad Samarnmitra, 22, 35–36
Preecha Khlaaylee, 99
Preeda Kanasutra, 121
Prem Chanarat, 140
Prem Tinsulanonda, 45, 208
Prince of Songkla University, 246

Princess Mother, 164–67, 248, 268, 276, 278
Princess Ying Yai. *See* Ubol-ratana
Private Secretary of HM the King, 50, 70, 116, 190, 204, 258
Private Secretary of HM the Queen, 243
Privy Council, 99, 145, 248
protests, 92, 99, 102, 171
provinces
    Ang Thong, 115, 172, 267
    Ayutthaya, 100, 114–15, 147–49, 172, 180, 266–67
    Bangkok, 17, 24, 27, 31, 39, 44, 47–48, 52, 63, 66, 72, 89, 92, 96, 99, 102, 114, 123, 129, 133, 135, 148, 158, 160–165, 172, 179–183, 187, 203, 206, 209, 217, 225, 233, 240, 246, 254–259, 266–69, 275, 280
    Buriram, 268, 269
    Chaiyaphum, 236
    Chiang Mai, 17, 23–24, 32, 46–47, 53, 57–61, 72–73, 100, 102, 116, 120, 124–29, 147, 151–53, 156, 158, 181–85, 217–20, 223–33, 250, 257–60, 271–72, 275, 278
    Chiang Rai, 15, 22–23, 28, 35–38, 58, 82, 155, 228, 231, 233, 259–60
    Chumphon, 104, 234
    Kalasin, 176, 206

Kamphaeng Phet, 222, 230
Kanchanaburi, 99, 186, 222, 236
Khon Kaen, 142, 176, 208, 267–68
Krabi, 38, 84
Lamphun, 45, 124, 153, 220–21
Loei, 82, 133, 177
Lop Buri, 82, 115, 149
Mae Hong Son, 53–54, 130, 156, 245, 273–75
Maha Sarakham, 176
Mukdahan, 206
Nakhon Phanom, 11, 38, 62, 68, 98, 142–43, 179, 206, 209–10, 253–54
Nakhon Ratchasima, 160
Nakhon Sawan, 49
Nakhon Si Thammarat, 38, 43, 103, 140, 161, 164, 183
Nan, 24, 27–28, 31–32, 35, 38, 82, 128, 158, 217, 226
Narathiwat, 8, 102, 108, 110–12, 133, 139–41, 167–70, 192–95, 198–200, 234, 243–44, 264
Nong Bua Lamphu, 177, 209
Nong Khai, 9, 10, 55, 205–206, 251, 253, 280
Pathum Thani, 206
Pattani, 108, 111, 197–98, 201, 236, 246
Phetchabun, 82, 223–24
Phetchaburi, 15, 48, 139, 234–35, 239
Phang Nga, 84
Phattalung, 38, 43–44, 160

Phayao, 233
Phichit, 63
Phuket, 38, 83, 84, 110
Pitsanulok, 14, 54–55, 99,
    132, 224
Prachin Buri, 146
Prachuab Kiri Khan, 2, 11–12,
    14, 36, 67
Ranong, 84
Ratchaburi, 236
Sakon Nakhon, 11, 38, 62,
    68, 102, 108, 112, 142–45,
    176081, 204, 206, 209–10,
    218–19, 229, 250, 253–54,
    268, 280, 285
Samut Prakan, 72
Samut Songkhram, 139
Sara Buri, 187
Satun, 108
Si Sa Ket, 268
Songkhla, 108–109, 135–36,
    203, 246
Sukhothai, 44, 151
Suphan Buri, 48, 276
Surat Thani, 38, 42–43, 46,
    74, 162–63, 183–84, 208
Surin, 158–60, 208, 268–70
Tak, 222–23
Thon Buri, 64, 66
Trang, 84, 161
Ubon Ratchathani, 11, 68,
    158, 179, 210
Udon Thani, 55, 142–43, 177,
    204, 208–209, 280
Uthai Thani, 46
Uttaradit, 54
Yala, 108–109, 138, 141,
    200–202, 242

Provincial Agricultural Exten-
    sion Office, 148
Provincial Police Special Opera-
    tion Division, 133
Rachadamnoen Klang Avenue,
    93
Rama I, King, 174–75, 216, 247
Rama III, King, 174–75, 205,
    216, 247
Rama V. *See* Chulalongkorn
Rama VI, King, 214
Rama VI Camp, 139
Ramathibodi Hospital, 98
Rambhaibharni, Queen, 114
Ramkhamhaeng University, 102
Ratchawallop Day, 85
Red Cross Day, 120
red zone, 48, 204
reforestation, 217
reservoir, 220, 222, 236, 238,
    252, 268–72
Revolution Council, 186–88,
    203–204
Reza Pahlavi II, Crown Prince,
    217
rice bank, 148, 230
Romklao School, 144–45, 209
Ronan, William J., 165, 188–89
Rougue Inspector, 284
Royal Aide-de-Camp Depart-
    ment, 26, 34, 104, 109, 186,
    224, 242, 250
    chief aide-de-camp general,
        35, 51, 60, 279, 282
    deputy chief aide-de-camp
        general, 85, 165, 176, 274
royal anthem, 212–13, 263

Royal Court Police Officer Act, 37

royal decorations, 75–78, 187–88, 213–16, 255, 278–79
   Ancient and Auspicious Order of the Nine Gems (*Nopharatratchawaraphorn*), 213
   Chula Chom Klao, 75–77
   Crown of Thailand (*Mongkut Thai*), 75
   Honourable Order of Rama (*Ramathibodi*), 214–6
   Royal House of Chakri, 47
   White Elephant (*Chang Phueak*), 75

Royal Guards Division, 56, 142

Royal Household Bureau, 85–86, 181, 192, 197, 204, 234, 245

royal medical unit, 55, 99, 121, 151, 161, 163, 198, 205–207, 229–30, 244

Royal Pages Division, 92

Royal Plaza, 93, 95, 171, 210, 254

Royal Ploughing Ceremony, 188

royal regalia, 113–14, 212
   Great Crown of Victory, 114
   Royal Fan and Fly Whisk, 114
   Royal Slippers, 114
   Royal Staff, 114
   Sword of Victory, 114, 116

Royal Thai Air Force, 9, 18, 55, 103, 152, 158, 161–62, 259, 275

Royal Thai Air Force Academy, 225

Royal Thai Army, 225, 259

Royal Thai Police, 9, 16, 23–27, 109, 115, 134, 138, 199, 261–63, 279, 283–86

Royal Thai Military Flags, 259

Royal Turf Club, 97

Rungruang Chulachat, 252

Sagai, 138

Sahathai Samakhom Pavilion. *See* Sala Sahathai Samakhom

Sai Jai Thai Foundation, 55

Sala Roeng, 4, 136, 262–63

Sala Sahathai Samakhom, 181, 259

Samak Sunthonrvet, 193

Samran Phaetayakul, 35

Samran Wangsapha, 181

Sanam Luang, 171

Sanam Suea Pa, 186

Sa-ngat Chaloryu, 171, 203–204

Sa-ngat Charnwathitanont, 31

Sangkhadit Diskul, MR, 166

Sanit Prangson, 236

Sanya Dharmasakti, 44, 96, 102–103, 106, 286

Sao Supharak, 118

Sapha Sanam Ma. See National Convention

Saranya Sasnupatham, 83

Sarawat Thuean, 284

Sawan Pracharaksa Hospital, 49–50

Sawang Wattana, King, 9

Sawat Srisakulmekhee, 163–64

Sayan Khampheeraphan, 85, 89, 105

SEATO (Southeast Asia Treaty Organization), 27

Senee Ronnayut Camp, 208

Seni Pramoj, MR, 132–33
Seri Thai, 22
Shaowana Na Seelawant, 62
Siam Cement Group, 161
Sirindhorn, Princess, 47, 53–54,
    83–92, 98–99, 104, 123–24,
    128, 130, 132, 139–43, 147,
    151–54, 158, 171, 182, 189,
    213–15, 219, 223, 228, 235,
    239–40, 243, 247–48, 252–53,
    259, 262–69, 273
Siwara Camp, 218
Soamsavali, Princess, 189, 215,
    259, 269
Social Action Party, 106–107
Somdej Base, 223
Somdej Chitralada, 2, 33–34
Somjit Dhanyachoto, 21
Somnuek Krisanasuwan, 21
Somporn Klinphongsa, 280
Sonchai Mountain, 43
Sophon Singhaplin, 54
South China Sea, 108
Special Branch, 1, 11, 19, 23, 36,
    75, 95, 109, 120, 155, 191
Special Warfare Task Force, 132
Sri Lanka, 43
Sri Nakarindra, Somdej Phra,
    164. *See also* Princess Mother
Sridej Poompraman, 35–36
Srinakharinwirot University,
    240, 246
Srisuriyawongse, Chao Phraya
    Borom Maha (Chuang Bun-
    nag), 76
Stockholm, 86
strikes, 99, 116, 153
Suan Amphorn, 240, 246

Suan Son Patiphat, 11, 21–22
Suep Rotprasert, 142
Sunan Khan-asa, 99
Sunit Panyawanit, 188
Suphot Khruthaphan, 274
Supoj Siripool, 132
Supreme Command Security
    Center, 61
Supreme Patriarch, 99, 155,
    247–48, 266
Suraphon Chulaphram, 134, 136
Surat Thani Hospital, 46, 184
Suthi Ob-om, 159
Suwanai Thongnop, 210
Switzerland, 16, 165–67
Talismans, 117
Taksin, King, 64, 66
Tan Yong Mountain, 8, 108, 169
Tat Tone Waterfall, 145
Teanchai Janmookda, 60, 61, 74,
    109–10, 177, 186, 217, 224,
    264
temples
    Wat Aphai Damrongtham,
        143–44, 280
    Wat Baan Pang, 124
    Wat Bang Nom Kho, 115
    Wat Benchamabophit, 183
    Wat Boromathat, 43
    Wat Boworniwet, 171, 177,
        248–49, 285
    Wat Burapharam, 269
    Wat Chetiyaram (Wat Phu
        Thok), 251, 280
    Wat Doi Thammachedi, 177,
        285
    Wat Doi Mae Pang, 116, 272
    Wat Don Pao, 157

Wat Don Sala, 44, 161–62
Wat Hin Hmak Peng, 62
Wat Indra Burapha, 269
Wat Jed Yod, 36
Wat Kai Fah, 149
Wat Kanta Seelawas, 62
Wat Khao Suwan Pradit,
    162–63
Wat Khatuk Chiangman, 221
Wat Khok Samankhun, 203
Wat Kosakaram (Wat Maha-
    chai), 67
Wat Lamphu, 264–65
Wat Mahathat, 140
Wat Mahawan, 272
Wat Nong Paphong, 179
Wat Pa Phurithattawat, 143,
    177–78
Wat Pa Sutthawat, 143, 177
Wat Pa Udom Somporn,
    145–46, 181, 218–19
Wat Pak Nam, 234
Wat Pathum Wanaram (Wat
    Sra Pathum), 66, 206
Wat Petch Wararam, 223
Wat Phanom Silaram, 268
Wat Phavana Phirataram, 66
Wat Pho Chai, 205–206
Wat Pho Sri That, 158–59
Wat Phra Buddhabath Khao
    Ruak, 63
Wat Phra Kaew, 158, 173,
    247. *See also* Emerald Bud-
    dha Temple
Wat Phra Nang Chamdhevi,
    272
Wat Phra Phut, 244
Wat Phra Yuen, 272

Wat Phrabat Huaytom,
    182–83, 220
Wat Phrathat Bang Phuan,
    253
Wat Phrathat Hariphunchai,
    272
Wat Phurithatthirawat, 253
Wat Pra Sing, 272
Wat Sam Kor, 115
Wat Sammanusorn, 117
Wat Sangkharam, 99
Wat Sattha Prachakorn (Wat
    Khao Ruak), 187
Wat Si Roi, 115
Wat Sirisukhaphibaan, 208
Wat Sri Khomkham, 233
Wat Sri Nuan, 267
Wat Suan Dok, 272
Wat Sukhonthawat, 163
Wat Suntharawat (Wat Son
    Sa), 160
Wat Suwandararam, 114
Wat Taa Sung, 46
Wat Takian Bang Kaew (Wat
    Kian), 43
Wat Tham Klongpane, 177,
    209
Wat Thepsirin Dharawat, 74
Wat Tri Thosathep, 158
Wat Tuung Khaow Puang, 46
Wat Umong, 218, 272
Wat Weruwan, 223
Wat Wiset Chai Chan, 115
Wat Yot Doi Kong Moo, 274
Term Wiphakpojanakit, 253
Territory Protection Volunteers
    Division, 253
Thai Lanna. *See* Lanna

Thai Rotary Club, 69

Thai–Burmese border, 58

Thai–Sino relations, 261

Thaksin Palace, 8, 108, 109, 133, 139, 141, 164, 168–70, 192, 197–203, 246, 264, 266

Thammasat University, 79, 92–93, 95–96, 171

Thammayut Nikai, 163

Thamrongrat Kaewkan, 265

Thang Sam Chang, 263

Thanin Kraiwichian, 171–72, 204

Thanom Kittikhachorn, 96

Thanom Premrasmi, 236

Thanying Vibha. *See* Vibhavadi Rangsit

Thaweesanti Ladawal, ML, 50, 70

Theatre Royal Haymarket, 91

Thep Suphasamit, 23, 26, 61, 109, 161, 172

Thewarat Mahesuan Gate, 212

Third Army, 23–24, 27–28, 31–32, 35, 224

Third Army Forward Headquarters, 23, 31–32, 35

Thongsuk Butsai, 165

Thung Lipa Sa Ngo Cooperative, 236

Thung Loeng, 258

Thung Luilai Cooperative, 236

Thung Samor Project, 223

Trai Phumi, 230

Ubolratana, Princess, 53

United States Operations Mission (USOM), 7

Usa Phanangkoon, 182

Uttarakuru Thaweep, 230

Vachira Hospital, 98

Vachiralongkorn Dam, 99

Vajiralongkorn, Crown Prince, 53, 58, 81, 104, 117, 139, 146–47, 151, 154, 174, 180, 183, 187, 189, 215, 217, 247, 254, 276

Veera Musikaphong, 92

Vibhavadi Rangsit, MC, 38–47, 56, 74, 85–87, 90, 92, 162–63, 182–84, 220

Vibhavadi Rangsit, Princess. *See* Vibhavadi Rangsit, MC

Vibhavadi Waterfall, 40

Viking Island, 84

Villa Wattana, 166

village defense volunteers. See also People's Assistance Teams

village scouts, 98, 139, 145, 147–48, 151, 160, 162, 164, 196, 200–201, 208, 221–22, 228, 234, 253

VIP Protection Branch, 61, 109, 186, 188

Visakha Bucha Day, 68, 158–59

vocational training, 273

Voice of America, 190

Wamathepmuni, Phrarajkhru, 193–95, 216

Wang Namkhang Tangerine Orchard, 123, 156

Wanit Chantara, 119

Waraphatphiman Throne Hall, 181, 266

Warin Wonghanchao, 164

Warorot Market, 272

Water Sources Development Project, 183
Westmoreland uniform, 280
white elephants, 192–195, 200, 230, 234–35, 239
Phang Khwanta, 235
Phlai Daorung, 235
Phlai Phrasri, 194–95, 235
Phlai Wanphen, 239
Winai Pansiri, 126
Wipas Wipulakorn, 41, 44, 207–208

Winter, Brigitte, 245
Withun Thasana Throne Hall, 180
Witoon Ya-sawasdi, 32, 134
Witthaya Kesornsaowaphak, 147
Wor Na Pramualmark, 38. *See also* Vibhavadi Rangsit
Xin Xiao Chu Temple, 263
Yingruedee Worawan, MC, 190
Yutthana Yaemphan , 215

(over)
Errata

PAGE	FOR	READ
216, line 17	King Rama III	King Rama II
248, line 37	King Mongkut	King Vajiravudh
265, line 8	mediation school	meditation school
266, line 21	to mediate	to meditate
280, lines 30-31	Na Silawat	Na Sailawan
281, line 10	Lt-Cdr. Chuladit Dejkunjorn	Sqn-Ldr. Chuladit Dejkunjorn
282, lines 2, 3, 10, 12, 17	Army Staff School	National Defence College of Thailand
284, line 6	deputy director-general	assistant director-general
285, lines 17, 30	deputy director-general	assistant director-general

Errata in Index

PAGE	FOR	READ
295, column 1, line 4	Chao Na Silawat, 280	Chao Na Silawan, 280
297, column 2, line 12	Kraisri Na Silawat, 280	Kraisri Na Silawan, 280
298, column 1, line 31	Mongkut, King (Rama IV), 1, 74, 104, 159-60, 174, 248	Vajiravudh, King (Rama VI), 1, 74, 104, 159-60, 174, 214, 248
302, column 2, line 11	Rama VI, King, 214	Rama VI, King. *See* Vajiravudh
303, column 1, line 23	Royal Pages Division, 92	Royal Pages Division, 56, 92, 142

Errata (January 2007)

PAGE	FOR	READ
1, line 4	King Mongkut	King Vajiravudh (Rama VI)
1, line 21	Ridhipachai	Ridhiluechai
1, line 22	Army Staff College	Command and General Staff College
9, line 21	Ridhipachai	Ridhiluechai
56, line 2	Royal Guards Division	Royal Pages Division
57, line 7	mediation	meditation
58, line 11	donkeys	mules
74, lines 4-5	King Mongkut	King Vajiravudh
81, line 16	rectors	deans
84, line 25	Pol. Lt-Gen. ML Jinda Sanitwongs	Lt-Gen. ML Jinda Sanitwongs
85, line 34	Pol. Maj-Gen. Chote Klongwicha	Maj-Gen. Chote Klongwicha
95, line 23	Special Branch	Metropolitan Police Division
104, line 8	King Mongkut	King Vajiravudh
105, lines 10, 28, 30	mediation	meditation
106, lines 3, 12	mediation	meditation
142, line 12	Royal Guards Division	Royal Pages Division
156, line 18	mediation	meditation
159, line 2	to mediate	to meditate
159, lines 34-35	King Mongkut	King Vajiravudh
160, lines 2, 8	King Mongkut	King Vajiravudh
165, line 8	dean of International Relations	dean of Public Administration
174, line 15	For example, one year	For example, in 2000
174, line 29	King Mongkut	King Vajiravudh
176, line 19	Captain Decha	Lieutenant Decha
179, line 4	Captain Decha	Lieutenant Decha
188, line 14	planning season	planting season
199, line 10	vice director-general	assistant director-general
205, line 32	a Laotian princess	three Laotian princesses